The Ultimate Triathlon

James Ketchell

Published by Ketchell Publishing
Copyright© 2015 James Ketchell
First published 2015

Printed and bound in Great Britain by Marson Book Services Ltd, Didcot, Oxfordshire. www.marston.co.uk

ACKNOWLEDGEMENTS

Writing this book has not been easy, but I was determined to see it through when I first put pen to paper two years ago. Thankfully, just like all three of my challenges, I eventually finished it. Here it is, I really hope you enjoy reading this as much as I enjoyed collecting these stories.

I need to thank a lot of people who, without their kindness, generosity and support I would not be where I am today. I need to say a special thank you to Richard Cribb, who has been instrumental in progressing many aspects of my life. Also Mike Rawlins for his coaching and patience with me since I met him back in 2010.

My thanks also go to the entire Pushing Limits Team who worked with me in 2012 to create a groundbreaking project. Sadly the project did not happen but the team's commitment and support is something I will never forget and I will always be grateful.

The following people made up the Pushing Limits Team: Richard Cribb, Mike Rawlins, Wendy Calloway, Clive Arkell, Tim Juby, Richard Carmen and Tom Macdonald.

Thanks to Pru Gayton, who worked with me to write this book and provided a huge amount of support when I experienced some very tough moments cycling around the world. Also, my good friend Claire Pitcher, for her contributions and support.

I also need to thank Bear Grylls for providing the foreword for this book, as well as Euan Blake, without whose support and hard work many things would not have happened for me. His belief and confidence in me is something I will always be grateful for.

To all of my friends who have supported me, thank you. You know who you are!

All of the 22,000 Scouts in Hampshire - thank you for your encouragement, I am proud to be a Scouting Ambassador to you all. And thank you to all of the Scouts around the world that I have met who have been incredibly friendly and typified the Scouting ethos.

My gratitude also goes to all those people who have read my blogs both during my triathlon and ever since. Thank you for taking the time to read about my exploits and being in contact to offer kind words of encouragement. I hope you will continue to follow me on social media and online via my website www.jamesketchell.net.

Last but by no means least, I need to thank my mum and dad for always putting up with me and generally supporting me whenever I come up with another hair-brained scheme. Not forgetting my brother Jeremy and his family for constantly reminding me that I'm a big loser.

FOREWORD

James Ketchell has shown great strength in the face of adversity, overcoming the prognosis of a permanent walking impairment from an accident that left him with a severely broken leg and ankle. His determination to undertake and complete many adventurous challenges, which most people can only dream about, is testament to his personality.

His struggle with gaining sponsorship and the task of simply getting to the start line is something that I can certainly relate to. In 2010, James successfully rowed single-handed across 3,000 miles of Atlantic Ocean, battling storms, near misses with container ships and eventually running out of food 230 miles from Antigua.

On 16th May 2011, James climbed to the highest point on earth, the summit of Mount Everest. As he neared the summit, battling a lung infection that was to put him in hospital on his return to the UK, he realised that the key to his success was simply just to keep moving and, step-by-step, he would eventually reach the top. Both James and I have walked the same steps as many great mountaineers have, which is something I will never forget.

James was also lucky enough to be led by the same expedition manager who successfully put me on the summit almost 13 years earlier, to the day, 26th May 1998.

In 2013, James cycled 18,000 unsupported miles around the world. He spoke in schools and at Scout groups, sharing stories of adventure and fun, inspiring thousands of young people to pursue their own goals. When he crossed the finish line on 1st February 2014, James became the first and only person to have completed all three challenges – the Ultimate Triathlon!

James is also a Hampshire Scouting Ambassador to over 22,000 young Scouts. Having seen him interact with many Scouts, I know that he is an exemplary role model for young people to show that anything is possible, while reinforcing the Scouting ethos of fun, friendship and loyalty.

In his book, James talks with candour and enthusiasm about how he defied the odds and rose to the challenges he faced. He describes his approach to these extraordinary tasks, continuously setting incremental yet achievable goals. As you read James's story, you will begin to believe that you too could achieve the extraordinary.

Bear Grylls

DEDICATION

In 2014 I supported my good friend Richard Cribb's charity dinner and auctioned a dedication page in this book on behalf of a wonderful charity called Kindled Spirit. Here is the page and a big thanks goes out to Simon Warwood for his kind donation and support.

This page is dedicated to the memory of Charlie Booth and the work of Team Charlie.

Charlie Booth was an outgoing young man who loved the outdoors and all manner of sports. His untimely death in 2013, when aged just 16, was a complete shock to all who knew him.

In early 2014, some of Charlie's friends visited Southern India and came across two children's hostels for orphans and those too poor to be looked after by their parents - the boys' hostel had no running water and only an open fire to cook on, while the girls' hostel was in a very poor state of repair.

It was here that the idea of 'Team Charlie – India' was born. Team Charlie could help renovate the two hostels and also build a multi functional sports centre on the land alongside – for use by the children of the hostels, the nearby high school and the wider local community, all in memory of Charlie Booth. Charlie, being such a keen sportsman himself, would have delighted in giving such opportunities to those who survive at or below the poverty line.

The synergies with Team Charlie and James Ketchell are numerous – the links with India, the shared love of sport for both Charlie and James and also the single minded determination of James to fulfil his dreams and Team Charlie to build a lasting legacy in memory of their friend that will benefit many thousands of young people in India.

'It's not the years in a life, it's the life in the years'.
Charlie Booth
28/10/1996 – 8/3/2013

www.teamcharlie.net

1

Everything happens for a reason

All I remember was accelerating out of the corner, gradually opening the throttle, just feathering it slowly as I felt the rear tyre biting at the tarmac for traction. At this point, I was doing just over 100mph with the bike still on its side. The next thing I knew the back of the bike broke away from me, losing traction. I was now flying through the air looking back at the bike, thinking, "Oh dear, this is going to hurt!" It's funny how time slows down - or you get that impression - when something is going catastrophically wrong. Of course, time is not slowing down, it's just your senses becoming heightened and you're mentally more alert.

I hit the deck hard; it was quite intense for a split second. I then found myself rolling around on the grass verge trying to breathe. The initial impact had knocked the wind out of me. Then an intense pain coming from my right ankle. Out of nowhere, a paramedic appeared in front of me asking if I was all right. By this point, the pain was excruciating. For some reason I still hadn't looked down at my leg. I remember it clearly: the paramedic said, "Don't look down".

So what do you do when you're told not to do something? You do it! I looked down and saw that my right foot was pointing 180-degrees in the wrong direction. It was quite a shock; blood was dripping out of the boot and it was still zipped up. When the paramedic slid the boot off, my white sock was soaked in blood and a piece of bone was protruding.

It's amazing what adrenaline will do for you. I'd say it's the best pain killer there is. As the adrenaline started to leave my body, the pain became intolerable. The paramedics really were first class, they could see immediately that I needed some pain relief and injected me with morphine. I would learn later that I'd actually broken my right leg, both the tibia and fibula, shattered and dislocated my talus bone and also broken the radius bone in my arm, as well as some of the bones in my hand. I did lose some feeling down the right hand side of my upper thigh and to this day, the feeling hasn't come back. Apart from that, I was fine.

I remember being put on a board and lifted into the back of the ambulance.

The paramedic asked me if I wanted him to call anyone for me. I managed to ask him to call my dad, so he dialled the number and my dad answered. "Don't worry dad but I'm in an ambulance," I slurred. At that point, my dad overheard the paramedic saying, "We need more morphine, quickly." I was dribbling and slurring my words so the paramedic took the phone off me and told my dad what had happened.

When I arrived at hospital, the morphine was wearing off, which meant I was able to talk more easily. A young nurse came out and helped the paramedics get me out of the ambulance and into the A & E ward.

The next thing I remember was lying on an operating table, looking down at a pool of blood on the floor. I asked where it was coming from. "You mate," the doctor replied, with a wry smile. He also said we needed to sort my ankle out as soon as possible. I don't know why, but I thought that he was just going to grab my ankle and twist it back into place. It was making me really nervous and anxious, so when I asked him if he was going to do that, he laughed, "No, you would go through the roof, it would be so painful."

After that, I vaguely recall asking the nurses if they could take off the leathers I was wearing without cutting them, but they said they had to cut them off. Next thing I knew, a mask was being put over my face.

It turned out that my ankle was in a pretty bad way. As luck would have it, however, the North Hampshire Hospital has some of the best orthopaedic surgeons in the country. Although the more experienced doctor, Nigel Rossiter, was on holiday at the time, he was called in to operate on me with two other surgeons, Dr Calder and Dr Wilson.

They managed to fix the ankle back in position without putting a bolt all the way through, which effectively fuses it.

In 2015 I was the guest speaker at a conference in Liverpool where Dr Rossiter happened to be in the crowd. He approached me afterwards and we chatted for some time. It was a great feeling to finally meet him, as I never got the opportunity to thank him when I was in hospital. He informed me that my injury was as serious as described to me and at one point amputation was a consideration. Thankfully a policy was in place that no doctor could chop off an arm or a leg without a second approval. Dr Rossiter felt quite strongly that it could be saved. I will forever be indebted to him, Dr Calder and Dr Wilson.

"Can I have a McDonald's?" were the first words out of my mouth when I woke up in the recovery room. Not the most poignant for such a lucky escape.

I was shocked by some of the negative conversations I found myself having with the doctors following my accident. They were constantly saying that I needed to understand the extent of my injury. Up until this point I considered myself a bit like Superman, but the accident made me realise that, actually, I wasn't invincible. According to the doctors, I was unlikely to get much movement back in the ankle and would be lucky if I would walk again without a limp. When I kept telling them that I'd be fine, I think it frustrated a few of them. I was very naïve.

A trainee doctor visited me and pulled out a model of an ankle and explained the extent of my injury. The talus bone is a particularly important bone in the ankle as it's what the foot articulates on and only has one major blood supply. I ruptured the blood supply when it was dislocated and smashed it into pieces, so it was likely that I was going to develop something called *avascular necrosis*, commonly known as AVN. This is where the blood supply is insufficient and the bone slowly dies, getting increasingly more painful as it deteriorates. However, I continued to stay optimistic.

After a few days, I got into the rhythm of hospital life. On a daily basis I would have to be washed by a nurse, as I was unable to do so on my own. Some of them were very young and attractive, so it wasn't all bad, I suppose.

JK

Many years ago, I met a very successful man who told me a story about how he owned a chain of gyms. Everything was going well until business suddenly started to slow down as other people were opening gyms nearby. He said he had two choices: either lie down and give up, or fight like a warrior to keep the gyms open and move things forward. He chose the latter and, over time, all his competitors shut down, leaving him with the majority market share. Eventually he became a multi-millionaire. I thought about this man during those first few recovery days and felt that I was in a similar position. I could feel sorry for myself or I could fight like a warrior to make a recovery.

I'd dreamt of rowing the Atlantic for many years and I knew that, if I had something to focus on, I would be able to bounce back from my accident. By telling people that I was going to row the Atlantic, it meant that I actually had to do it. However, it also gave me the structure and discipline of working towards something tangible. I already knew from past experience that if I set my mind to something, I could be pretty successful.

When I was 23 years old, I competed in a body building competition. This fascination with growing stronger and bigger stemmed from a young age. When I was a teenager, I had no confidence at all and was extremely skinny, with very bad acne. I couldn't speak to girls at all and when I did, they would call me pizza face. I was never bullied as such, just considered to be very average. It was about the time that I was leaving school that I discovered the gym. I started to learn how to change my body and build strength. I became fascinated with lifting weights and gradually became stronger, bigger and, eventually, even the spots cleared up.

I'd go into town on a Saturday night and people from school didn't recognise me at first, saying: "Oh my God, James Ketchell, you have muscles, you look so different." By this stage, I had ditched my glasses and was wearing contact lenses. I could only wear them for short periods as they would make my eyes sore, but it meant I was no longer that skinny, spotty little kid. Girls were approaching me, asking to feel my muscles and chatting me up, it seemed crazy, I just wasn't used to it.

I knew that if I put the same amount of effort into my Atlantic campaign, I could succeed. A few weeks went past and I eventually left hospital. I remember telling people that I was going to row the

Atlantic and they would just laugh. I even took myself off to the Southampton Boat Show, still on crutches and hobbling around.

I went armed with some business proposals and starting touting for sponsorship. One stand I approached was a big company called International Paint. I told them what I was planning to do. "You must be crazy," the guy said, looking at me on my crutches like I'd gone mad. "It's just a minor setback," I insisted. He said that he loved my style, so they agreed to sponsor me – as well as help paint the boat. So there I was, only a few weeks out of hospital, and I'd got my first sponsor for the project. Although it was only a load of paint, it was a sponsor nonetheless and proof that someone believed in me.

It was fairly easy to get free kit, but a totally different ball game trying to get funding. I needed to do something quite drastic to take the project to the next level. I decided to borrow the money from the bank to buy a boat. I rang up Barclays, and they said they would loan me £22,000; two weeks later, it was in my bank account. Now I could buy a boat and people would start taking me seriously. It meant that I would have something tangible to show people so they could physically see what I was going to row the Atlantic Ocean in and where they could potentially put their sponsorship logos.

I was taking a big risk really but it eventually paid off. Buying an ocean rowing boat wasn't like buying a car: you can't just pick up a copy of Auto Trader. On a specialist website selling boats I came across the perfect vessel. The guy selling it, Anthony, had rowed the Atlantic in this boat. He was asking £23,000, slightly over my budget, but I thought I could knock him down a bit. I drove up to Manchester with my friend Matt to see it. It instantly felt right and I could see myself rowing in it. The boat was called *Albatross* and was bright yellow.

After a bit of negotiation, I paid Anthony £22,000 for the boat. It was fantastic, and had actually crossed the Atlantic three times before. The first was with a chap called Stuart who was a paraplegic, then it was sold to two ex-Gurkhas who called it *Gurkha Spirit*, and then to Anthony. I was the new, very proud, owner.

By this point, I was walking and getting around pretty well. I'd been working hard on my physio and doing all I could to help myself recuperate. I was trying to stay positive about my ankle but it was playing up a lot and quite painful at times. Understanding my injury and what had actually happened interested me so I started reading medical documents online, trying to find case studies from people with similar injuries. I did manage to find people who had sustained major talus fractures and dislocations and generally it was not good news. They were all reporting major movement issues and increasing pain and some had even developed *avascular necrosis*. My injury was playing tricks on my mind: one minute I thought it was healing well and then the next minute, it felt worse. I was still determined to not feel sorry for myself.

At a routine check-up, I saw a different doctor. Usually the doctors were quite chatty and, I think, probably admired my motivation to try and make a good recovery. However, this particular doctor was - I could only assume - having a bad day. I asked him about a couple of things I'd researched, to which he replied: "Look, unless you are going to spend five years studying to become a doctor, just don't bother wasting your time trying to research this and asking me questions about something you will never understand." I was really taken aback by his response and it knocked my confidence that day.

Looking back, I understand the pressure he was under to see patients and get things done and you never really know what's going on inside someone's head, or what he had been dealing with before he saw me. I never saw him again.

The up and down movement in the foot is called dorsiflexion and plantar flexion. My plantar flexion was fine so I could point my toes towards the ground but my dorsiflexion was reduced by about 40 per cent so it was difficult to point my foot up. Thankfully, I still had sufficient movement to walk around without a limp.

I went for another check-up at the hospital and also to look at the results from an MRI scan. I was excited to get the results, as this was about six months after the accident and around the time you would see if there are any signs of *avascular necrosis* setting in. I was met by the doctor and we chatted about the results. He warned me it wasn't the best news, and then showed me little spots on the MRI scan that were early signs of AVN. This was perhaps why I was getting pain in my ankle. I came away feeling devastated and very low. I felt like the work I had put in with my physio and rehabilitation exercises had been a waste of time.

2

Finding my sea legs

For a few weeks I had no motivation at all and was generally feeling very sorry for myself. One evening, I was watching a TV programme about a soldier who had stepped on a land mine and had his foot blown off. He was still doing amazing things despite missing a foot. It hit me that I was being quite ungrateful and that, in comparison to others, my injury was really nothing at all. I was in fact very lucky to even have a foot, even if I had reduced movement. From that day on, I was determined not to feel sorry for myself again.

The previous owner of the boat had painted it bright yellow but, for my project, I already knew that I wanted to paint it red and white. I'd never really worked on a boat before but I had worked on cars in the past so had a reasonable aptitude for working with my hands. It was actually quite simple and the only help I needed was with rewiring some electrics.

I was going to be rowing solo as part of the Woodvale 2009 Ocean

Rowing Race and the organiser, Simon Chalk, was holding a training weekend in Cornwall. Rowing from Newlyn to the Isles of Scilly is approximately 35 nautical miles and the weekend would prove to be a very steep learning curve.

I had wanted to row the Atlantic with someone else as, generally, most people row as a pair or a four. For some reason, I just couldn't find anyone who wanted to do it with me, which surprised me, as I thought it would be an amazing adventure. I decided to row on my own and that was one of the best decisions I've ever made. However, for the Scilly Isles row, I was going to need a partner, so I drafted in my friend Matt to come with me. The drive to Newlyn took six hours and on arrival at the harbour we were met by five other crews who would also be rowing across.

We got the boats off the trailers and into the water and tied up on a berth. That night we went to the pub and chatted with the other rowers before returning to the boat where Matt and I slept in the cabin. We were all due to set off at 5am so we could catch the tide that would pull us offshore, giving us a helping hand to get away from land. My boat was actually a pairs boat but was set up for a solo rower with just the one seat position. The plan was for us each to row two hours on and two hours off.

This worked fine for a few shifts until we got a little further out to sea and the conditions started to get a bit rougher. The inevitable seasickness crept in. It hit Matt very hard initially and then I started to feel ill. We carried on but things got a lot harder when a thick sea fog came rolling in and soon visibility was down to about 100 metres. What made things even worse was the VHF on the support rib failed so we lost contact with them. By this time, all the rowing boats had separated and every single crew that was rowing across was completely debilitated by sea sickness.

At this point, I was quite worried as Matt was in a very bad way, lying in the back of the boat. I've never seen anyone look so green before. It became clear very quickly that we were never going to be able to get across to the Scilly Isles in this sort of state. What made it even harder was that the tide had turned, pulling us closer to the shore, no matter how hard I tried to row against it.

We didn't know it at the time but some other crews were in exactly the same position and decided to call for help on the VHF. I heard a noise off to the port side and, through the grey murky cloud, a bright yellow rib was approaching. It was Simon, who told us that he had lost contact with the other crews. I could also hear a helicopter getting closer and closer until it was hovering over the top of us. I then heard communication on our VHF between a Royal Navy Search and Rescue Sea King and an RNLI lifeboat. The helicopter passed over and then, a few seconds later, an RNLI lifeboat approached us.

I told them that Matt needed to be taken off the boat as soon as possible. They suggested towing the boat back to shore and taking Matt with them. I was still feeling okay at this point, although slightly sea sick, so I went on the rib with Simon to help round up the other boats. I felt quite relieved after that, as I knew my boat was being safely towed back to shore. At £22,000, it was an investment I really didn't want smashed on the rocks.

I had a hand-held VHF that I took with me onto the rib and, with the Sea King above us, they quickly found all the other boats and relayed their position to us. Simon and I went about rounding them up and by the time we had four boats in tow, we realised that it was going to be easier to keep going to the Scilly Isles, as opposed to turning back. We were over half way there.

While we were looking for the boats, I took control of the rib and Simon rested up for a bit. We were pretty tired by now but at least the fog had cleared and the sun had come out, making for quite a pleasant day. It was a pretty powerful rib, with two 150 horsepower outboards on the back. A small rib with 300 horsepower makes for a lot of fun. When all the boats were under tow and we were heading into the Scilly Isles, I felt sorry for a lot of the crews, as they were severely seasick. Seasickness is extremely unpleasant and will bring down the toughest of people.

Eventually we made it to the Scilly Isles, all utterly exhausted. When we arrived, there was nowhere open to buy any food apart from a small newsagent that sold pasties and ice creams - not the best sustenance, but certainly good enough for a dozen starving rowers. I managed to find a boat to sleep on for the night and I have never slept so well in my life. It's funny, you really can sleep anywhere if you're tired enough.

The next morning, we all took the rib back to Newlyn and I got the train home. When the RNLI recovered my boat the previous day, they very kindly pulled it out of the water and put it back on the trailer. When he was feeling better, Matt was able to drive my car back home and get the boat safely back into the warehouse.

In hindsight, we were all rookies but it was certainly the best training weekend we could have hoped for. The next day, our weekend escapades were all over the BBC News in Cornwall, and I had numerous reporters calling me for interviews. I made quite a significant donation to the RNLI about a month later as I was so impressed by their amazing, selfless work, with most of the crew being volunteers.

JK

The year went on and I carried on doing as much promotion and fundraising as I could with the boat. The boat was a major asset in my campaign for sponsorship as the project became real when people could actually see what I was going to row the Atlantic in. I even had the boat outside Twickenham rugby ground, promoting my row at an England versus France Six Nations game.

Eventually, the time came to pack the boat with all the supplies needed for the crossing: 100 days worth of food and gas. I drove the boat up to Tilbury Docks where it would be put in a container and shipped out to the Canary Islands, then transported to La Gomera, about 15 miles west of Tenerife. My route across the Atlantic was quite a historic route as La Gomera is the same island from which Christopher Columbus departed in 1492 when he discovered the Americas. The final destination was Antigua in the Caribbean, a distance of just under 3,000 nautical miles.

The row was scheduled to start on 4th December so I flew out about two-and-a-half weeks beforehand to get the boat ready. As I was part of a race, it was also mandatory to be there two weeks before the start. I remember saying goodbye to my parents and friends before I took the flight out to Tenerife. It felt like it went pretty quickly, despite the butterflies in my stomach. The hardest part was over though. I had made it to the start line, although the trip wouldn't turn out to be that simple.

I spoke to a good friend of mine over the phone as I was getting the ferry from Tenerife to La Gomera. His nickname was Romeo, but his actual name was Clive. I'd met Clive 10 years ago when I was weight-training on a serious basis, day in, day out. When I first met him, I was just starting out and was very skinny, and Clive was always very supportive. In the gym, he was such a smooth operator with the women and I was in awe of his confidence. I'd never seen anyone able to chat to women so easily. From then on, he was known as Romeo and I still call him that to this day.

We chatted for the entire ferry crossing and he told me that I really deserved to be there, undertaking the row, which meant a lot to me. He also told me something else that I will never forget: "Remember, when you think you're working hard, there will always be someone working twice as hard!"

I got off the ferry in La Gomera, checked into my hotel, then decided to go out and meet up with some of the other crews. Just as I walked out of the door, an English chap who was in his late 20s asked me if I could keep the door open for him. I chatted to him briefly and found out his name was Rob and he was another rower taking part in the race. You never know what's around the corner but Rob was to become an extremely good friend of mine and he has opened many doors for me that have effectively changed my life.

It didn't take me long to realise that a big part of the Woodvale Ocean Rowing Race culture was the banter with other crews and drinking almost every night was pretty much par for the course. There is a particularly famous bar with ocean rowers in La Gomera called 'The Blue Marlin', which is famous for some serious drinking sessions. Ocean rowers have a reputation for being able to drink, which in most cases is true. It's also a tradition to write your boat name and signature on the wall of the pub.

Most of my time on the island was spent working on the boat, making sure everything was packed and rechecking equipment. The race organisers had a pre-race scrutinising examination that every boat had to pass before it was allowed in the water. It turned out I had to fit another vent on the bulkhead in order for the organisers to pass my newly-renamed boat, 'Speedo'. It was a real pain to fit but I eventually managed it and the boat passed with flying colours. When Speedo was put into the water, it really was a magical feeling, seeing all of the hard work that I'd put into the project sitting there, sparkling in the sun, on the beautiful blue water.

Most of my time over the next few days was spent rowing and going through some sea drills, like deploying the para anchor. The race date was getting closer and there was talk going round the rowers that impending bad weather could possibly delay the start. This made a lot of crews restless, as they had only been able to get a certain amount of time off work and before they'd even set off, it was looking like they were going to fall behind schedule. A meeting was called with the rowers and the race organisers to discuss the issues with weather and the impact of a delay. A new date was set but sadly most families who had come out for the start of the race were going to have to fly home without seeing off their loved ones, due to the unforeseen delay.

My family and friends who had come out to the start also had to go home so I made the journey over to Tenerife to see them off. On the way back, I was waiting for the ferry and, as it docked, there were some other rowers on board who asked me if I had heard 'the news'. I didn't know what they were talking about until they told me that the race had been postponed again until after Christmas due to further weather issues. When I got back over to La Gomera, I spoke to some other crews and the organisers and they confirmed that the race would go ahead at the end of December or very early January. Some crews stayed on the island but most people decided to go home for Christmas.

I wasn't sure if I should stay on the island or go home. Flights were relatively cheap so I made the decision to fly home for a couple of weeks. It was really strange getting on a plane and flying home; something just didn't quite feel right. I arrived back into the UK to find snow on the ground and winter in full swing already.

3

A close call

I flew back out to La Gomera, refreshed mentally and physically, ready to row an ocean. When I arrived, I bumped into Rob who I had met on the first day in La Gomera over a month earlier.

Rob was a very accomplished high altitude climber, having summited Everest five times, and had numerous other 8,000m peaks under his belt. He was an all-round lovely guy. We became good friends, along with another solo rower called Leo. He was an American living in Boston and was an ex-US Marshall who had the most fantastic stories of how he bust mafia drug dealers in his 'bad-ass cop' days. The three of us spoke about going out to Everest and decided that the best thing to do was to pick the conversation up after the row. I was about to row across the Atlantic, thinking about how I could raise the funds to get out to Everest. I should just be concentrating on the task in hand.

The morning of the departure rolled round, 4th January 2010. I wasn't as nervous as I thought I would be, considering that I was about to row across the Atlantic. I said goodbye to some of the crews that I had become friends with after my time in La Gomera and sent a few last-minute emails. There was a good feeling of camaraderie between the crews and all the banter was put aside, with everyone wishing each other good luck.

I got into my boat, left some stinking trainers on the dock to be disposed of and pushed my oar into the dock. I slowly drifted out and rowed through the marina where there were quite a few people around, waving and whistling. Simon was on a rib with a megaphone, announcing the countdown. The start line was between a rock and yacht called 'Aura'. I didn't think there was much point in getting too close to the start line as this was going to be a marathon as opposed to a sprint, for sure. The klaxon went off and that was it - I was on my way across the Atlantic.

I rowed for about four hours before I became hungry and needed to stop for some food. There was a lot of adrenaline running through my body and the time passed very quickly. It started to get dark and the wind started turning so it was blowing from the northwest, which meant it was effectively blowing the crews towards North Africa. I decided to deploy the para anchor *(a device designed to be deployed to minimise the loss of ground and slow the boat down if you're being blown the wrong way. It works exactly the same as a parachute but instead of air, it's the drag of water that slows you down).* For the first 24 hours, all the crews were on the para anchor, basically going round in circles.

Most crews were suffering very badly with sea sickness but as luck would have it, I wasn't suffering at all. Not because I was a tough guy, it was just pure luck, although I did take an anti-sickness tablet before I left and had a good stash of them on the boat. It took about three days for me to fully clear the island of El Hierro, which is situated south west of La Gomera. The next stop after that was Antigua: there is nothing in between, apart from 3,000 miles of Atlantic Ocean.

It only took about six hours from leaving land to losing mobile phone signal and then it was just the sat phone, which I was using for all communication. I'd checked and rechecked all my electrics before I departed but for some reason, my battery was already at 50 per cent, which was not good at all, considering that I'd not yet used the water maker or anything that draws a lot of power. A quick call to my dad on the sat phone for advice and we'd decided to turn everything off and just let it charge.

It's funny how human beings are able to adapt to their surroundings quite quickly. After about five days, I felt pretty comfortable being on my own in the Atlantic. I wasn't really fussed about the race, I just wanted to get across safely. That said, it was quite disheartening when I spoke to my dad over the sat phone and he informed me that the faster crews were pulling away from me by the day and I was the second to last boat in the race. For the first few days, I could see other boats on my chart plotter as I had AIS (Automatic Identification System). It's basically a radar system that shows other commercial shipping vessels my position and details.

It took around five days to get into a good rhythm and find a shift pattern that worked for me. If you are rowing as a pair, you would generally row two hours on and two hours off, so one person would be rowing all the time. There is no right or wrong way for a solo rower and obviously you can't row all the time. In the end, I found the following shift pattern worked quite well for me: rowing four hours on, one hour off for lunch, another four hours on, and then an hour off for dinner. Then I would finish the day with either a four-hour shift to make 12 hours or just finish with two hours, depending on how I felt. I stuck to that routine religiously the whole way across the Atlantic.

It only took a couple of weeks to realise that routine is your best friend when away on an expedition, or at least it was for me. It's funny how missing a simple task like brushing your teeth at night is much more important than you think. It's actually got nothing to do with brushing your teeth, it's all about the routine. If you don't have the willpower to brush your teeth, you'll soon become lazy and start missing other jobs and then it can be a downward spiral.

After a few weeks at sea, I finally started to have some better weather. The waves were getting bigger but not too steep or choppy, just nice, long, rolling waves that the boat could surf down. I was coming across a lot of commercial shipping as I was going through major shipping lanes. At first, it was quite intimidating having massive vessels passing but, after a while, it became fun as I would chat with them on the VHF radio. Quite often, they would ask if I needed assistance, as I appeared to be demasted as far as they could see. I told them that I was okay and that I was rowing solo across the Atlantic. Some of the reactions were quite funny: "You're doing WHAT? Are you out of your mind?" I was getting used to large ships passing me until one day I came a little too close to being hit.

It was a rough day and the wind had changed direction, which meant I was getting pushed back by the winds. I deployed the para anchor and lay down in the cabin, just relaxing and watching a DVD on my laptop, since I was unable to row. As I lay in the cabin, which is only about seven feet long at its maximum, I could see out of the hatch window. The boat would move up and down as it rolled over the crest of the waves. As I was coming up to the top of the wave, I could see right out across the ocean. It was like being lifted 20ft up into the air. As you come down into the waves, all you can see in front of you is a wall of water approaching. Then it just picks the boat up as if it's as light as a feather.

All of a sudden, something caught my eye just over the top of the laptop screen as the boat came up over the crest of a wave. It was an oil tanker coming straight towards me. My heart has never jumped out of my chest quite like it before. I jumped up and grabbed the VHF radio and immediately started to try and make contact with the tanker, "This is Speedo, this is Speedo, I am directly on your bow, do you see me?" There was no answer from them and the colossal, 300m long vessel was getting closer and closer.

I jumped on the oars as quickly as I could and tried desperately to row out of the way although, with the para anchor still in the water, it was very difficult. As the tanker got closer, I realised that it wasn't going to hit me head on, but pass very close by. I held on tight as the monster ship passed me with about 50m to spare, which is extremely close. The wake of the vessel nearly rolled Speedo as it passed me. I could feel the vibration and smell the fumes from the gigantic engines that powered it along at over 20 knots.

I'm often asked what the most dangerous thing is about ocean rowing and, of course, there are many things. However, for me, the answer is commercial vessels. There are instruments on rowing boats to prevent collisions such as early warning systems, a bit like a radar, but they are not foolproof.

I'm not a religious or spiritual person at all but I had so many close calls on the trip that I just felt that someone must have been looking out for me. A few months before I was due to set off, my grandfather was taken ill and sadly passed away before I departed on my row. He was very sick but I was really hoping that he would stay alive long enough to see me row the Atlantic. Before he passed away, I showed him photos of Speedo. His eyes were glazed over as he lay in hospital and he couldn't talk, but I knew he was taking in and understanding what I was saying.

Before I set off on the row, I decided to put his name on the boat as a way of remembering him. His name was Rocky Rochelle. He was a very tough, working-class man in his day and had a short temper at times. He did however have a very big heart and would often buy gifts for friends and family. I decided that I should put the name of my other grandad on the boat too, Henry Ketchell. He had sadly passed away many years before the row when I was much younger. I had some times on the boat, late at night, when I really felt like someone was sitting there with me. I felt very calm and the temperature around me would go up slightly. Perhaps they really were looking down on me.

JK

The Atlantic Ocean can make or break people and I believe I was lucky to make it across. Rowing an ocean has got very little to do with actually rowing, in my opinion. For me, it's about staying strong and not panicking when things stop working, which inevitably happens all the time. One of the most important bits of kit on the boat is the water desalinator, which turns salt water into drinking water. It's not possible to take enough fresh drinking water to cross an ocean so the water maker is critical.

One morning, I turned the water maker on and the noise it was making was quite different. Within a few minutes, I realised that it wasn't sucking in water; effectively, it wasn't working. I spent about half an hour looking at it, turning it off and on. The pump head had failed and needed to be replaced. This is the part that is connected to the pump and is made up of two gears that turn and force water through the system. It should have been a fairly easy fix however it was a slightly rough day, so sitting in a cabin (which is on a par with sitting in a sauna in the day while moving up, down and side-to-side), was not a nice thought.

I grabbed my tool kit and set about trying to make the repair. The first few screws came undone and it was coming apart fairly easily. I then had to remove a panel to get to the bolts that were holding the pump in place. This is where things started to get a little tricky and every nut and bolt was seized up and rusty. They were particularly awkward to get to and every time I tried to undo the bolts, the spanner would slip and round the head of the bolt off.

I began to panic slightly, knowing that I would have quite a serious problem on my hands if I couldn't fix it. I decided to take a break and have a cup of tea as by this point, I was dripping with sweat and feeling quite nauseous from being in the cabin. Above the water maker was a selection of photos that I had put on the side of the cabin to remind me of my family and friends when I was feeling low. There was one particular photo of my dad with me on his back and my younger brother, Jeremy, on my back.

I've always admired dad, as he is mentally very strong, despite not having an ounce of physical fitness or strength. I have never once in my life seen him feeling sorry for himself. He has the ability to stay strong and focused when things are not going well and is excellent at solving problems. He completed his apprenticeship at London Transport when he was younger, building bus engines, and is an excellent mechanic, despite working as a SAP architect now. I knew if he were here, he would easily be able to remove the bolts that were giving me so many problems and fix the water maker. I looked at the photo of me, dad and Jeremy and said, "Okay, I'm struggling, I need some help with this," - a bit silly really, as I was talking to no one. I persevered and managed to free the bolts, change out the part for a new one and the water maker was as good as new. I was so pleased with myself!

One thing I will never forget from my time in the Atlantic Ocean is the incredible wildlife. Some crews that rowed across claim they saw nothing for the whole crossing. I, on the other hand, was incredibly lucky with the abundance of wildlife I witnessed. Fin whales would swim right next to the boat and underneath it. You just can't grasp the size of them, they were gigantic - the size of a bus. Sometimes the whales swam underneath the boat and then lifted the boat up on their backs and the boat would slide off the side of them. It's quite amazing when they swim close and on the surface as you can hear them breathe from the blowhole in their backs. Water would shoot high up into the sky. You could see and hear a whale breathing from over a mile away. If they were close to the boat, the smell of the water spray that shot up as they breathed stank of fish.

I also found out that flying fish really do fly. It was one o'clock in the morning and I had been rowing for 13 hours. I had just pulled the oars up out of the water to store them while I slept. It was an eerily dark night with a lot of cloud cover and the moon wasn't out. Without my head torch, I couldn't even see my hand in front of my face. All of a sudden, a white object came flying up out of the water and hit me in the face. I was so tired, I had no idea what was going on and at first I thought I'd just been hit by a golf ball. Ridiculous, there was no one playing golf out in the ocean. I had in fact been hit by a flying fish. The left side of my face was covered in scales and fish slime, which left a rather unpleasant smell on my face.

I looked down on the deck to see this little fish flapping up and down trying to escape. I decided to throw him back into the Atlantic so he could hit someone else in the face another day. I can only surmise it was attracted to the light from my head torch.

It was quite a common occurrence to have flying fish jumping into the boat. I would often get out of the cabin in the morning to find half a dozen dead fish on the deck that had jumped into the boat and were unable to get out. Sometimes at night I could hear them hitting the side of the boat as they made a little thud. Every now and then, one or two would jump into the boat and I wouldn't notice them as they had fallen behind the life raft. A few days later, there would be an awful smell and I'd find a rotting fish, which wasn't very pleasant at all.

Being hit in the face wasn't the only close encounter I had with a fish on my voyage across the Atlantic. Every week, I would get out of the boat to clean the bottom of the hull. This was quite a dangerous thing to do as a solo rower, as the boat was my lifeline and without it, I would almost certainly be going to a watery grave. I needed to clean the hull, as growth would build up and slow me down, sometimes cutting my speed in half. So if I could make the boat go just half a knot faster over every hour, every day, every week, this small marginal gain would become quite substantial. Underneath the boat there would be a fantastic ecosystem of fish: small fish taking shelter from the sun's rays and bigger fish coming up to eat them, and so on. At any one time, there could be hundreds of fish swimming around the boat.

One particular day, I was cleaning the hull and a small fish, about six inches long, bit me on the nipple. I couldn't believe it. It didn't really hurt as such, it was like being pinched, but just a bit of a shock. Being out of the boat in the water in the middle of the Atlantic was quite an amazing experience. The water was crystal clear and as I looked down, I could see the water getting darker and darker as it disappeared to the depths of the ocean. The ocean floor was roughly three miles below me at any one time, so I was never that far from land; it was just in the wrong direction.

When I got out of the boat, I would always tie myself on with a floating line, as it was quite frightening how fast the boat drifts away from you when you let go of it. One day, I lost a T-shirt over the side and, without thinking, I jumped in to retrieve it. Upon surfacing, I expected to be beside the boat but I was shocked at how far it had drifted away from me. I had to swim incredibly hard to get back. That was probably one of the most irresponsible things I've ever done, and I was very lucky to get back to the boat at all.

There was one particular fish that fascinated me, and that was the Oceanic White Tip Shark. These amazing creatures would swim around the boat but never come that close. I would find this frustrating, as I wanted to take pictures and film them. I decided that if I tried to feed them, perhaps they would come closer, but that wasn't the case. I even had a theory that if I jumped in, they would probably swim off, but I didn't want to try it out. There is something magical about the way they swim so gracefully through the water with their fins protruding like something out of *Jaws*.

It wasn't just fish who followed me all the way across the Atlantic. I was amazed to find so many birds in the middle of the ocean too. I thought that I would see birds a few hundred miles out of the Canary Islands and then a few hundred miles from the Caribbean but it wasn't the case. I saw little birds flying around in the middle of the Atlantic on an almost daily basis. When they needed to rest, they would just sit on the surface of the water and bob up and down. Most of the time they would actually come and sit on the boat and fight each other for the best position. Most would sit on the bow of the boat and some would actually sit on the oars. Occasionally, they would hop into the cabin; one particular bird stayed on the boat for two weeks. It was quite a sad day when it finally flew away.

One thing I do regret is not taking an Atlantic Ocean wildlife reference book with me as I saw so many wonderful creatures that I was unable to identify. I did discover that the majority of birds I saw were Brown Noddys. Having these little birds flying around the boat was quite therapeutic. I often sat there wondering what it must be like to be able to soar above the ocean waves, covering huge distances in a relatively short space of time.

I was about a month into my Atlantic row and still nowhere near the halfway point. I'd been quite unlucky as I'd been hit by a massive area of low pressure which usually shifts the winds blowing from the east to the west; it meant that I had to spend almost 10 frustrating days just sitting on a para anchor. I lost over 200 miles and it was probably the most depressing time of the entire row. All I could really do was lie down in the cabin as it was too rough to be on deck as the para anchor pulls the boat hard and makes for quite an uncomfortable ride. The best way to describe being in rough seas in a rowing boat and sitting on a para anchor is like being on a rollercoaster ride. No matter how loud you scream, you can't get off. After a while you get used to it, but it's not a particularly pleasant experience.

Most of the time, the currents and winds will assist rowing boats across the Atlantic, certainly the mid trans-Atlantic route from the Canaries to the Caribbean where the currents are strong.

The mid Atlantic is by far the most common ocean that is rowed today. As you come out of the Canary Islands, you quite quickly pick up the Canary current that flows down the side of Africa. As you start getting to a lower latitude (closer to the equator) you then start picking up the North Equatorial current which flows all the way to the Caribbean and will funnel up to become the gulf stream.

This is a massive advantage when at sea in a rowing boat as you can ride on the currents for most of the time. That said, it's not easy, as it's quite common to have little micro-currents swirling round that can push you back. For the most part, you'll always be drifting the right way. Some nights, I'd sleep for about six to seven hours, wake up in the morning and find that I'd drifted over 25 miles closer to Antigua. Now that was always a good start to the day. Sadly, there is always the opposite possibility and some mornings I'd find that I'd drifted back over 10 miles.

JK

I remember on day 45, I was in the cabin having my breakfast and drinking a cup of tea. It was about 7.45am and I would usually start my first rowing shift at 8am so I was just getting ready to get out on the oars. All of a sudden, I heard a loud foghorn go off. This is not the sort of thing you want to be hearing and I thought I was about to get run over by a colossal container ship. I jumped up to look outside at what was about to run me over and, to my surprise, it was a tiny, little sailing boat with four guys on board. Initially I was relieved, as it wasn't a container ship, then I became really excited to see these guys waving and shouting at me. It was just my luck though to stumble across a boat in the middle of the Atlantic and find that its crew was all half-naked German men who couldn't speak a word of English.

After the panic had subsided and I knew I was safe, I looked down and realised I was wearing no shorts. In fact, I was standing there waving at them stark naked. I quickly jumped back into the cabin and made myself half decent. They circled Speedo a few times, although they didn't appear to be particularly competent with their boat as they were getting in a right mess with the sails. At one point, they were coming far too close for my liking and had they hit me, they would almost certainly have ended my row.

I soon forgot about my encounter with the four German guys. On the side of my boat, I had the name 'Atlantic Adventurer' which they obviously took note of and Googled at some point, because a few months after the row, I had an email drop into my inbox from one of the crew. They had taken some pictures of my boat and thought it would be nice to send them to me. Thankfully, none of them featured me standing there naked.

On a calm day when there is no wind, the middle of the Atlantic can look like a mill pond, completely still and not a ripple in the water. Days like that are perfect for a little dip in the ocean and a good body scrub. Washing off the boat can be a lovely refreshing experience, which is something I tried to do every few days.

The challenge you have when you're in a rowing boat and being so close to the water is salt: it gets everywhere, and I mean *everywhere*. To really get the salt off the body after it has dried (which after a while becomes the worst exfoliating experience you'll ever have) takes a fair bit of fresh water. Most of the time I didn't have enough battery power to run the water maker for long enough to create washing water as the water needed for drinking and mixing with rations was my top priority.

A quick wash would involve jumping in to get wet and then coming back on board to lather up with soap and then jumping back in to rinse the soap off. I would then have to dry myself and rub all the salt off which was sometimes quite painful. I did take two bottles of shower gel with me as well, which I used for a treat.

One of the best feelings was rowing all day and taking the evening off before the sun went down and it was still warm. It's funny what I missed when I was at sea and it wasn't what I'd imagined. After I'd cleaned and dried myself, I would put on a clean T-shirt. I took about 10 T-shirts with me so I could pretty much wear a new one every 10 days. The feeling when you put on clean clothes was just magical: the soft fabric running over your skin and the fresh smell as if it had just come out of the wash was fantastic. I missed the feeling of wearing nice, clean fresh shirts and smart clothes. It's something that most of us don't think twice at doing every day but when it's taken away, it makes you realise it's the simple things you miss.

I did take a solar shower with me, a device you fill with water and place in the sun for a few hours to warm up. Most bags hold 25 litres of water. I'd managed to source a metal pole that I thought was going to be excellent at holding the solar shower up, effectively meaning that I could stand under it and, 'job done'.

My mistake was not thinking about the weight of the bag when it was full of water. I'd been saving drinking water over the course of a few days and was making a bit extra so that I could have a shower.

I was really looking forward to trying my solar shower and pole out and waited for a calm day to try it. I lifted the bag full of water up on to the top of the pole and it initially stayed there. I turned around for a few seconds to get the shower gel and all of a sudden, I heard a crack and then, splash. The pole had snapped in half and the solar shower had fallen into the water.

I was devastated and annoyed at myself and was about to jump in to retrieve it but something in my head stopped me. There was a particularly strong current that day and I couldn't believe how quickly the bag drifted away from me. I stood there watching it float away; it was almost like the scene out of the Tom Hank's film *Cast Away* when he loses his volleyball, Wilson. I had spent so much time engineering the onboard shower and it had failed miserably.

Going to the loo could be an interesting experience; it was a case of 'bucket and chuck it.' This was fine when it was a calm day but unfortunately you still need to use the bucket, no matter what the weather is doing outside. Imagine sitting on a toilet seat doing what you need to do, while being violently thrown from side to side. Only, you're not sitting on a seat, you're squatting over a bucket. Let's just say, it could get quite messy.

I'm often asked if I rowed naked. Having tried, I can say I didn't find it that comfortable and in the height of the day, the sun is extremely powerful and sunburn can be a real issue. I rowed in Lycra shorts, which I found to work perfectly for me. It's not uncommon for ocean rowers to suffer with blisters on their bum and extreme soreness. I was lucky as I only started to get a sore backside and chafing between my thighs around day 95, at which point I was almost finished.

I discovered that rowing in wet Lycra shorts was very soothing. Another great discovery I made was just how good Sudocrem is, an antiseptic nappy rash cream. Occasionally, I would get rashes and little blisters on my feet where they had been in the foot straps all day. At night before I went to bed, I'd plaster Sudocrem on anything that was sore and the next morning, it was healed. Most of the day I rowed topless but I needed to put a T-shirt on at around midday for a few hours as the sun really made me feel awful. Sunstroke can be seriously debilitating. Another thing that can really make rowers' lives a misery is something called 'claw hand', when your hand is in a permanent state of closure and it's agony to open your hands and fingers out. Thankfully, apart from a few minor blisters, I was very lucky not to have any problems with my hands at all.

4

Testing times

By now, I was approaching the halfway point, which felt amazing. It had seemed like such a massive task to row 3,000 miles across an ocean that I couldn't really comprehend it. I looked at my crossing of the Atlantic as a mountain, which is quite ironic, considering that I went on to climb Everest. When I left La Gomera, my goal was to get to the halfway point. I knew that if I could do this, the currents and winds would take me into the Caribbean. In my head, I always knew that I didn't need to do anything special, apart from keep rowing and don't row in circles.

I was supposed to be out in the Atlantic for Christmas but the bad weather before the start put an end to that. I did however decide to take my Christmas presents (that were meant to be opened on the boat) with me and open them at the halfway point. It was lovely opening gifts and cards from friends and family. Every year, mum makes a fantastic stocking and this year was no exception. It was filled with sweets and chocolate. Reading so many nice cards really lifted my spirits and the fact I was half way also really motivated me to finish.

The race fleet, including my boat, was being tracked all the way across the Atlantic, meaning supporters and family at home could log on and see how far I had or hadn't gone. It also gave them the race positions of all the boats and, for the vast majority of the race, I was one of the last boats with two other solo rowers, Leo and Sean. There were also three other great solo rowers who were a lot further ahead. South African adventurer, Peter Van Kets, was rowing the Atlantic for the second time, and Dave Brooks was another solo rower. Both guys were very strong and had great personalities. Pete spent a fair bit of time helping me programme my Garmin chart plotter with all the waypoints for the crossing in La Gomera before the start. He had a very calm, relaxed presence about him, which made me feel at ease with the task ahead.

The other solo rower was a guy called Charlie Pitcher, a very driven man with an eye for detail. He had spent a lot of time and effort designing his own ocean rowing boat. It was a risk but his hard work and planning really paid off as the boat worked really well for him, and he was the fastest solo rower by a long way.

When Charlie finished, I had only just crossed the halfway point and I remember getting a text message from him on the sat phone, basically saying well done and don't worry too much about being at the back of the race fleet. He said he wished he was still out rowing as the prospect of going straight back to work was not much fun. When I did eventually finish, I knew exactly what he meant. It's quite a come down getting back to normality again after the initial excitement of seeing your friends and family subsides.

I did feel slightly embarrassed that I was one of the last boats because physically I was one of the strongest rowers in the fleet. I eventually learnt that it doesn't matter how strong you are, as no human being can compare to the power of an ocean. Pretty much everything that happened on that ocean was out of my control. That said, I learnt that preparation is everything, and if you fail to prepare, you really will need to be prepared to fail.

Once I was beyond the halfway point, knowing in my head that I was closer to Antigua than where I had started from, made me incredibly motivated. Every day I would wake up and become obsessed with how many miles I had drifted overnight and how many miles I could row that day. Time started to pass very quickly.

It was at the halfway stage that it became apparent to me that my food supplies would get pretty low if it took the same amount of time to complete the last half of the row. I tried to ration food down but found it incredibly difficult to row for 12 hours a day and cut down on my calorie intake. I decided to keep to my set meal plans and just try and row harder and then worry about the food situation as I got closer to shore. This actually proved to be a mistake.

On day 80, I remembered that I'd packed some food into one of the lockers underneath the cabin which I'd totally forgotten about. I lifted up the mattress and opened the lockers to see about 10 ration packs sitting there, all sealed and ready to be eaten. It felt like Christmas had come early because at this point, I knew my food supply was running really low. One thing I still laugh about now, looking back, was how important the food was. It wasn't just your fuel; it was your morale as well. Certainly for me, coming off a four-hour rowing shift and looking forward to a good meal really lifted my spirits.

By day 90, it was obvious that I was probably going to run out of food before I finished the row. I decided to try and ration the food down, despite the consequences on my rowing ability. If I didn't row for such long shifts, I could cope with the reduction in calories, but it also meant that I wouldn't row as far, therefore I'd be out at sea for longer and would still need more food.

I tried to catch fish to see if I could fry them and add some extra calories into my diet but was amazed to find that the fish would simply pick the bait off the hook. I couldn't believe it when I saw them doing it. A harpoon gun would have been ideal, as Yellowfin tuna would swim right up to the boat on the surface, so close that you could almost grab them if they weren't so fast.

Despite my optimism of finishing before I ran out of food I eventually ran out with about 300 miles to go. When I look back as this time, it was such a silly thing to have let happen and I'm sure if I had pushed myself harder, I could have made the food go further.

I was left with no choice but to call for some outside assistance. I decided to call Simon and he kindly arranged for a support yacht to sail out of Antigua to make an emergency food drop. The yacht would have to beat back into the wind in order to meet me. This was pretty simple as the yacht used for my resupply was an open 60 ex Vendee Globe boat called 'Ocean Planet'. It took two days for the yacht to reach me and by that time, I was physically and mentally drained because I'd still been trying to row every day, despite only having water and no food.

I remember the day clearly. I had a call on the sat phone from the captain of 'Ocean Planet', a guy called Pete. He was a real sea dog and had many ocean crossings to his name, and was, in general, a very experienced yachtsman. He asked me for my position and said he was about six hours away. I carried on rowing, as I hated lying around doing nothing, despite being very hungry. Eventually I was able to pick them up on my AIS radar and, after a few hours, I saw the mast appear over the horizon coming downwind from behind me.

The support yacht had actually sailed past me and turned around in order to make the food drop going downwind so it would be easier. Once they got a little closer, I picked up the hand-held VHF and called them up on the radio. It was great speaking to them but I realised that I was probably trying to talk too much when Pete asked me to be quiet over the radio. As they got closer, I could make Pete out as he and another guy were standing at the helm.

Once they were close enough, I could hear them talking and they both shouted my name. They reduced the sail on 'Ocean Planet' so that it just sailed gently up to the starboard side of Speedo. I was wondering how they were going to get the food to me but it was quite simple: Pete's deck hand threw some floating line to me, which I managed to catch first time. Once I had the line, they placed the dry bag overboard. I pulled the line in and retrieved the bag. It all happened quite quickly, from seeing the support yacht on the horizon, to collecting the food and then watching them sail off into the distance.

It was quite a calm day, so for the next few hours I sat down and started to go through everything that was in the bag. I thought I would have found some chocolate or a few sweet things but there wasn't much in the way of treats. However, I needed the food to fuel me effectively so it was more about having the 'right' food, not the 'nice' food.

I was so hungry by the time the food drop came that I experienced a level of hunger that I'd never experienced before. It was horrible. At the time, I didn't have the energy to do anything. Due to the lack of food and general nutrition, my body was really starting to show signs of fatigue. My gums were cracking and my nails were starting to lift up. I have never used the word 'starving' since my experience of running out of food. It was good, character-building stuff now I look back on the experience and it made me appreciate the simple function of being able to eat when I was hungry, which most of us take for granted these days.

I often thought about the people in the world who aren't so fortunate to be able to call for a food drop when they run out of food. The physical and mental difference was instantaneous as soon as I started eating again. My morale picked up, I started feeling happier and my energy came back straight away. I realised that I had more than enough food to make it into Antigua, which was about 230 miles away. I stowed all the food away and started rowing with a newfound energy and enthusiasm.

JK

As soon as I had sorted one problem out, I was thrown another challenge. This time it was completely out of my control as the wind and currents were pushing me south of Antigua. I was anxious about this as another race competitor who was ahead of me missed Antigua completely and ended up almost 200 miles south, and he had to be towed back up to English Harbour. It didn't really matter that he had still successfully rowed the Atlantic Ocean, it just wasn't really the dream finish that I'd been imagining.

I was getting closer to land and, on my current trajectory, I was on course to arrive south of Guadalupe. I remember panicking as I spoke to my dad on the sat phone, wondering what I should do and how I was going to deal with the situation. Life in an ocean rowing boat can be quite strange at times as things can be going really well then, all of a sudden, your good fortune can be turned on its head in no time at all. With this in mind, I decided not to get too down about the fact I was more than likely going to overshoot Antigua. After all, I had survived almost 3,000 miles of ocean.

I remember going to sleep on the evening of the 107th day. I'm not religious at all but I said to myself as I was falling asleep, looking up at the roof of the cabin, "I pray that everything works out okay". The next day was quite calm as the winds had dropped overnight so the boat was very still. I turned the chart plotter on and it updated my position and showed that I'd drifted northwest overnight, almost 20 miles in the exact direction I needed to be, heading for Antigua.

I sat and watched my position on the chart plotter and, despite very little wind, the currents were very strong and pulling me up to Antigua at around two knots, which was amazing. I couldn't believe how dramatically things had changed in 10 hours, when I was very despondent, thinking that I wasn't going to make it to Antigua at all. Now there was a real chance that I would be able to make some northerly progress and get back on course. I rowed for 16 hours on day 108 and by the time I stopped, I'd covered 55 miles and had only 100 to go.

One thing that really got me excited was seeing aircraft overhead, that I can only assume had taken off from Barbados and were flying north, as they were still quite low. For the entire crossing, I didn't see one aircraft in the sky, not even the white vapour trail that you so often see when you look up. As I started getting closer to the Caribbean, I noticed more debris floating around in the ocean. Bits of fishing net and the odd bit of rubbish would float past. At night you could start to make out an orange glow on the horizon in the night sky. It really was a magical feeling as I started getting closer to Antigua; the adrenaline and excitement was just rushing around my body. In my head, I started playing out different scenarios as to what I thought it would be like when I finished.

On day 109, I was rowing and listening to my iPod, when I heard a noise like a drone that you'd get from an engine or something mechanical. This was certainly not normal. When it's a calm day in the middle of an ocean, you experience a silence like you've never experienced before. I quickly turned around, expecting to see a giant container ship about to run me down, but instead I was greeted by a scene that you'd expect to see on *Miami Vice*. It was a speedboat heading straight towards me at a serious rate of knots.

At first I was relieved that it wasn't a commercial vessel about to flatten me, then I started to feel anxious, as I was alone and very vulnerable. The speedboat was travelling extremely fast, bouncing out of the water as it hit the waves, heading straight for me. As it got closer, I could make out two men who were of local origin wearing bandanas and one of them was holding a machete. My heart started racing and I experienced a huge surge of adrenaline. I honestly thought that these guys were the real *Pirates of the Caribbean*, perhaps wanting to take me hostage and demand a ransom for my return. I just stood there and watched helplessly as they got closer. There was nothing I could have done to prevent them from doing whatever they wanted to do to me.

By now, they had slowed down and I could hear them talking to each other. They were speaking French, which is not uncommon in the Caribbean. They pulled up to within about 30ft of me and I was so nervous, I wasn't sure how to act. I decided to try and come across very confidently so I started waving and trying to speak to them. One of them leant over in the boat and I was wondering what he was going to pull out. He then stood up, smiling, holding a massive Yellowfin tuna. It turned out that they were just fishermen – I was so relieved!

They circled the boat for a few minutes, showing off their fish and then just disappeared. They could have at least given me one of their catch, but they didn't. Sadly, we couldn't communicate as I don't speak French and they didn't speak any English, despite it being the international language of the sea.

As I dipped below the magical '100 miles to go' marker, I was really excited. I was on exactly the same latitude as English Harbour and the currents were pushing me into Antigua. I had been warned about the strong currents that whip around the Eastern coast of Antigua and the harsh coral that was renowned for catching out inexperienced sailors. One of the boats participating in the same race as me was wrecked on the coral a few miles offshore. The currents are extremely strong coming in off the Atlantic Ocean and accelerate as they make their way around the island. The advice from past rowers and sailors who have made the crossing to Antigua was to arrive in the daytime so you can see exactly where you need to be positioned. English Harbour is hidden behind a headland so as you're coming in, you can't actually see the harbour until you are almost in it.

So, knowing that I needed to arrive in the daytime, or at least in some kind of daylight, I worked out that, at my current pace, I would arrive in the middle of the night. As I could see it, there were two options: one would have been to stop rowing and arrive a day later, or try and row non-stop through the night. Rowing through the night would mean I would arrive in the afternoon the next day. I was so excited to get there that I opted to row through the night to try and make it in the following day. I wasn't going to be able to sleep anyway, what with all the adrenaline.

That night went quite quickly and by morning, I was about 55 miles out and could just make out an orange glow in the sky, which would have been the lights of Antigua. The first glimpse of Antigua was at around 45 miles out and I could just make out a bright red light flashing on the horizon. It was very faint but it was the top of a radio mast. I'd heard reports from other rowers that you can see Antigua from 90 miles out, but that certainly wasn't the case for me. If you were on a yacht and higher up then that might be the case. Ocean rowing boats sit very close to the surface so you really can't see that far ahead.

I happened to have an FM radio in the boat that I used to try and pick up BBC World Service on the crossing but I could never really tune anything in that was good enough to listen to. When I saw the red light flashing, I turned the radio on and for the first time throughout the crossing, I picked up some radio stations. The first was a local Antigua station that was playing reggae music. I stopped rowing and listened to the music and the DJ was promoting a local event on the island. It was at this moment that I thought to myself, "I've done it!"

JK

That night passed pretty quickly and every hour I was rowing, I could see the sky above Antigua getting brighter and brighter from the lights shining up at the clouds. Eventually I was able to make out the lights from the buildings and streetlights. It was a beautiful night, with thousands of stars illuminating the sky and just a few fluffy clouds dotted around. It was also a full moon and it happened to be a Friday night. I wondered what my friends and family were doing with their Friday night as I sat there, rowing my last ever night shift.

I stopped to have something to eat on deck and accidentally fell asleep. I woke up about two hours later and saw that the lights of Antigua looked a lot closer. While I had been sleeping, the currents were pulling the boat into the island at almost 2.5 knots, and I wasn't even rowing.

By now it was about 5am and I could start to see the sky to the west getting a little brighter. Eventually the sun made an appearance and just tipped over the horizon and started to climb up into the sky. There wasn't one recreational vessel around but there were a few commercial tankers that passed me.

I really didn't know what to expect when I arrived in Antigua. My parents were not able to make it as their flight was cancelled. About a week before I was due to arrive in Antigua, a volcano had erupted in Iceland, which sent a massive plume of ash into the earth's atmosphere. It was such a vast ash cloud that it was picked up by the jet stream and blown around the world, causing global chaos with airlines having to cancel flights. The ash was dangerous as it could have potentially been sucked into the plane engines. For this reason, there were no flights coming in to or out of Antigua.

I started to see some sailing boats coming out of Antigua at around 8am, so I knew it wouldn't be long until I had some form of contact with people. I heard my sat phone beep as a text message came through. I stopped rowing and went into the cabin to check the message. Just before I picked it up, the phone started to ring. It was another rower who had arrived almost a month earlier, asking me what my position was. I was a bit taken aback as I wasn't quite sure why he was asking me. He told me he was still on the island along with another rower and they were on a sailing boat on their way out to meet me. About an hour later, a yacht was heading my way on my starboard side. As they got closer, I heard people shouting my name; it was two rowers, Dave Brooks and James Denniston. They jumped off the boat, swam over to me and asked to climb aboard.

Dave did extremely well and crossed in a much faster time than me, and James had rowed as a pair with a guy called Sam. I was the second to last boat to finish the race so apart from Dave and James, the other competitors had gone home, as most of them had to get back to work and were running behind schedule anyway.

When they came on board, Dave handed me a beer and we chatted for about 20 minutes. They couldn't believe how much weight I'd lost, as I was quite stocky before I set off in La Gomera. I had to apologise as my bucket, which I'd used as the toilet, was sitting on deck with some pretty nasty stains inside it. I quickly threw it out of the way.

Dave and James told me that everyone on the island knew I was arriving and it was going to be crazy, as it was also Antigua Sailing Week. I didn't really have any idea what they were talking about or how people would know that I was arriving.

Antigua Sailing Week is a regatta with crews coming from all over the world to race their yachts around the island. It's mostly made up of wealthy Americans who come down to the Caribbean for their vacation. James and Dave drank their beers and then jumped off to swim back to their yacht. By this time, there were quite a few boats out and about and I was only around 10 miles from land.

I was now getting yachts coming by quite close, waving and cheering. Most of them were asking how long I had been at sea for and generally congratulating me. One chap on a boat was asking me if my parents were here and would they like to jump on his yacht so he could bring them out to see me row in. When I explained they weren't on the island, he couldn't believe it, and invited me to stay in their villa with them. He couldn't have been friendlier.

With around six miles to go, a local Antigua and Barbuda Search and Rescue rib came out to guide me in. Simon was on board and it was great to see him as we had got on quite well, especially after the fiasco in Cornwall on the training row when the RNLI were called out.

The strong currents could quite easily have pulled me in to shore so it was nice to have them keeping an eye out and passing the local knowledge on. Luckily for me, the weather was perfect on the day I arrived. There was a very calm, light breeze so conditions were good. One thing that really struck me was just how blue the water was. I've never seen an ocean or sea as blue as the Caribbean.

For the whole crossing, I'd not really used the GPS much as I just couldn't stand looking at my speed, which was so slow. A few days before I left La Gomera, my fellow rower from South Africa, Peter Van Kets, helped me upload my waypoints into the chart plotter. When we loaded the last waypoint in, which was actually the finish about three miles out of English Harbour, I always wondered what it would be like to watch the GPS as I crossed the finish line.

So I had the GPS running with less than one mile to go until 1 crossed the finish line. My eyes were fixed on the GPS repeater that was mounted on the deck. Slowly, every few minutes, 0.1 of a mile would pass. I was looking around at all the other boats and suddenly heard a loud claxon go off. It was Simon on the support rib shouting, "Well done, you've crossed the finish line!" I looked at the repeater and sure enough, I had crossed the finish line and the count down to the waypoint was at zero! I had completed the 2010 Woodvale Atlantic Ocean Rowing Race in 110 days, four hours and four minutes.

All the other yachts started sounding their horns and cheering. I still couldn't see the main harbour as it was around the headland. There was still about three miles to go into English Harbour from the finish line and technically, once I'd crossed the finish line, I could have taken a tow into the harbour but I just didn't like the thought of that. I wanted my crossing to be land to land.

There was so much activity going on in the water and people cheering for me that the three miles passed in the blink of an eye. I rounded the headland into Nelson's Dockyard and couldn't believe my eyes. There was a mass of luxury boats and super yachts moored up with palm trees all around the harbour; it was a truly beautiful sight. I then saw flares going off, being waved in the hands of people standing at one of the pontoons.

When I looked around, there were hundreds of people everywhere. Simon was next to me in the support rib with a big smile on his face, "They are all here to welcome you in, you've arrived at the best possible time – Antigua Sailing Week." I now knew what Dave and James were talking about earlier. All of the super yachts started to sound their horns and people were cheering and clapping everywhere. I rowed up to the pontoon and started to take my last few strokes on the oars. I deliberately slowed up, just drifting into the dock while looking at all the faces of people who were standing there, cheering for me.

As I took the last stroke of a 3,000-mile row, something quite surreal happened. I thought to myself, this is it: the last stroke of this incredible adventure and all of this will be over. I took the stroke and halfway through, with the blade in the water, the gate that holds the oar in place snapped. I couldn't believe it – that truly signified the end of the row. I did have a spare one but obviously I didn't need it. What were the chances of that happening? Of all the millions of strokes that I'd taken over four months, it broke on the last one.

As the bow slowly touched up against the dock wall, there was an incredibly loud cheer. Simon had already got off the rib and was there to moor the boat. I then heard "Three cheers for Speedo!" and the crowd gave me three cheers. It was a feeling that I don't think I will ever experience in my life again.

I saw Pete in the crowd; the guy who'd sailed out to make the food drop. Simon told me that everyone on the island had been tracking me on the race website and had come down to support me, as I was one of the last rowers to finish. He then spread the word that my parents were not able to make it (which I had told him on the sat phone a few days earlier) and the support and kindness that was bestowed on me was incredible. I stepped out of the boat and was greeted by a woman who I had never met before. She lived on the island and apparently knew my aunt. What a small world it is. She was very friendly and familiar with me, as if she'd known me for years. I was then passed a bottle of rum by a local woman who I can only assume was from the Tourist Board, as she officially welcomed me to Antigua. I looked up and there were so many people staring at me, it was like being a celebrity for a few hours. Guys were coming up to me asking if their wives could have their photo taken with me. It doesn't happen any more for some reason, but it was quite good fun at the time.

5

Returning in style

There was a hotel in front of the pontoon where I had landed and they offered to cook me any meal of my choice. For the whole crossing, I had a crazy craving for a BLT sandwich but at that moment, I really fancied a cheeseburger and chips, as well as a glass of ice cold Coke. It was almost impossible to keep anything cold on the boat, especially water, so most days I would end up drinking warm water, which didn't taste great. So the thought of something cold was like heaven to my taste buds.

The waiter returned quickly with a glass of ice cold Coke. It was so refreshing, I will never forget that moment. A few minutes later, he came out with the burger and I sat down at a table right on the water's edge. By now, most of the crowd had dispersed but there were still people chatting with me and taking photos of the boat. I guess they thought it was a big deal to row across the Atlantic.

The burger looked absolutely fantastic and I couldn't wait to tuck in. I took a bite and to my utter disappointment, it was stone cold! My first meal on land, which I had spent almost four months dreaming about, was cold - I couldn't believe it. I didn't have the heart to tell the waiter because it still tasted pretty good, so I carried on eating.

Later on, Simon gave me a lift to the hotel my parents had booked for me. It was set back about half a mile from Nelson's Dockyard and was up on a hill, with the most stunning views of the marina. The next thing I was really looking forward to was a decent shower. I did have a wash about 24 hours prior to arriving in Antigua but my hair was thick with grease and I think I probably smelt quite bad. I guess I was used to my own smell, spending so long alone. I had saved some Hugo Boss shower gel that I'd only used on the row at milestone markers. I was looking forward to using it at the hotel but when I stepped into the shower and turned the water on, nothing more than a cold dribble came out.

That evening, I managed to catch up with Dave and James who were staying on the island as they were planning to sail back to Europe. Simon also came out and we went to the local nightclub. It was a very surreal situation, as 10 hours earlier, I was in the same boat that I had been in for almost four months, and now, I was in the middle of a packed nightclub, with people jumping up and down around me. My legs were not really up for dancing as they were pretty weak; I hadn't been weight-bearing or walking around for quite a while. I was chatting to a group of girls who were asking me why I had a massive beard, when I heard the DJ talking about a guy called James who had just rowed across the Atlantic. "Massive respect to James Ketchell who has just spent 110 days rowing across the Atlantic and is in here with us all tonight!" Everyone started cheering and he went on to say, "After 110 days at sea, your balls must be massive! Let's hope that there are some lovely ladies who can help you sort that out later." The crowed just roared with laughter.

It came round to about 2am and things were pretty lively. I was still taking everything in and trying to digest what I had just completed. It was time to head back to the hotel and to my amazement, Simon pulled up in the car outside the club. It turned out that there are no real rules around drinking and driving in Antigua. It's not something that I condone but if you can drive straight and stay on the road, that appeared to be good enough and the police were not interested, or had other things to worry about.

That night, when I got into bed, it felt quite strange lying there flat with no movement at all. I woke up several times to find myself in a braced position, similar to how I had slept on the boat.

Over the next couple of days, I chilled out, waiting for my parents to arrive who had finally managed to get their flights rearranged, after the ash cloud had subsided. I managed to borrow a car and drove up to the airport to collect them. I'd deliberately kept my beard for them to see. I parked up and stood by the exit, waiting for them. To my amazement, they came out and walked straight past me! I then went and stood in front of them – they couldn't believe what I looked like and didn't recognise me at all, until they looked into my eyes. My hair was completely blonde and I was tanned beyond recognition: quite different from the last time they had seen me in the Canary Islands.

That evening, we went out to have our first family meal together on the island. As I was just about to sit down to eat, a dark-haired chap with a big smile on his face came over to me, "Excuse me, are you the guy who just rowed the Atlantic?" he asked. "You arrived a few days ago, right?"

"Yes, that's me," I replied. These were his exact words: "Fuck me, can I buy you a beer?" My parents and I laughed and asked him if he wanted to join us for a drink. His name was also James and he was in Antigua for a corporate sailing event with some business partners.

A friendly chap, he asked if I would speak at his daughter's school in Putney when I returned home. We chatted for a while and he handed me one of his business cards before heading off with his colleagues. I didn't think anything of the meeting until I received a £500 donation on my Justgiving website page. I instantly dropped him an email to thank him for his generosity, and to float the idea of his company sponsoring my next project. James asked me what charity I would be doing it for and I said it would be for a children's charity but I hadn't decided which one yet. He then told me about a wonderful charity called the ELIFAR Foundation. It's a very small charity that helps and supports families with disabled children, by providing specialist kit to help improve their quality of life. They only turned over around £80,000 a year, which is nothing in the charity sector. The charity was also formed and managed by James' business partner who had two severely disabled children who tragically died.

When I rowed the Atlantic, I raised £10,000 for a major children's charity but was treated in an appalling way by the charity representative at the time. I was quite naive to charities and how they operated and, although I certainly wasn't expecting much from them in terms of support, their engagement (or lack of) with me was quite eye-opening. It wasn't really the charity's fault, just the unprofessionalism demonstrated by that representative.

Early on in the project, I received a shocking email saying how she had heard that I wasn't happy with a few things, and went on to tell me how lucky I was to be raising money for them. If I didn't like it, I could go somewhere else. I was then told I would have to sign a contract that the charity's lawyers would put together, if I still wanted to use their name as my chosen charity. This was a real shock and I had no idea where this had come from. The contract never appeared and I questioned if I should carry on supporting them as my charity, as this was very early on in the project. I decided that I wouldn't let the actions of one person tarnish the reputation of a charity that was doing some much-needed work.

I'm a true believer that, if you work hard and push yourself outside your comfort zone, doors of opportunity will naturally open. I'd certainly pushed myself out of my comfort zone on many occasions for the past 110 days. I was sitting in a bar in Nelson's Dockyard one lunchtime, eating a large bowl of chocolate ice cream, when a friendly woman approached me and asked me how I was doing. She said she had seen my arrival a few days ago and congratulated me on what she said was an amazing feat. I asked her if she wanted to join me for ice cream and we started chatting.

Her name was Tina and she was on the island with her husband, Tony. They had sailed over a few months ago from the Canary Islands to St. Lucia in an organised crossing called the ARC (Atlantic Rally for Cruisers). They had sailed over to Antigua for Sailing Week and they happened to be dockside as I arrived.

She asked me how long I spent in the shower when I got to the hotel and joked that apparently I stank when I arrived but no one had the heart to tell me. We laughed about it. She then asked me how I was getting home as there was still a large backlog of people trying to get off the island due to the ash cloud which had grounded so many flights.

Tina told me she was sailing back to Europe with her husband and they were short-handed and asked if I fancied joining them. At first I thought she was joking. I didn't really know what to think as I'd just spent almost four months on my own in a 23ft long rowing boat. But I realised it would be a fantastic way of dragging out an already amazing adventure. I said I didn't have a great deal of sailing experience apart from a few weekends on the Isle of Wight. She laughed and said that rowing the Atlantic solo was more than adequate experience, in her opinion.

Tina asked me if I wanted to have a look round the boat so we walked over and I met her husband, Tony, who I could instantly tell was a very friendly guy. The yacht was a 54-foot Sun Odyssey, which is a fairly high-end yacht, capable of circumnavigating the globe. I stepped up on to the back of the boat and Tony offered me a drink, while we sat on deck and chatted for a while. Tina showed me around the boat, starting with the bow cabin, which was the master bedroom with an en-suite shower.

It really was an incredible boat and I couldn't believe how lucky I was to be given the chance to sail back to Europe on it. We finished the tour with another drink on deck, "So, James do we have another crew member then?" asked Tony.

"You sure do," I replied.

I couldn't wait to get out there again but I still had a week of holiday left in Antigua. I told my parents that I intended to sail back across the Atlantic and to my surprise, they thought it was a great idea. We spent the next week relaxing and I took the opportunity to have a haircut and shave. It was quite funny as I was unrecognisable after I'd been to the barber.

Over the past few days, I'd forgotten that I'd actually left a lot of personal items (some of which, like my camera and laptop, were very valuable to me) in Speedo, which was still tied up in English Harbour. It was quite stupid of me to leave these items lying around in the boat as there was no lock on the hatch and anyone could have taken them, but luckily they hadn't. After I had cleared Speedo out, it was time to arrange and prep the boat for shipping back to the UK. It was quite a simple process: I just had to secure everything in the boat and lash the oars down, then the boat would be lifted out of the water on to a cradle and pushed into a container.

After an amazing 10 days relaxing with my family and catching up with friends over Skype, the time finally came to leave Antigua and sail back to Europe with Tina and Tony. There were also two other crew members, John, who was one of Tina and Tony's friends, who had a fair bit of sailing experience, and Artar, a young German lad in his early 20s who had been sailing in the Caribbean and was on his way back to Europe. He was a smart young man who carried himself with confidence. He was fluent in English and spoke very good Spanish and Portuguese.

The first day was spent in a place called Jolly Harbour, stocking the boat up with food and supplies for the crossing. We then went out for a meal in the evening and socialised over a few beers. The next morning, we were up at around 7am to have time for breakfast, which consisted of a trip to Subway, and then to clear Immigration before making our way home. We sailed out of Jolly Harbour and headed north, coming up the west side of the island which is protected by the winds and currents from the Atlantic.

It was a beautiful day with a light breeze and the sea had a magnificent glimmer, as the sun's rays were beating down on the water and reflecting on our faces. The route that we were going to take heading back to Europe would be quite different to the route I'd taken from La Gomera to Antigua. On the way across, I was being carried by the winds and the currents. It would have been possible to sail back into that but it was not the ideal route. It would be slow and very rough, so we planned to sail north up to Bermuda following the Gulf Stream and southerly winds that would take us north.

At this point, we would start to pick up the Atlantic current, which moves from the West across to the East, as well as the prevailing westerly winds that would blow us back to the Azores and then on to Portugal. The first few days were really exciting as we had some great weather which was taking us north and we were covering around 150 miles per day, which wasn't bad, considering our leisurely pace. It was still very warm with lovely blue skies and a crystal clear ocean but it wasn't long before that changed and the sky became more overcast and the temperature dropped quite considerably. We were now almost 400 miles north of Antigua and only 100 miles from Bermuda.

We hadn't planned on stopping over in Bermuda and passed to the east of the island. As predicted, the winds started to turn and we made good easterly progress until we hit an area of high pressure, where we had no wind at all for two days. As John and I were on a bit of a tight schedule to get home (I was already a couple of months late going back to work), Tony decided to use the motor. I was amazed at the range the boat had on one full tank of diesel – almost 1,500 miles – which would be half of our crossing. One of the support yachts from the rowing race was an ex-global challenge boat designed to sail around the world the wrong way into the winds. It was made of steel and had a range of 3,000 miles on a full tank of diesel. The theory was that if de-masted, it would be able to motor to safety, no matter where it was.

We broke the sailing up into two shift patterns: Arta and I would be with Tony and we would usually be on watch through the nights. Tina and John would take the other shift. I remember there were times when we would be out in the middle of the night and the sky would look amazing. "I have no idea how you were able to row the Atlantic," Tony would often say to me. We were crossing in absolute luxury in comparison to my rowing boat.

Tony was an incredibly kind person who had made his money after he sold his architecture business. He was very wise and we'd talk for hours about all the things I wanted to do and all the things that he still wanted to do. For everything that he wanted to achieve, he seemed to have some kind of entrepreneurial angle for how he could make his idea not only possible, but profitable. One of them was setting up a sailing school in the Mediterranean; he had it all figured out in his head as to how it would work. He asked me what I was going to do when I got home. At the time, I was working for a large American IT distribution company as an Account Manager. Luckily, they had granted me a sabbatical and put some money into the rowing project so I was obliged to go back to that job.

I explained how I used to be a personal trainer and accidently fell into a sales role. I was made redundant from my local gym where I worked for five years, and needed to find some other employment. I wasn't bothered what it was; I just needed money to pay for my food and supplements as my whole life revolved around the gym at that time. I found a job in a warehouse, which was fairly standard and not very well paid but it put money in my pocket. One of the products they sold was folding bikes. We would get lots of returns coming back into the warehouse and I loved anything on two wheels, so I would make up complete bikes from faulty ones and put them back into stock. I was then asked if I wanted to attend a trade show to promote and sell the bikes. It sounded like a good deal, as I was only really interested in the overtime. I went to the show and ended up selling twice as many bikes as anyone else, without really trying. Consequently, I was offered a job in sales the very next week and never looked back.

JK

I made sure I took my satellite phone with me when I sailed home so I could stay in contact with the people who needed to know my whereabouts. I had it up on deck with me one day as I was using it to download some grib files. These are used to overlay weather information on a chart. Suddenly, my phone started ringing and a number came up I didn't recognise. I wondered who on earth it would be, as everyone who had this number was saved on to the phone. I answered it tentatively and was greeted by a deep, male voice: "Ketch, when the bloody hell are you coming back to work?" It was my boss, Andy, an all-round good guy. He was the Sales Manager and had been instrumental in arranging for me to have a sabbatical so I had a lot to thank him for. Whenever the phones rang more than twice in the office, he would shout, "Phones!" basically telling someone to answer it immediately. He was an old school salesman who had been in the industry for a long time.

As my schedule was so delayed and I should have been back at work nearly two months ago, he was getting slightly concerned. I told him that it was all under control as I was on my way home. I was expecting him to ask me where I was but, to my amazement, he had no idea he was speaking to me from the middle of the Atlantic Ocean.

About half way between Bermuda and the Azores, we experienced some slightly bigger seas as the wind picked up. I thought it was really good fun and secretly wanted the wind to pick up and the seas to become bigger. By this point, I felt very at home at sea and was craving some excitement. One thing that did strike me was, if you're looking to learn how to sail, an ocean crossing is not really the best way to go about it. Tony and Tina's boat was quite a serious bit of kit and had a sophisticated autopilot system, so most of the time, you didn't even need to be at the helm, as long as someone was keeping a watch. Once the boat is set up and the wind doesn't change direction, there is actually very little to do and the autopilot will adjust to the changes in wind direction.

Most of the time we didn't use the autopilot and manually helmed the boat instead to stave off the boredom. Also, for anyone suffering with sea sickness, the best place for them would be at the helm because looking at the horizon and concentrating on steering the boat would help take their mind off the sickness. Thankfully, I was never sick and would quite often volunteer to go down in to the galley to make food or wash the dishes when it was rougher, and the boat was rolling all over the place. If you were ever going to succumb to sea sickness, it would be in the galley. I guess 110 days at sea already meant that my equilibrium had adjusted to the roll of the waves.

We were averaging around six hours' sleep a day, which was enough, as the watch systems were not physically difficult. One particular evening, I came out of the shower all fresh and clean, wearing a new T-shirt, which had that new smell that I'd craved after nearly four months of wearing the same dirty clothes. The other guys were all up on deck having a barbecue and enjoying some beers. As I poked my head up through the galley, the smell of the barbecue sent my senses crazy. Tony was frying some steak! Arta threw me a beer and I sat down, looking up at the sky, which was absolutely beautiful, as the sun was starting to set. I thought to myself, if you're ever going to cross an ocean, this is the way to do it. We started to get closer to our first destination, which was Horta on the island of Faial in the Azores.

Arta and I were discussing what we were going to do when we arrived and we came to the conclusion we would find a bar and have a few drinks and chat to some locals. We didn't physically see the island of Faial until we were about 20 miles out as it was a very foggy day.

The next day, Tina, Tony, John, Arta and I hired a car and went for a drive around the island. That evening, John and I started to chat about the idea of flying back to Lisbon from Horta so we could get home quicker. I was starting to run out of time as I'd been away from work for over seven months and was lucky they were still holding my job open for me. John was also running short of time. If we sailed from Horta to Lisbon, it would take around seven days, which was making things very tight for me.

Tony and Tina also weren't sure when they were going to leave Horta. I worked out that if they left the next day, I might just have time to make it all the way to Lisbon. However, there was a storm front of low pressure arriving, which didn't look too good. It was looking very likely that they would not be sailing anywhere for at least four days. John and I made the decision that we had to leave and fly back to Lisbon.

We started looking at available flights and booked one for the next day. The adventure really had come to an end and it felt slightly strange packing all my kit away that evening. The next morning, we got up and had a nice breakfast and then said our goodbyes. John and I had managed to get on the same flights from Horta to Lisbon and back to London Gatwick. It was quite surreal when the taxi arrived at the dock to collect us for the airport. To think back on the journey I'd experienced since I was last in the UK was quite crazy.

I personally believe that people come in and out of your life for a reason, and meeting Tony and Tina was something that was meant to happen I think. We waved goodbye and headed to the airport. Sadly, for no particular reason, I've never spoken to Tony and Tina again and they probably have no idea what I've been up to since leaving them.

It was only a quick 90-minute flight to Lisbon, and John and I managed to sit next to each other. We changed planes at Lisbon and two hours later, we were back in the UK.

Above: Before: Hard at work on the preparations for a new paint job.

Below: After: The boat is ready for packing and shipping to La Gomera for the Atlantic row.

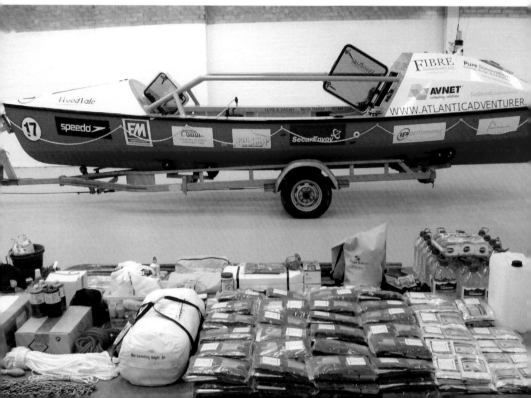

Above: Selfie in the middle of the Atlantic, just after opening my Christmas presents.
Below: The beard at 80 days in.

Above: Arriving to cheers and applause in English Harbour, Nelson's Dockyard, Antigua.
Below: Sailing back across the Atlantic. From left: Tina, Arta, John, myself and Tony.

Above: Feeling tired about to start our descent from Camp 4.

Left: Ladder crossing at the Khumbu icefall at the foot of the Western Cwm, 5,500m.

Below: Charles at Base Camp after successfully summiting.

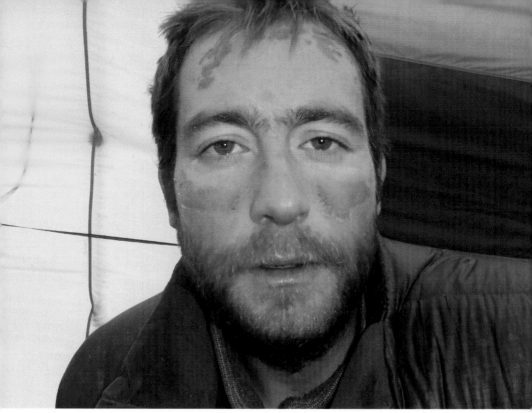

Above: My weather damaged face at Base Camp after summiting.

Right: Camp 4 – above 8,000m in the 'Death Zone'.

Below: My Sherpa, Dorje, to whom I owe my life.

Above: The scarily short runway at Lukla airport, Everest.

6

Acclimatisation

It was quite odd being back; I couldn't stop thinking about everything that had happened over the past seven months. It was nice sleeping in my own bed again and catching up with friends. The day I got back, I went to see my best friend, Andy. Apart from a quick chat over the phone in Antigua, I hadn't spoken to him the whole time I'd been away. After a few days at home catching up with friends and running some errands, I went back to work. It was quite weird for the first few days as everyone was congratulating me on the row and wanted to know all about it. I was teased quite a lot as I was one of the last boats to cross the line and everyone in the office had been tracking me on the race website. They wanted to know why I was so slow, but it was only in jest. One of the directors, Dave Park, was a great supporter of the row and managed to get one of the vice presidents to donate £5,000 to my chosen charity, on behalf of the company. A lot of my work colleagues were also very generous with their donations.

After a few weeks back, with the novelty of the row inevitably wearing off, I was quite restless and struggling to concentrate. I still turned up to work and did my job every day, as routine and structure are very important. As soon as I slipped out of a routine during the row, which happened while I was on para anchor, I really struggled to get things done.

The question I was being asked all the time was, "What's next?" I knew secretly in my head that it was going to be Everest, following on from the conversations I'd had with Rob, who I stayed with in La Gomera prior to the row. I didn't want to say anything to friends and family though as it was too soon. I just knew after I finished the row that things had changed for me but I still couldn't quite put my finger on what that change was.

I'd been back a few months and decided to get in contact with James, the guy I'd met in Antigua, who'd put the large donation on my fundraising site and who had asked me to speak at his daughter's school. We caught up and chatted about things in general and he introduced me to his business partner, Paul, who set up and ran the ELIFAR Foundation, supporting disabled children. I alluded to the fact that I was probably going to climb Everest but agreed nevertheless to align ELIFAR to whatever my next project was going to be. I didn't talk too much about Everest at this point.

A few weeks later, I received a call from Rob. The last time I'd spoken to him was in the Atlantic and he was being picked up by one of the support boats, as he had run out of time to finish his row due to a guiding commitment on Everest.

"Ketch, it's Rob here. So tell me, are you coming to Everest then?"

"Yes, I'm in!"

"Great, you have six months to find £30,000."

"Damn! How on earth am I going to do this?" I thought to myself. But it was like I couldn't help myself. My natural reaction was to say yes.

I quickly realised that if I could row an ocean on my own, I could at least have a go at raising the funds to get out to Everest. I truly believe that I didn't do anything special in the Atlantic, I 'just kept going'. If I just kept approaching companies and individuals who I thought might be able to help me, then surely at some point I would get lucky and stumble across the funding?

Rob also said that I should head out to Nepal with him to get some experience at altitude and climb Island Peak, a very straightforward, 6,000m peak. I needed about three weeks off work and suspected that I wouldn't be granted any more time off. I was expecting to have to leave my job. I spoke to my parents and they were surprisingly supportive.

The next day I went into work and asked to speak to my boss, Andy. I thought, well, if you don't ask, you don't get!

"Ketch, on your bike son. Have you gone mad? You can't surely be asking for more time off?" I will never forget his face; I always chuckle when I think of Andy's comment.

As I'd expected, I ended up leaving my job, but when I explained the situation, not wanting to let the opportunity to get out to Everest slip away, everyone completely understood and they were incredibly supportive. I didn't need to leave until I was due to head out to Nepal in October so I had a couple of months left to prepare. I started with the sponsorship campaign and, at every opportunity, I would promote the climb and seek funding and support.

On my return from the Atlantic, I was asked to give talks at local Scout groups and networking events. I couldn't stand the term 'motivational speaking'. I thought it was cheesy, so I took the perspective of just telling my story, from having the accident to rowing the Atlantic, with supporting videos and photos.

There was a local event in a village called Odiham, just outside Basingstoke. It was a networking event in a pub and the organiser told me it would be a good place to look for potential sponsors. I gave my talk and got chatting to a few people afterwards. One of them was a guy called Mike who said he didn't know how he could help at this stage but he really liked my story and wanted to do something to support me. He would prove to be invaluable and he became a good friend, as did someone else in the audience that night, a guy called Richard who had masses of enthusiasm and was very friendly. He was the MD of a website design company and offered to build a new website for my Everest expedition.

I was still finding my feet in the world of speaking and did a lot of talks for free to begin with. Depending on the audience, every time I was up on stage, I looked at it as a great way to promote Everest and seek out potential sponsors. I really enjoyed speaking as I was sharing my own story and it was something I was passionate about; public speaking also came quite naturally to me. I was then asked to speak at other events and people were offering to pay me for my time.

I started to try and get the money together to go out to Nepal and a friend mentioned to me that he delivered Chinese takeaways in the evening for the local Chinese restaurant. I said I'd be very interested in doing that too if he could introduce me to the right person. I started the following weekend.

It really wasn't much money but if I was out delivering food on a Friday and Saturday night, it also meant that I wasn't out spending money either. It wasn't the most glamorous job and I soon discovered that most people in the large houses on the nice estates, who clearly had money, were by far the tightest when it came to tips. Those people who didn't have the big houses and flashy cars were actually far more generous. The money wouldn't really make any difference to the Everest project but it just made me feel like I was going that extra mile and, after all, doing something is better than doing nothing.

I had some A5 brochures produced to promote the climb and

the ELIFAR Foundation, and I would hand them out to people as I delivered their takeaway food to them. I did wonder if it would ever get back to the restaurant but nobody complained. One generous guy gave me a £200 donation to the project. I gave half to the charity and put the other half into the project. Fundraising is tough and not for the faint-hearted, because it can be mostly rejection. My sales background certainly stood me in good stead, as I knew it was just a numbers game.

JK

October rolled around and it was soon time to head out to Nepal for some acclimatisation and climbing with Rob. Another solo Atlantic rower, Leo, was also coming with us, as he'd been part of the original conversation about climbing Everest in La Gomera. Leo was an incredibly motivated and determined man despite being in his 60s. He had already tried to row the Atlantic, before he successfully crossed in 2010 on his second attempt. The first time, he'd had to be rescued by the Spanish coastguard, as five days into his row, he was incredibly seasick and started vomiting up blood. He was in no state to continue and was deteriorating quickly. Most people would have given up completely on the idea but, with dogged determination, he tried again and made it.

Leo was living in Boston and was going to meet Rob and I in Kathmandu. I was really excited to see Rob again; he just had an aura about him that was amazing to be around and he was a fine example of selflessness and kindness. He was also an incredibly strong-minded individual, which I really admired. We booked ourselves onto the same Virgin flight so we could travel to Nepal together.

At the time, I had a friend who was working for Virgin as cabin crew and she had changed her roster to be on our flight, so would try and upgrade us if she could. I really talked her up and told Rob that my friend who was working on the flight would move us up to First Class. I met Rob at Terminal Three Heathrow and, in his typical style, he was late but we just made the flight. Rob was always running around doing something or other and was late for most things. He's either terrible at balancing his commitments or he is simply doing too much, I still can't decide.

I called my friend at Virgin about an hour before we were due to board, but I didn't get a reply, so I just assumed she was busy. We boarded the plane and I sat down and looked around for my friend: there were plenty of cabin crew milling about but I couldn't see her. I asked one of the cabin crew if she could tell my friend what seat I was in, as I figured that maybe she was working in First Class. She looked at me as if I'd just fallen out of the last rain cloud and said she had no idea who this person was and that she was in charge of all the crew on this flight. My heart sank and I felt like such an idiot. I'd been telling Rob how great the flight would be as my friend was running the cabin. Rob just laughed when I told him. I don't think there have been many times when I've felt so embarrassed.

We arrived in Delhi, which was our first stopover, as we couldn't fly direct to Kathmandu. We had just over 24 hours in Delhi so we checked into a cheap hotel called Hotel Rak in the city centre. It was Ramadan at the time, so most people were fasting and alcohol was not available legally. The first thing the guy behind the counter told us was that, if we wanted to buy some alcohol, he could get it for us. We declined the offer and went to our room. It had two beds and a shower and it has to be one of the filthiest rooms I've ever stayed in. There were blood stains all over the sheets, so we stripped the bed and just slept on the mattress. It was a very cheap hotel, around £5 a night, so we didn't complain. That evening, we went out to explore the city and decided that the best way to get around was to hire a Tuk Tuk. We asked the driver to take us on a guided tour of Delhi, which he took great pleasure in doing.

After about three hours in the Tuk Tuk, and several times where I thought we were going to crash, due to his crazy driving, Rob and I were getting slightly anxious. We asked him to take us back to the hotel but he refused and insisted that we finish the tour. He then drove to a really rough-looking area where homeless people were living. We were wondering what to do at this point as it was dark and we had no idea where he was taking us. We concluded there wasn't much we could do so we decided to go with the flow; it turned out that he was just taking a short cut to another attraction. An hour later, we arrived back at the hotel and the driver insisted that we take a photo of him standing proudly by his tuk tuk. He used a large walking pole to get around, as one of his legs was a lot shorter than the other. It was a real relief to make it back safely after one of the craziest tuk tuk rides we'd ever experienced.

The next morning, we flew into Kathmandu. It wasn't dissimilar to Delhi, just a whole mass of people everywhere and intense heat. We broke into a sweat as soon as we stepped outside. I had never travelled to India or Nepal before and it was a real eye-opener when I saw how most people were living their lives. Children were playing in sewers and on piles of rubbish that had been tossed into the street; wild dogs were roaming around, while cows just stood in the road, totally oblivious to the fact they were blocking all the traffic. Cows are sacred in both India and Nepal so traffic would be extra careful not to run them over. What struck me most was the noise: it was just a constant barrage of horns beeping, as people tried to negotiate the roads without crashing into one another.

Rob and I arrived at the hotel where we met Leo and four others who were going to join us. They all seemed lovely people and I was really looking forward to what lay ahead. The next day, we went for a tour around Kathmandu to the Monkey Temple and to the famous Bagmati River, considered to be the source of Nepalese civilisation. The Bagmati River also runs parallel to one of Nepal's most important Hindu temples. Along the side of the temple, plateaus are made for open-air cremations to be carried out as Hindus are cremated on the banks of the river. The locals believe the river purifies their souls. It's quite a strange sight: locals bathe in the water for spiritual purposes and to clean, yet the remains of those cremated will be swept into the river only metres away from them.

I remember when I was told that there would be open-air cremations, I didn't really know what to picture in my head but it was quite an interesting experience. The family of the deceased gathered around the body, which would be wrapped in cloth. A platform of wood and straw makes up a frame that the body lies on and more wood is then placed over the body. One of the family members - usually the eldest child of the deceased - will light the fire. It's very smoky to begin with as a layer of hay is placed on top of the fire, which is soaked in water from the river, for spiritual purposes. It takes a good couple of hours for the body to burn away to ashes. It wasn't the gory sight that I'd imagined and you actually can't see a great deal through the smoke and flames. Occasionally, the wooden frame that the body is placed on would collapse and a half burnt limb would protrude out of the side.

After the day trip around the local sights, it was time to head back to the hotel, as we had to catch our flight to the Himalayas at 6am the following day. We arrived back at Kathmandu's Tribhuvan International Airport to a mass of chaos, with people everywhere and porters stacked high with luggage. The company Rob was using for the logistics, Himalayan Guides, was brilliant and the Managing Director, Iswari, was there to sort everything out. There was a local man passing through the security check-in in front of me and, when the guards checked his rucksack, they pulled out a large hunting knife. To my amazement, they put it back in the bag and let him pass through. It was only a domestic flight so I guessed that their laws on security were not that tight.

The flight was only an hour from Kathmandu into Lukla, which is the start of the Everest trail into the National Park. We flew in a small twin-engine plane, which could only hold about 20 passengers. It was quite an adventurous flight, thanks to a lot of turbulence. Rob had told me to sit on the left-hand side of the plane, as the views up over the Himalayas were simply awesome. He wasn't wrong: it was one of the most stunning sights I'd ever seen.

The Himalayas are home to the planet's highest peaks, including over 100 mountains that exceed 7,200m in elevation. A lot of them are actually unclimbed and will probably remain unclimbed, as most of them are sacred in both Buddhist and Hindu religions. It really was an incredible vision – you just can't grasp the sheer size of the mountains; protruding high up into the skies, unless you're witnessing them with your own eyes.

The breathtaking views made the flight pass in a flash and it was soon time to land. It was a small plane with a single aisle for passengers to get on and off and one seat on either side. I peered out down the aisle into the cockpit and could see the entire flight deck. In the distance was a tiny strip of tarmac that had evidently just been cut into the foothills of the Himalayas at Lukla. It was getting closer and closer. As we dropped altitude, the mountains and hilltops were now standing high on either side of us as we flew down into the valley. The pilot was almost wrestling with the control wheel as the plane was bobbing up and down in the turbulence. As we got closer, I realised just how skilled these pilots really were. There was no room for error whatsoever: overshoot the runaway or come up short, and you'd be straight into the side of the mountain.

7

Reaching the peaks

There was a loud thud as we touched down. Set at 2,800m, the Tenzing – Hillary Airport is so small it can only accommodate twin Otter or Dornier aircraft. The runway is set at a 12 per cent incline so gravity helps slow things down as the aircraft touch down. Only a couple of minutes after landing, we were disembarking and ushered out of the bustling airport. In the height of the trekking season, there can be up to 100 flights a day landing and taking off at Lukla.

The first thing that really hit me was the altitude, as we were at almost 3,000m. The air was cold and thin and I noticed just how out of breath I was simply from walking up some steps and round the back of the runway. We headed for a local lodge where Rob knew the owners and had breakfast. Lukla appeared to be mostly made up of lodges and shops, selling trekking equipment and souvenirs. It had a real frontier feel to it as lots of people were either coming or going, at the start of the Everest trail. Lots of new trekkers with their shiny boots and new rucksacks were waiting around for their guides and porters, having their photos taken. For as many people that were about to embark on their trek, there were just as many tired but happy faces coming back down off the trail.

All of our kit was divided up in to larger bags and would be collected for the porters to carry. We always had a day sack with us that would hold water, food and spare clothes. The idea being that if you got stuck on the trail, you had enough provisions and equipment to survive the night.

I was standing around, waiting for the rest of our group to set off after our breakfast and I noticed a couple of young boys picking up our main kit bags which had been left for the porters to carry. Rob walked over and could see me looking at the boys. "It's okay, they're our porters."

I couldn't believe these young boys were going to carry our bags, which must have weighed about 40 kilograms. I felt pretty embarrassed that they were carrying our main bulk of kit but Rob reassured me it was completely normal and they were very grateful for the work. Mount Everest is situated in the Khumbu Valley of Nepal and most of the children start to carry things on their backs as soon as they can walk.

We started our day slowly and walked at a very gentle pace. It was quite an odd experience, just walking up a simple set of steps, of which there were plenty, on a trail that would completely take your breath away, leaving you panting like a dog for oxygen. The key was just to take oxygen in nice and slowly. Rob was quite amazing and didn't appear to be affected by the lack of oxygen at all.

The first day was over after about five hours of walking and, to celebrate, we all had an ice-cold beer. The following day, we were up at around 6am and were on the trail just after 7am. We were heading to the village of Namche Bazaar, about 600m above us. The route winds its way around trees, hillsides and across rivers. It was also the day I saw Everest for the first time with my own eyes and not as a postcard or on TV. It stood high above the other peaks and was slightly set back, with vast amounts of snow being blown off its summit. From afar it looked like cloud but Rob pointed out that the winds would have been upwards of 200mph on the summit, so what looked like cloud was actually snow being blasted off the top.

Rob and I were slightly ahead of the others so we stopped and waited for them. When Leo caught up, he was panting hard and complaining he was too hot. He was wearing a pair of trekking trousers that he thought had a zip on them to turn them into shorts. We pointed out there was no zip and they were in fact a normal pair of trousers. I will never forget what Leo did after that, as it was incredibly amusing to watch. He shouted in his loud New York accent, "Right, I'll solve this, I'm too damn hot!" He pulled out a pretty hard-looking flick knife and began to hack at the knees, cutting his trousers into shorts. Bystanders couldn't believe their eyes that this lunatic was wielding a knife and frantically cutting his trousers up. "There you go, that's better," he said. It was one of those times where you had to be there but it still makes me laugh now.

A few hours later, we arrived at Namche Bazaar where we would take our first rest day. Namche Bazaar is the central hub of the Khumbu and Everest trekking route. Its streets are packed with souvenir and trekking shops, not dissimilar to Lukla, but on a larger scale. Most of the local villagers come together to buy and sell produce. The next day was a rest day so we had plenty of time to explore the village and go for a few acclimatisation walks.

Everyone was very friendly, as most of the people in the Khumbu Valley rely heavily on tourism from trekkers and climbers as their main source of income. I was amazed at the facilities that Namche had to offer, such as bars, bakeries, restaurants, Internet cafes, even massage parlours (legitimate ones). Almost anything you wanted you could get, or find someone who could get it for you. I met some wonderful people in Namche including a lodge owner called Paldon, a friendly guy who was born in the village and who had lived there all of his life with his family. Namche did however appear to have a side that you needed to be mindful of, and that was petty crime.

Some locals had nothing, apart from the clothes they were wearing and a small wooden hut to live in, which would resemble something I would have built as a teenager, pretending to be an adventurer building camps. They were at one end of the scale whereas some of the lodge owners had absolutely amazing homes with Internet, satellite TV with a massive LCD screen taking pride of place in their living room. That's just life wherever you go: there will always be people who have far more and people who have far less. What surprised me the most was that, even in the Himalayas, where everything had to be carried or helicoptered in (there were no roads), the latest technology and fashion trends were *still* finding their way in.

There were a lot of people passing through the village on their way up and on their way down. There were also a lot of sick people, some too sick to carry on up the trail and some who had been rushed down from higher villages with altitude sickness. The one thing that I really didn't like was the amount of people who would cough and splutter every evening in the guest houses while we were trying to eat our food. I tried to sit away from people who had stinking colds but gave up in the end. Luckily, I didn't get a cold or any kind of sickness for the whole trip.

The following morning started at around 6.30am and we headed down for breakfast, which consisted of porridge, toast and eggs, as it did most mornings. It was a good day's trek up to the next village of Pangbouche, which sits at 4,000m. I was carrying very little but was astonished at the weight some of the porters were carrying up the steep steps and navigating around the rocky, rugged terrain. Some of the trails were littered with loose rocks and it would have been very easy to slip and damage or break your ankle.

Most of the porters were just wearing sandals or flip flops and carrying massive loads on their backs. Some porters would be carrying building materials such as wood and large building stones, while others would be carrying food produce such as rice, beer or soft drinks. The porters were paid per kilo they carried, so as you can imagine, they would carry as much as they were physically able to. Their ethos was, if it can be picked up, it can be carried.

I was astounded to see that some of the porters who, bear in mind were only small in stature themselves, were carrying more than 100 kilograms on their backs. These were known as 'double loads' and would therefore benefit from double pay. I was shocked at how young some of these porters were and it wasn't just men; lots of women were doing this work too.

We arrived at the lodge, which was owned by the sister of our local guide, a guy called Ang Nuru. He was in his mid to late 20s and was a very strong climber with several Everest summits, and many other peaks, to his name. He stopped climbing when a relative was killed in an avalanche on a mountain called Ama Dablam. A few years later, I would find myself on that same mountain. The lodge was called Sonam Lodge and had a large metal fire burner in the middle of the communal lounge. It really heated the room up in the evenings if it was cold. I wondered what it was that the owner kept putting into the fire as it didn't look like wood and certainly wasn't coal. It turned out to be yak dung which, when dried out, burnt well and gave off plenty of heat. That did explain why I could see women in the fields during the day picking up what looked like cow poo, flattening it out and placing it in the sun to dry out.

Yaks are long-haired, bovid animals and are found throughout the Himalayas and Tibet. Most of them are domesticated so they are used for carrying large loads up and down the trails. They are also bred for meat, although they are not butchered in the Khumbu Valley for spiritual reasons. They look a bit like bulls, with large horns and a thick coat of fur. Most of them have bells around their necks that the owners tie on so they can be heard as they are walking along the trail. They're not the kind of animal you want to get too close to when you walk past them, as they are known to regularly head butt the legs of trekkers who get too close. With their weight and power, they can easily break a leg with one swift blow from their horns as they thrash their heads around.

The following day was another planned rest day but, instead of sitting around doing nothing, we decided to walk up to Ama Dablam Base Camp, as the village of Pangbouche sits just at the base of the mountain. Ama Dablam means 'Mother's Necklace' in Nepali and it's a truly breathtaking mountain. It's not particularly high at just below 7,000m, but it's quite technical.

JK

Over the next five days we slowly worked our way up the valley until we arrived at Gorak Shep, which is the last village before Everest Base Camp. Gorak Shep sits at just over 5,000m and is below a trekking peak called Kala Patthar, meaning 'Black Rock' in Nepali. It looks more like a hill than a mountain, although it is classed as a mountain.

Most trekkers take the walk up to the summit to watch the sun set over Everest, which is an incredible view. We all decided to walk up to the top to see the sun set and, although it didn't look particularly steep or far, it was deceptively further than we thought. As the mountains are so big, they can appear closer to the eye than they really are. We got to the top and sat for about an hour, taking plenty of photos. We then walked slowly back down to our lodge at Gorak Shep. We didn't stay long in the communal lounge where we ate our food as it was filled with people coughing incessantly. You could almost see the germs circulating around the room.

There were five of us sitting around a table: Rob, myself, Leo, Penny and James. All of a sudden, a chap on the table next to us turned and asked if we had been up Kala Patthar. Before any of us could answer, his wife interjected and said it was extremely hard and that we mustn't be disappointed if we can't make it. She said that her husband was really strong and managed to climb up in a staggeringly fast time. He grinned at Rob and said, "Yeah, I'm pretty fit", then asked Rob if he had done any climbing before. We just smiled; he had no idea he was talking to a seven-time Everest summiteer and one of the strongest Western guides around.

Kala Patthar was something Rob could just walk up before breakfast to stretch his legs, as his ability to deal with altitude appeared super human. He was also an extremely polite, humble and modest man and, instead of telling this chap that he was one of only a handful of people who had actually summited Everest twice in the same season, he chose simply to acknowledge the man's efforts, "Well done, I have done a little bit of climbing myself." We chuckled to ourselves and headed off to our rooms for the night.

The following morning we were due to walk up to Everest Base Camp and then over the valley to climb Island Peak the next day. It's a relatively flattish walk from Gorak Shep up to Base Camp and we walked quite slowly, taking about three hours to get there. Eventually, we saw a mass of people standing by a large rock in the distance taking photos.

"This is it, Everest Base Camp," Rob said.

Although most of the expeditions for Everest would set their camps up about half a mile further up the glacier. At some point, somebody had carved *Everest Base Camp* into the rock and prayer flags were flying from its side. We only stayed for about 20 minutes to take some photos and admire the view.

We then walked back down to Lobuche to stay the night. Another early start saw us head out over to Dingbuche, which was a fairly easy day. We would be climbing with Rob, Ang Nuru and Ang Nuru's brother–in-law. All of the equipment was taken over to Base Camp by yaks and porters who went ahead of us so everything would be set up when we arrived. We ate noodles, drank tea and got our heads down in the tent for some kip.

To climb Island Peak, there are a couple of options: starting from Base Camp, which is around 5,000m and starting the climb at about 3am or, ascending to a higher camp at around 5,600m, to reduce the amount of effort and time needed for the summit.

We decided to go from Base Camp and leave in the night. I remember waking up and it was freezing outside. I was sharing a tent with Leo and I told him that we needed to get up as my watch was reading 2.30am. It felt so cold outside of my sleeping bag. It didn't take too long to get ready and before I knew it, Ang Nuru was unzipping the tent and passing us through a hot lemon tea. A few minutes later, he came back with a welcome bowl of porridge. We came out of the tents and I could see the rest of the guys getting ready with their head torches flickering in the darkness.

Right on schedule, we left at 3am and started to trek very slowly up to the higher camp. It was about 600m in elevation so took quite a few hours, as we were moving slowly. Leo was having some difficulty with his breathing and tiredness. I felt slightly sorry for him when Rob told him that he was going to need to speed up. He was trying his best but it wasn't fast enough. Leo then needed to go to the loo, which can be a bit tricky when it's pitch black and extremely cold. Ang Nuru took him off behind some large rocks. Luckily there were no other climbers around at the time so he didn't have the embarrassment of people walking past him. About half an hour later, Leo was like a different person and was having no trouble keeping up. God knows what difference it made but whatever had happened, it worked. Rob thought he would have to send Leo back down again and I really didn't want that to happen, so I was pleased he had started to speed up.

The hours passed and eventually we started getting closer to the next part of the climb where we would stop and put our boots and crampons on. Crampons are devices that attach to the bottom of your boots, which have spikes on to bite into the snow and ice to provide grip. They have been around for years and without them, it would be almost impossible to get around on the ice.

The sky was starting to give off an orange glow to the east as the sun was slowly making its way round the earth and getting closer to us. The very second the sun inched its way over the jagged mountainous horizon, the temperature instantly rose – not by much, but just enough to feel the difference. We had now reached the point where we were going to stop and change from trainers into boots. The last hour had mostly been scrambling over rocks but now it was a combination of snow and ice on the glacier. We quickly swapped our footwear over and got going.

It was a little more risky being up on the glacier. Although unlikely, it could just collapse in certain parts. Rob decided that we should all lash onto a rope and walk together at the same pace so if one person fell, the idea was that we could all take their weight. If we all fell, then that was that, I suppose.

It didn't take too long to get to the last section before the summit, which was a fairly steep wall of about 100m. This was a very popular mountain to be climbing so there are permanently fixed ropes to scale the last section. By now, we had caught up with a few climbing teams but there was no rush. We got to the face of the wall and took off our rucksacks for a quick rest and food break. I have to admit that by now, I was actually really exhausted, but I didn't want to show it. Leo clipped onto the rope first and started to ascend, followed by Rob, James and myself. Penny decided that she didn't want to tackle the last bit and was very happy with her efforts to get there, which was a good achievement. Ang Nuru took her back down to Base Camp.

It was actually quite simple climbing up as the rope was fixed into the slope and I was using a device called a jumar (a climbing tool that has a handle and allows the rope to slide through teeth. It's designed in a way that it can be clipped onto the rope and it slides up the rope but, when pulled, the teeth grip the rope tight). So, not only could I use my legs to lift me up, I could pull myself up as well on the rope. The fixed rope ran in sections fixed in place by a climbing guide to the top of the face, with anchor points about 10m apart. Along with the jumar, I had a carabiner that was attached to a rope and my harness. This was my safety line, so no matter what I was doing I would always be clipped into a line. If I fell, I would have only fallen to the next anchor point where I would be brought to a violent stop as the carabiner hit the anchor point.

It was really just a case of taking a few steps, stopping for a rest and repeating it all over again. The trick was to move very slowly, trying to conserve oxygen and move as efficiently as possible. This does come with time and experience though. Most males are driven by testosterone and of course, every guy on the rope wanted to be the quickest. Multiple ropes were set up so people could get up quicker and abseil down without bumping into anyone coming up.

I ascended as quickly as I could but was completely shattered. I think I looked better than I felt as Rob was shouting down to me, "Looking strong, Ketch." I felt exhausted but was determined to get to the top. Eventually, I made it up over the top of the wall where there was one last part of the climb left. It was an easy walk up a slight incline to the summit. There was still a fixed rope to clip my safety line into but the last part was quite straightforward. As I was walking up, the others were standing on the summit waving to me, as I was the last one to climb. It was a great feeling, as if it was just the five of us standing on the summit. The view was breathtaking and we all took some photos and chatted for a few minutes.

It was soon time to start descending. We abseiled down the last 100m of the face and were back on the glacier quite quickly. "It's on the way down that accidents happen," Rob kept reiterating. The gravity was really pulling at me so I had to concentrate and pay attention as I was changing my figure of eight into the next rope (*a figure of eight is a device used to abseil and control the speed of descent on the rope passing through it via friction*). It's very simple to use after you have abseiled a few times.

When we were back on the glacier, we lined up and clipped back into the same rope so we were all connected to get back to the safety of the rocks. We made it back over to the point where we would change from boots back into trainers or walking boots.

Apart from Rob, we were all absolutely shattered and still had another 600m to descend. With each step taking us lower, the air around us was becoming richer in oxygen and that was certainly starting to make a difference. Rob appeared to be a bit of a mountain goat as he quickly navigated his way down through the loose rocks. James, Leo and I decided to take it slightly slower coming down and let Rob go ahead. When we arrived back at Base Camp, we were greeted with some hot noodles and tea. Leo and I just crashed out in our tent and didn't wake up until early the following morning.

JK

We woke up bright and early, ready to start our descent back down to Lukla. By the time we were up, the team that had set up camp for us had cleared almost everything down and packed everything up, apart from our tents. They had some tea ready for us and we would head back to Dingbouche for breakfast. We would then trek down to Pangbouche where we would stay for the night. We were all feeling quite tired at this point. Rob pointed out that if we wanted to, we could fly back to Kathmandu a day earlier so we had another day to chill out. At first, it sounded like a good option but it meant trekking from Pangbouche to Lukla, which would have been a very long day. It was doable but we decided to have a more leisurely walk back to Namche.

The following day, we reached Namche and stayed with Paldon again. That evening, we went out to the local bar called the 'Pub Danphe'. It's a small place with a pool table and interesting decor inside, mostly made up of flags and T-shirts all signed by the people who have passed through as they have been climbing and trekking. Some people had dated their flags and I noticed that a few of them were almost as old as me.

The place had a really happy party atmosphere since most people who were there drinking were on their way back down and only had one more easy day left before they flew back to Kathmandu.

This meant that pretty much everyone was celebrating their efforts by getting drunk. It's a real multi-cultural environment with a complete mix of nationalities. I remember trying to play pool but there was a foreign chap (I can't remember where he was from) who was staggering around and kept falling onto the table and moving all the balls around. Obviously this was quite frustrating and the atmosphere got quite heated but I didn't think it was worth getting into a fight over a drunk guy moving some balls around the pool table. I suggested to Rob that we leave but as soon as I turned around again, the drunk guy had gone. I have no idea what happened to him but I'm guessing he was probably kicked out.

There are police in Namche but I got the impression that the locals pretty much policed the area themselves. I had seen first-hand how some of the police deal with criminals and it wasn't anything like you'd see in the UK. As soon as someone stepped out of line, they would have a baton smashed around their head to keep them in check, something a police officer could go to prison for in the UK. We carried on playing pool and drinking and, at about 2am, we decided we really should leave and get some rest. We were pretty hungry and really fancied something to eat but there was nowhere open. Ang Nuru said he knew the owner of the local bakery and, before I knew it, he had climbed in through an open window and reappeared with a handful of cakes and doughnuts. I told him we should leave the money on the counter but he said it was okay. I felt slightly guilty but Ang Nuru assured me that it was fine, and who was I to question? We were all hungry and they tasted great.

We crashed back into the lodge trying not to wake anyone else up. As soon as I closed my eyes, if felt like I was opening them immediately and it was time to get up. I instantly knew that I'd drunk too much and was already regretting it. We had some breakfast and thankfully, I started to perk up a bit. We walked pretty slowly back to Lukla and I was completely shattered and ready for a good shower.

We arrived late in the afternoon and checked into the place we'd had breakfast at when we'd first arrived in Lukla. By that stage, all memories of the previous night's hangover were gone, so we thought we should go out to the local pool bar one last time, as it was our last night in the Khumbu. Rob had sorted out all of our tickets so that was the most important job done. We were booked on the first flight the following morning, scheduled to depart at 6.30am. We stayed out until about 1am and then went back to our room. I was sharing a room with Leo and Rob, who were not too impressed with the smell of my trainers by this time, so I was made to put them outside in the hall.

Early next morning we caught the flight back to Kathmandu and were back in our original hotel, Hotel Manaslu. It was a lovely place and, compared to some of the lodges, it was complete luxury: hot, powerful showers, comfy beds, fast Internet and plenty of food to keep everyone happy. I hadn't had a shave for the past few weeks and was looking pretty messy, so I decided to find a barber. Next to our hotel was the Radisson Hotel and they had a salon for men where you could get a full grooming service. I booked myself in for a shave, hair wash and haircut. I was incredibly impressed with the attention to detail and effort the chap was putting into what he was doing. I'd never had a cut throat shave before and I remember looking at the blade when he took it out of the packet and thinking back to a horror film I'd watched years ago, where a guy was having the same type of shave and the barber sliced his throat open with the blade.

When he had finished, he massaged my shoulders and head. It still remains to this day the best haircut I have ever had. I asked him how much it cost and I couldn't believe it was only 500 rupees, equivalent to £3! The same service in a London barber would easily have cost about £50, so I gave him the same again for a tip and he was over the moon.

Leo also used the barber for a trim up then we headed to the Thamel district where we were due to meet Rob at a local café, 'Fire and Ice'. We handed some kit back that I'd rented from one of the trekking shops and had a look around the North Face shop. Something that instantly caught my eye was a massive picture of Everest that was about six feet tall and three feet wide, covered in signatures. Rob said this was the Everest summiteers wall and, if you had summited Everest, you were entitled to sign the picture.

"Ketch, your name will be on here next year," he said.

This trip was part of the plan for getting me out to Everest in 2011 and Rob said there was still a little more work required but he didn't think I'd have a problem going back with him to climb the following year.

I'd really enjoyed the trip and, although it had been tough at times, it wasn't too bad really. Things are generally never that bad when you look back, even when you're struggling at the time. I was extremely motivated to get back out to Everest. I knew that the hard part wouldn't necessarily be the climbing itself but raising the money for the climb. I had to think carefully about how I was going to do this.

That evening, we all went for a meal at a local steak house recommended by Rob. It was called 'The Everest Steak House' and had a great reputation for incredible steak. There was one particular steak on the menu that jumped out at me. It was a foot long and sounded incredible, even though I had no idea what cut it was. When I ordered it, everyone looked at me as if to say, you're really going to eat *that*? The waiter brought everyone's meals over and mine just dwarfed the table. I did eat all of it but I have to confess,

I was pretty stuffed by the end.

Everyone was due to fly home the next day and we said our goodbyes. Rob and I were flying back together and would fly home via the same route. We grabbed a lift to the airport and flew back to Delhi. We only had about a two-hour turnaround time before our flight to London departed. For some reason, there was a delay when we were sitting on the plane waiting to leave Kathmandu. We didn't know what was going on but we sat there on the tarmac for over an hour-and-a-half. That had eaten into our turnaround time and we realised that we would not make our connecting flight in Delhi. When we eventually touched down in Delhi, we didn't even bother trying to make the connection as the plane was taking off just as we were landing.

We headed over to the check-in area to explain what had happened, expecting to be sleeping on the airport floor. They were incredibly helpful and put us up in a local hotel, a few minutes away from the airport. We were scheduled to be on the next flight the following day. We checked in to the hotel and opted to just eat in the hotel and chill out. We felt that we'd seen enough of Delhi a few weeks earlier. I fell asleep on the bed and Rob went down to the gym. I joined him about half-an-hour later but I was still shattered and had no idea why Rob wasn't as tired as me. I guess everyone's tolerance to lack of sleep is different.

The following morning, we went back to the airport to catch our flight home. At the entrance to the airport, there were armed guards who checked everyone's ticket before they entered the building. Anyone who wasn't flying was not allowed into the building. For some reason, Rob didn't have a print out of his ticket, which the staff had given to us the previous day. Getting into the building turned into a bit of a nightmare, as the guards wouldn't let him through. They were like robots, programmed to do their job: if you didn't have a passport and ticket, you were not allowed in. Rob tried to tell them that he was booked on the flight but the guard just stared blankly at him. Eventually, a senior officer arrived and told Rob he could get a ticket print out from a desk around the corner. He eventually got through and we made it home.

8

'Chicken with altitude'

When I returned home, I immediately started putting a plan together for the next six months, working out how to raise enough money to get out to Everest and also have enough money to live on. As it stood, I had no money to my name and no job, so I needed to make something happen fast. Most people around me thought I was crazy and didn't think I'd be able to raise the money.

I did wonder at times if they were right, but something inside me was telling me that everything would work out okay. I kept thinking back to the fact that when I rowed the Atlantic, I didn't do anything special – I just kept going. I thought that if I continued the principle of just keeping going and applied it to my fundraising efforts, surely someone would eventually sponsor me? I did have the credibility of having rowed single-handed across the Atlantic, which I guessed was a fairly significant achievement.

It's funny how things happen and how people come in and out of your life. I was training in the gym with Andy and I got chatting to a guy called Mark, who I'd known for years. He was a pretty big guy who worked for a security firm. I'd asked him in the past what he did for a living and he was a little cagey about the details. When someone says, "this and that" when I ask them a question, I generally take the hint that they don't want to tell me more. So I was having a conversation with Mark and mentioned that I was desperately looking for some work. He said he might be able to help me out. I wasn't actually asking him, it just came up as we were chatting while passing weights. He suggested we meet up for a coffee and he'd bring me up to speed.

I was pretty pleased, as this spot of luck couldn't have come at a better time. We met up a few days later and it turned out that Mark ran the security contract for a large vehicle manufacturer at Southampton Docks. The brand-new cars would be kept in a massive compound and be driven on to the ferries for export by the logistics company that ran the docks. My potential job would be to sit in the security hut by the entrance and monitor the cars going out and the transport lorries bringing them in. It seemed very easy work and I would be paid cash in hand, so it really was a no brainer.

I started a week later and it would be just a few shifts a week and some weekends, which worked perfectly for me while I was trying to raise funds for Everest. There were two shifts available: the day shift, which could be quite busy, and the night shift. The shifts were standard, 12-hour security shifts, which felt quite long to begin with, but which actually passed quite quickly once I got used to them. The bonus was that it was just a one-man role, so if there was nothing going on, I was at a loose end. I needed to work out how I could start to use this time constructively, as I found myself sitting around far too much.

There was another lad who worked the night shifts, called Fernando and he would work on his university studies at night. At that point, it occurred to me that the day shifts were no good and I needed to move onto night shifts. I could basically get paid to sit there for 12 hours while profiling potential sponsors and sending out mass emails. A few night shifts came up, so I started taking them, from 7pm through to 7am. At 7pm, the day's activities would be coming to an end, which meant that from around 9pm to 4.45am, when the first drivers started arriving, there was no work to be done. I bought an Internet dongle for my laptop so I could get online and off I went.

Other people who worked the night shift basically slept, although they would swear blind they didn't. Fernando once fell asleep at night when an intruder broke in, who started joyriding a car around the compound without him even realising.

At the weekend, there was no work going on in the compound at all so I would take my bike with me and put it on the turbo trainer and train for hours at a time. I also had a 'Concept 2' indoor rowing machine that I would put in the back of the van I was using and sometimes sit there rowing in the evenings to get fitter.

Most of my time would be spent sending out sponsorship emails. I would drive home absolutely knackered most mornings and crash out in bed as soon as I got home. When I woke up, I would check my emails to see if I'd had any replies from the previous night's efforts. Sometimes I would have emails saying they were potentially interested but more often it would be rejection emails. Some would be quite harsh and others would be standard rejection emails, which were probably sent out every day.

Whenever I told people I was looking for sponsorship, nearly everyone would say, "Have you tried Red Bull or Richard Branson? I'm sure they would love to be involved." Well, guess what – that's what the other 10,000 people thought who were trying to obtain funding for some kind of project. I realised that, unless you had a fairly senior contact within a prominent organisation, it was nigh on impossible to get a foot in the door. Every now and then, you might get a reply from these big companies but the simple fact is, they are approached by people just like me every day. I was having much more success with the slightly smaller companies as opposed to those on the *FT 500*.

One morning, after a night of sending out 300 emails, I woke up to a bit of a surprise. I had over 20 email responses and I was excited to see if any of them were positive sponsorship offers. Sadly, none of them were, but there was one that caught my eye. It was a direct reply from a CEO of a technology company who said he was incredibly impressed with what I was doing but just wouldn't be able to get board approval to sponsor me. He attached a spreadsheet and simply said, "You might find the attached useful." I could see that it was an Excel spreadsheet but I was pretty despondent at that point about the amount of rejections I was getting, so I didn't look at the attachment for a few days.

That was a very foolish decision, looking back, because when I did open it, I was amazed to find a list of over 1,000 Managing Director and CEO email addresses for various companies. Some were large enterprise organisations and others were much smaller but this data was like gold dust and I couldn't believe this chap had sent it to me for nothing. I had produced a standard email that I would send out to potential sponsors, accompanied by a very slick PDF document outlining the most important factors of the project I needed to convey: what I was doing, why I was doing it, what I was looking for and what I could give back in return. I had a friend called Malcolm who I met while speaking at a networking evening. He is probably one of the best graphic designers I've ever come across and he kindly designed the PDF document for me. I gave him the text and relevant photos and he worked his magic, creating what I thought was a masterpiece of a proposal.

The next night, I drove down to Southampton, ready to start another security shift and another night of churning out emails. I was really motivated to try and send out all 1,000 in one hit. Each email was technically the same but I obviously had to change the name of the person I was sending it to and I always dropped their company name into the mail so it didn't seem like blatant copying and pasting. I began sending the emails out one by one; this was the easy part and didn't actually take that long.

I was also trying to train during the day and, because I was staying up all night working and sending emails out, it was starting to take its toll on my energy reserves. I felt like a walking zombie and almost crashed my car driving home one morning, so I took the evening off to get some rest.

By now, I had emailed thousands and thousands of companies and I still hadn't really got anywhere with any responses that looked like they might turn into something positive. I was starting to panic slightly and was questioning myself, wondering if this was really meant to be. Every human being, no matter how mentally tough you think you are, will start to question themselves when things are consistently not going your way. With hindsight, I did come close to thinking that the project wouldn't happen. This feeling really scared me as I'd told people what I was doing and had met up with the person who was going to take me to Everest with his expedition. I couldn't let them down but I was running out of options for sponsorship. It felt incredibly frustrating and demoralising.

I still had another batch of emails to send out but I was finding it very difficult to motivate myself. I just didn't see the point anymore, as I wasn't having any luck. I went back to work the following night with the objective of sending out the final emails I'd prepared. It didn't take long to get through them and I was on the last few, which were all contacts in the food industry. There was one contact name that stood out for some reason and it was the Marketing Manager for Nando's, an incredibly popular restaurant chain in the UK. I just couldn't see any connection between Nando's and climbing Everest, so I skipped it and continued emailing. All of a sudden, an incredibly strange feeling came over me as if someone was saying, "What the hell are you doing? You're making all this effort so why are you cheating yourself by not sending this *one* email?" I went back to the Nando's email and sent it out, then gave it no more thought.

At 9am the following day, my phone rang. I was shattered as I had only been home for about an hour after my night shift. I answered it, as I didn't recognise the number (I always answered numbers I didn't recognise in case it was a potential sponsor). An enthusiastic voice came through the speaker, "James, it's Andrew from Nando's, I'm just following up on your email." I quickly started to pay attention, as I knew I was going to need to be in 'sponsor mode' and really sell the project.

Andrew thought the project was great but he had one important question for me.

"So James, do you actually eat Nando's?"

I swiftly replied that I loved Nando's chicken and ate it almost every day. I did joke with him that I can't eat their Peri Peri hot sauce and said that I could only eat their lemon and herb chicken burgers. He thought it was hilarious that I could row the Atlantic Ocean single-handed and was planning to climb the world's highest mountain, but I could only eat Nando's lemon and herb burgers.

"Actually, I like this angle, why don't you come up to our head office and we can discuss it further?" So Andrew and I arranged a date to meet.

After the phone call, I was absolutely ecstatic. It was the lucky break

I really needed and to think that I wasn't even going to send the email to Nando's. Their head office was based in Putney, so I travelled up to meet him and Keri, their PR Director. I thought we were going to have our meeting in an office but we actually had it in their local restaurant, which apparently was the first Nando's in the UK. They teased me about how I ordered the same thing every time I went.

Keri and Andrew listened to me for almost an hour while I brought them up to speed on the project and went through my sponsorship pitch. I paused to take a breath and Keri looked into my eyes and said, "You're probably the most driven and determined person I've ever met. This is amazing but you need to eat your food, it's almost cold now." My chicken burger was stone cold but I didn't care, I needed to get my message across, and I think I had. Andrew chatted to me about what I could do in terms of marketing and Keri started discussing all the PR angles. They were both getting excited by the idea, which was a good sign.

Around the time of the meeting I was training a lot and happened to be in pretty good physical shape. I was doing a lot of gym work and had solid 17-inch arms that were toned and muscular. As Keri was talking to me, I noticed that her eyes kept flitting to my arms, which made me chuckle. I had a fitted T-shirt on that day and had trained my arms that morning, coincidentally, so they were still quite pumped. The meeting eventually came to an end with Andrew saying they would most likely sponsor me but needed to run through some of the finer details first.

A few days later, they asked to see me again and they confirmed that they would like to sponsor me. I was thrilled that they believed in me when so many others had ignored my requests. Their offer wasn't anywhere near enough to cover the cost of the whole project but it was a very good start. They became one of the most proactive sponsors I've ever had. They built a separate Nando's page on their main website that was going to track me up and down the mountain. I would be represented on a map by Nando's mascot 'Barci' the chicken.

In my local restaurant in Basingstoke, they made up posters that showed the detailed route of my climb with a link so people could follow me and also donate to my chosen charity. All of the staff were wearing T-shirts that said 'Chicken with Altitude'. They really got behind me and when it was time to depart, they even laid on a massive good luck party with all my friends and family. I also got to know Andrew and Keri quite well.

It seemed my luck had changed and all of a sudden, in the space of a week, I had quite a few replies from my nights spent sending out hundreds of emails. I had responses from DHL, House of Fraser and Internet giant AOL, all wanting to meet with me to discuss my Everest plans. I met up with someone from House of Fraser at London HQ and a week later, they had agreed to sponsor me too.

I was starting to realise a very simple equation: proactivity equals positive results. I really did spend hundreds of hours chasing up any leads and contacts for sponsorship and it was finally starting to pay off. I still had a fair way to go as I appeared to be having much more success asking for a sponsorship figure of around £5,000 than any more. I did propose sponsorship packages of varying amounts but £5,000 seemed to be the most popular take-up. It wasn't a vast amount of money for most companies and could be signed off by a director most of the time, without needing corporate approval from the top.

I had a conference call with AOL, based in New York. Two weeks later, I had them on board too and had secured another £5,000 towards the project. The guys at DHL were in Germany, so again, I never actually met them face-to-face, but they also confirmed they would like to sponsor me. I was constantly trying to think outside the box, coming up with new sponsorship angles. With DHL, I was trying to set a record for the world's *highest* delivery, by effectively just giving a small package to another climber, which, in reality, was a small, empty DHL box. I thought it would be quite a cool record to break. Initially, Guinness World Records processed my application but later declined it, saying it wasn't valid because someone could climb Everest twice and say they had gone higher.

I decided to leave the world's highest delivery but did try and pursue another idea for a sponsor who came on board, called Optimal Payments. They had a prepaid card called Neteller and are very well-established in the online gambling world, handling most of the online payments. I was going to try and set a record for the world's highest online transaction, which would have been marketing gold for Optimal Payments, but again, it was declined by Guinness World Records.

JK

By this time, it was January 2011 and I was due to fly out to Nepal in April, but I was still around £10,000 short. The plan was to head out to Everest with Rob, who I knew very well by this point, and then meet up with our team manager, Henry Todd, who had a wealth of experience, leading and managing expeditions on Everest for the past 30 years. Henry had successfully put over 300 people on the summit of Everest including Bear Grylls, when he became the youngest Briton to stand on top of the world.

Henry had a tough reputation but was extremely pleasant to me, forthcoming with advice and offering to lend me any kit I didn't have. When I told him I was slightly short with the funds, he actually told me not to worry about it. As long as I could get the rest of the money at some point, he was sure it would all come together. He knew that the hard part for me, and most people, was getting to the start line.

I did have a few friends who owned their own companies and were doing very well financially. One friend, Ian, owned a company called Fiber Technologies and they were my first ever sponsor. I'd met Ian a few years back when I had my boat on display outside London Olympia, raising funds and awareness for the Atlantic row. I was mindful of the fact that I couldn't keep going back to the same people asking for more money; that's the quickest way to lose friends. However, I explained that I was short and Ian kindly agreed to put some money into the project in exchange for a photo of his company flag on top of Everest. I was extremely grateful for his ongoing support.

However I was slightly concerned, as I had about seven or eight flags to lift when I did eventually make the summit. There was a lot of pressure on me as some of the sponsors were making a big deal about it. Most people aren't going to part with money without getting something back, which I was learning very quickly.

I remember chatting to my friend Mike Rawlins when I got back from the row. At the time, he said he wanted to help me but he wasn't sure how. Things had progressed since then and he had been helping me with various aspects of the project, including utilising some of his contacts to try and secure funding for me. One of his colleagues was a guy called Richard Cribb who worked for National Grid. His job was to manage the relationship between National Grid and the Indian IT outsourcing companies that they used and with whom they spent hundreds of millions of pounds every year. Richard was planning to do a joint sponsorship with National Grid and Wipro who are one of India's largest IT outsourcing companies. National Grid agreed to donate £2,500 if Wipro would match the other half. I didn't actually realise that Richard was doing this on my behalf because Mike didn't tell me until he was fairly sure that it looked like it would happen. Mike used to work at National Grid so understood how the company worked and what hoops Richard would have to jump through in order to secure the funding.

It turned out that National Grid were happy to donate the money to the project but didn't want any public acknowledgment, making them a silent sponsor. This wasn't unusual as a similar thing happened when I rowed the Atlantic. A large networking organisation gave me £5,000 but said I wasn't to advertise their sponsorship. They actually didn't want anything to do with the project as they thought it was incredibly dangerous but needed to spend the money or the marketing department would lose it the following year. For me, it was just a case of being in the right place at the right time I guess.

I didn't meet Richard before I left for Everest but I was grateful for his support. I didn't know it at the time but he would end up playing a major part in my life moving forwards.

By now, I had a vast array of companies on board with the project, ranging from family-owned businesses to multi-billion dollar corporations. I'd left it a bit late as I only had about three weeks to go before I was due to fly out to Everest and I needed to find a company that would make up all the logos for my jackets and flags. Keri at Nando's introduced me to a small, family-run business called Clothing for Events. I spoke to Rob who ran the business with his wife and went to see them the following day. They were so excited to meet me and hear about what I was doing. They were very good to me and had no problem getting all the logos made up and applied to the jackets. The bill was around £1,000 and I remember when I went to pick up the kit, they said to me that they wanted to sponsor it as their way of supporting me, which was a truly wonderful thing to do. They asked if it would be possible to get a photo with their flag somewhere on Everest for them. I made sure I got a good photo for them and they were so pleased with it, they used it for the front cover of their company catalogue the following year.

About three weeks prior to my departure for Everest, I received a phone call from Rob who was working in Canada at the time. I was excited to hear from him, as his enthusiasm was infectious.

"Ketch, I've got some bad news," he told me.

I paused and my heart sank as I thought he was going to tell me the trip was off. He said that he wasn't sure if he could come now, as he was unwell and having a few problems at home. I was absolutely gutted as I was really looking forward to heading out to Nepal with him again; retracing the steps we'd taken in October the previous year.

I was however relieved that the trip was still going ahead, as I'd raised all the money and it would have been a nightmare if it wasn't going to happen now. Rob did say that he might still be able to get out and he would know nearer the time but it was looking like I wasn't going to be climbing with him. I spoke with Henry who was very reassuring and said it wouldn't actually matter if Rob was climbing with me or not, as I would be climbing with a Sherpa. I'd really been looking forward to sharing the experience with him.

The next couple of weeks passed quickly and I just focused on my training and last minute testing with my technical kit, which I planned to use to update my website while on the mountain. Most of my training consisted of cardio work with the aim of increasing my aerobic capacity and dropping some weight. Typically, a lot of my training over the years (and certainly prior to the row) had been geared more around weight training. When I went out to Nepal on my previous trip, it became very clear to me that the lighter I was and the greater my cardiovascular strength was, the easier it would be. All I wanted to do was increase my chances of a successful summit.

Some weekends, I would don my rucksack with a little bit of weight in it and spend the day walking up Snowdon and various peaks in the Lake District. I wanted to try and replicate what I'd actually be doing while on Everest. I did mix it up with some cycling, which was good for endurance. I knew I had the mental strength to be out there but it was impossible to know how my body would cope with the oxygen deprivation.

I didn't have any problems on my previous trip to the Himalayas but that was only up to 6,500m. Everest stands at 8,848m, which is a big difference. I'd spoken to some people who had successfully summited and I had mixed feedback from them. Some would say that it was relatively straightforward and only really difficult for the last few days as you reached the push up to the summit, and that as long as I took it slowly and carefully, I had nothing to worry about. Other people made out it was basically six weeks of hell and I'd be very lucky to make it to the top at all because it was so difficult.

I was certainly apprehensive as the time came to fly out, but there was one thing left to try and do. Ever since I was six months old, I'd been wearing glasses and had terrible eyesight. I was long-sighted with astigmatism, meaning my eyesight was particularly poor. I'd got used to wearing glasses but they were such a pain when I was racing motorcycles and one pair went rusty when I was rowing across the Atlantic. It would be such a nightmare with glasses underneath goggles with an oxygen mask on Everest that it would be advantageous to not have to wear them. I couldn't really use contact lenses either, as I suffer from dry eyes and they cause irritation.

Laser surgery had been around for quite some time and, by all accounts, was pretty much risk-free. It was still pretty expensive though at around £4,000. I had this idea that perhaps I could try and get my eyes lasered as part of a sponsorship deal. This would demonstrate how good laser surgery was and also promote the company who performed the operation. I could lift a flag at the summit and it would be the ultimate case study for successful laser eye surgery.

There were two market leaders offering the treatment at the time, Optimax and Ultralase. I sent out a proposal to both companies, detailing my ideas. I wasn't expecting a reply from either of them; it was more of a punt to see if I could pique their interest. To my amazement, I had a reply in less than 24 hours from Ultralase, saying that they thought it was a fantastic idea and they would do the treatment for me. I couldn't believe my luck. Just over two weeks after sending out the proposal, I no longer needed glasses. It was an extremely strange feeling to begin with, as I felt completely naked without them. The procedure was completely pain-free and was over very quickly. A few weeks later, I had a call from the Marketing Director at Optimax, asking if they could also perform the surgery for me. When I told them that Ultralase had beaten them to it, he wasn't surprised. It was an absolutely fantastic marketing and PR opportunity and he was quite annoyed that his team hadn't picked up on it sooner, as they'd missed out to their biggest rival.

9

Base Camp life

The day came when I was to fly out to Nepal and I was slightly anxious but excited at the same time. I was still waiting for the last £5,000 of funding to come through from DHL. I knew I was going to get the money but I didn't really want to be chasing it while I was in Nepal. The day before I flew out, I spoke to my contact, a lady called Maxine who headed up the marketing for DHL Europe. She had been very supportive and really bought in to the project, despite never having met me.

She said not to worry about it and she would make sure it was transferred before I left. I was flying with British Airways from Heathrow Terminal Five to Mumbai, where I would make the change to Jet Airways for the last leg into Kathmandu. This was a journey I had made before but this time, I had managed to get a very good deal on my flights, thanks to a very friendly, glamorous blonde woman called Romey who worked as a personal trainer at my local gym. She was ex-cabin crew for British Airways and had worked for them for the past 20 years.

I got up quite early on the morning of departure and my flight was around midday. I still hadn't received the DHL funds and it was very much playing on my mind. I cleared security and customs very quickly and grabbed some food. I wanted to check my bank account one last time before I boarded. Suddenly, I heard a boarding call for my flight and I just managed to access my bank account in time. Much to my delight, the money was there. It was a massive weight off my shoulders and I could now concentrate on the task at hand without having to worry about getting the last instalment to Henry. I quickly made my way over to the gate and boarded the plane.

Including the stopover in Mumbai, I arrived in Kathmandu about 12 hours later. I was met by Henry as I came out of the terminal at Tribhuvan International Airport. As I'd remembered from my previous trip, it was organised chaos: there were people everywhere, horns beeping and just a general mass of people waving and shouting. It was also very hot and within a few minutes of being outside, I was sweating profusely. One of Henry's support staff from Himalayan Guides came over and took my bags from me, loading them into the van that would take us to our hotel.

When we arrived, I just crashed out, not waking up until the following morning. I had a few days in Kathmandu to settle in and sort out any kit issues with Henry before heading into the Khumbu Valley. I was fairly well prepared so I didn't need to do a great deal. Most of my time was spent chilling out and eating in the great café 'Fire & Ice' in the Thamel district, the central tourist hub of Kathmandu and where most climbers and hikers congregated.

The day after I arrived, Becky was due to fly in and Henry went to the airport to collect her. Becky was an 18-year old trainee doctor who I'd been in communication with for the last six months. She was trying to become the youngest British female to summit Everest. Becky was not your average 18-year old girl; she was incredibly motivated and driven towards reaching her goal. I could tell this just by chatting with her on the phone before I met her in Kathmandu. We'd talked a lot as she was struggling with her sponsorship and only just managed to raise the funds in time. As I'd had a fair amount of success with raising the funds required to climb Everest, I wanted to help her. Becky didn't really have any experience in the corporate world, which is certainly beneficial when negotiating sponsorship deals. Short of getting on the phone and calling people on her behalf, there wasn't that much I could do. I decided to share some information with her that would ultimately lead to her securing a title sponsor.

I still had the database of contacts that I'd been given, which had resulted in a lot of positive responses. I told her to email everyone on this list as a last ditch attempt to obtain some funding. Becky was quite grateful, as she knew how valuable this data was. A few weeks later, she emailed me to say that DHL were going to be her title sponsor and would fund everything. I couldn't believe it as I too was sponsored by DHL but it turned out that we were speaking to different people within the organisation. I was slightly anxious as I wondered if DHL were going to pull my funding to give it all to Becky but thankfully, that didn't happen.

When Becky did arrive in Kathmandu, it was good to finally meet her, after months of chatting. She had travelled to Kathmandu before so knew her way around, so we all just got on with our own thing. Henry spent most of his time in meetings with oxygen suppliers and generally organising climbing permits and last minute details.

On my third day in Kathmandu, we were due to fly up to Lukla but Henry was informed there was a delay caused by the weather so we flew the following day. This time, I was a little more anxious arriving at Kathmandu Airport to pick up the little twin engine Otter that would fly us into the Himalayas. It was no different to the last time I was at the airport, except that Henry was shouting orders at me to move on through the queues. We passed through the security checks and were soon out on the tarmac boarding the plane. I knew I wanted to sit on the left-hand side again to appreciate the stunning views over the Himalayas. Most people who were boarding had the same idea too but luckily I managed to get a seat.

It's only a small plane but they still have an air stewardess who hands out sweets and checks the seat belts. As the plane took its position on the runway and powered up to full throttle, it sent a shiver down my spine. As the plane hurtled down the tarmac, shaking and creaking, I thought to myself, "This is it, I'm really on my way to Everest!" I was particularly nervous about this flight, more so than on my previous flight into Lukla, as there had been a fatal crash a few weeks earlier, killing everyone on board. I prayed that wouldn't happen to me. Thankfully, after a hard bounce, we touched down safely.

Becky and I jumped out and made our way out of the airport. Our bags were collected by a porter and taken to the lodge where we would have breakfast and meet Tim, a guy who would be trekking with us part way to Base Camp. Henry stayed in Kathmandu as he had other meetings and errands to run so he was going to meet us at Base Camp. Tim was an experienced climber and already had several summits of Everest under his belt. He worked with Henry and uses his logistics on the mountain to take his own paying clients up. We could have made our own way up independently but it was quite nice chatting with Tim and his clients for the first few days.

We had been on the first flight of the day so we had breakfast in the lodge when we arrived at 7am. Afterwards, we all took a slow walk to Monjo where we would stay for the first night on the trail.

Next morning at around 6.30am, we washed and went downstairs for breakfast, and were on the trail by 7.30am.

Tim and his clients were going slightly further than Becky and I intended to walk that day as we were just heading to Namche. It's a good hike up to Namche with around 500m of height gain. It's also the first time that trekkers actually see Everest far off in the distance. Becky and I stopped to take some pictures and I remember looking up and seeing the summit of Everest with a huge white cloud of snow being blown from its summit, battered by the jet stream. It was a strange feeling of déjà vu and I had butterflies in my stomach this time. The last time I'd had that feeling was looking out at the Atlantic Ocean for the first time when I arrived in La Gomera. It was a particularly rough day and I wondered what I'd let myself in for. That exact feeling came back to me when I stood looking up at Everest in the distance. I stood and stared for a couple of minutes, wondering what it would be like to be standing on that very spot, before moving on.

I arrived into Namche about 20 minutes ahead of Becky so I perched myself on a wall and waited for her. Tim and his gang were a little way behind but were going straight through Namche to another small village, so we didn't bother waiting for them. It was in Namche that Becky and I would meet our final team member, Charles. We tried to book into the same lodge but with it being the height of the trekking season, everywhere was fully booked. I went to see Paldon, the lodge owner who I'd met on my previous trip but he was also fully booked; he did however get us booked into another lodge.

Charles was trekking up to Base Camp with his wife and two other friends who were also husband and wife. They would return to Lukla, leaving Charles at Base Camp to continue with the expedition. Charles was an experienced mountaineer and had already tried to climb Everest once before but had to turn back only a few hundred metres from the summit, due to bad weather. He had also climbed other 8,000m peaks, including Manaslu. We would now all trek up to Base Camp together over the next week. The plan was to take around 10 days, including rest days, to get up to Base Camp, which would be sufficient time for our bodies to acclimatise as we trekked higher.

The following day, we trekked up to Pangbouche. The pace was incredibly slow but I was in no rush, so it was quite an easy day, arriving at our lodge at around 4pm. Charles wanted to meet Lama Geshi so he could bless us before we headed up into the mountains. Lama Geshi is one of the highest ranking practicing Buddhists in the Khumbu Valley and he has been blessing climbers for decades. He was educated in Tibet before the Chinese occupation when he crossed the border into Nepal. Our Sherpa guide, Lhakpa, managed to organise a meeting with him the following morning.

I remember that Lama Geshi had a very gentle nature and looked quite frail. He was sitting in a down jacket, which he wore over his crimson robe. We were lucky enough to be invited to his house where the blessing would take place. Lama Geshi's daughter was present so, along with Lhakpa, they could both translate.

I was amazed at how detailed the ceremony was and it went on for quite some time. Becky, myself and Charles were all blessed separately. Firstly, he took a thin red string and passed it around my neck. I then passed him a folded silk scarf, which I was given upon arrival, for which I gave a small amount of money as an offering. He said a brief prayer, took the money and placed the scarf around my neck. He then started to chant prayers for my safety and for permission to climb and pass through the mountain. At the same time, he was tossing rice into the air, occasionally ringing a small bell. He was also flicking water over my head. This lasted for a good 15 minutes and it was quite a surreal experience. Everyone was silent and Lama Geshi had this calm aura about him that was almost hypnotic. We all left feeling motivated and privileged to have met and been blessed by him.

JK

Over the coming days, we trekked slowly up the trail, getting closer to Base Camp by the day. It was also getting significantly colder, with snowfall becoming a daily occurrence. It was all fairly straightforward as we had ascended quite slowly so were all well acclimatised by the time we made it into Base Camp. I was very impressed at how well organised and comfortable it was at Base Camp. Henry's logistics were excellent. There was one large, communal mess tent that was used for eating, relaxing and chatting. It was heated by a gas heater so it was always warm despite being around -20°C outside on the colder days.

Then there were around 15 two-man tents set up, which would be home to the climbers at Base Camp. Everyone had his or her own tent, which was quite nice. The Sherpas had their own tents as well but spent most of their time relaxing in the kitchen, which was a massive marquee-style tent that food was stored in and cooked in. There was also a toilet tent, which was basically a hole in the ground with a large oil drum container at the bottom to catch the waste. All of the waste, including human waste, was actually taken out by porters and disposed of further down the valley.

I was quite amazed at the scale of Base Camp itself. We were just one expedition and there were many others on the mountain, making up around 300 climbers, all with the aim of scaling the world's highest mountain. I'd heard horror stories of how dirty Base Camp was and how there was rubbish everywhere. This mainly came from people who had never set foot in Nepal, let alone Base Camp, but I was amazed at just how clean, tidy and organised it was. Perhaps other climbing expeditions were different but I saw very little, if any, waste or rubbish lying around.

After a few days relaxing at Base Camp and chatting with other people, I was surprised to find that most of them had been saving for years and some had even remortgaged their homes to get the chance to fulfil their dream. It was refreshing to see, as there is often a lot of negative criticism about people who try to climb Everest. It is mainly portrayed by the media that anyone who wants to climb Everest is a self-glorified, selfish individual, taking advantage of the local Sherpas to carry them to the top. The media has also alluded to the fact that everyone out there are simply rich play boys with nothing better to do with their time than ticking Everest off their bucket lists. There may have been one or two people that fitted that description, but I certainly didn't cross paths with anyone like that.

Henry finally arrived at Base Camp a few days after us and went about setting himself up in his tent. From there he would command all the movements up the mountain. He was very much at home at Base Camp and had spent many years of his life there over the best part of three decades. He suggested that Becky, Charles and I should go for an acclimatisation walk back down to Gorakshep and then hike up Kala Patthar.

The following morning, we had breakfast and headed out of Base Camp, back down the frozen trail that was littered with boulders and stones that slip away under foot. A common injury on the Base Camp trail is a twisted ankle, so I was mindful not to let that happen to me. We arrived back at Gorakshep and I popped into a lodge to grab a bottle of Coke and some chocolate. We then made our way slowly up Kala Patthar where the views were simply stunning. On the way back down, I was quite surprised to see that Charles was beginning to fall behind as we descended. I asked if he was okay and he said he was just a little tired.

I realised that something was wrong when I turned around and saw him slumped on a rock, resting. I walked back up with Becky and he told us he was light-headed and thought he just needed to have something to eat. I was really surprised, as he was an experienced climber, but I also knew what it felt like to run out of energy and let your sugar levels get low, as it had happened to me while training. I offered to take his rucksack and at first, he was reluctant. He was losing his motor skills as he struggled just taking his rucksack off. I gave him my Coke, which he sipped and we all walked slowly down. As quick as he had felt faint and weak, he was okay again and asked for his rucksack back. The energy boost from the Coke was almost instant and he put it down to just not eating enough, which was probably the case.

We arrived back at Base Camp a few hours later and spent the rest of the day relaxing. By now, I was starting to feel very comfortable and settling into Base Camp life quite nicely. When I'd first arrived, I was out of breath just walking to the toilet, but now I was moving around like I was at home and didn't really notice the altitude.

I was writing a blog in the communication tent and I heard Henry shouting my name. Henry was the type of guy who commanded your attention: when he said, "jump", you asked, "how high?" I went over to his tent and he called me in. He had been speaking to Rob on the phone and he wasn't going to be coming out after all. I pretty much knew this but there was a slim chance he may have been able to get out. Unfortunately he was still unwell and had things at home to take care of that took priority over climbing. He sent me a lovely email a few days later, wishing me well and reassuring me that I would be fine. I was absolutely gutted that Rob wasn't able to make it out; he was the person who really made it happen for me and had personally recommended me to Henry. I didn't want to let Rob down so, in a strange way, not having him there motivated me even more to push hard and see the expedition through.

The next morning, Henry would be coming up to Camp One with Becky, Charles and myself. It was to be my first time in the infamous Khumbu Icefall. We would have breakfast at 4am and head into the icefall at 4.45am, just before dawn. This was the best time to be going through the icefall. I'd heard lots of horror stories about how dangerous and scary it was and I quickly realised that it *was* very dangerous. However, for some reason, I didn't find it scary, it just really felt like I was on an adventure. It was still dark so we were moving under the light from our head torches. It took a good 15 minutes to get off the rock of Base Camp into the ice where we would put our crampons on.

As we made our way into the Khumbu Icefall, I could hear the ice cracking and moving around me. Henry kept reminding us that this was the most dangerous part of the climb. Many people have been killed over the years when large crevasses open up with little or no warning, causing large seracs (blocks or columns of glacial ice) to collapse. These can range from the size of a car to a large house and would take no prisoners when gravity is pulling them down.

As we climbed higher, we came to one of the first ladder crossings over a large and very deep crevasse. I watched Charles cross first with confidence and then Henry said it was my turn. There were three separate ladders that had been lashed together to form one long, continuous ladder.

"The key is not to look down, take your time and don't panic. Panic will kill you, nothing else will," Henry advised.

Those words stuck in my head. There were two ropes that ran either side of the ladder, which were fixed in at each side, acting as a support rope that I could hold for support and balance as I crossed. I was wearing my harness and unclipped my carabiner and clipped it onto the safety line that ran across the crevasse. If I did fall, in theory, it would save me, but I certainly didn't want to find out.

I stepped slowly onto the ladder with the spikes of my crampons slipping on the bars as I walked across. I looked where I wanted to go, held the support ropes taut and, before I knew it, I'd crossed. I thought it wasn't that bad and I'd quite enjoyed crossing the ladders that were strategically placed through the icefall trail. It didn't take long before I started to feel quite confident and the hours drifted past as we made our way up through the treacherous terrain. Charles asked me what I thought of the icefall and the ladder rope crossings. "So far so good," I replied. He started to explain that the exposed crevasses that we could see were not that dangerous compared to the hidden ones. Snow bridges can form over a crevasse and to the untrained eye, they appear to pose no danger until walked over and it collapses.

(A crevasse is a large opening in the ice that can be just a few metres or hundreds of metres deep. Most of the crevasses we were crossing were so deep that we couldn't see the bottom; it was just one giant, black abyss. If a climber was to fall, it would be almost certain death and no attempt would be made to rescue them.)

There weren't many climbers in the icefall; it was mostly Sherpas carrying large loads of equipment up to Camp Two. I was amazed at just how much they were carrying in these tricky conditions and the fact that we were now at a height of 6,000m. The altitude just didn't appear to affect them as they so nimbly moved through the icefall, making it look so easy. Most of the Sherpas were locals who were born and raised in the Khumbu Valley and were following their relatives' footsteps by working in the mountains. It was dangerous work but could earn them over 10 times what they would earn in a normal job in just a few months of the year. It's expected as the younger generations grow up and become independent that they look after their parents and family. One salary from a skilled Sherpa can quite easily look after an entire family for some time. Because of this, there are a lot of young Nepalese boys trying to get in to mountaineering.

They would typically start out as a porter, hauling supplies up the trail to Base Camp. Then they may be employed as a Base Camp assistant, helping out with the cooking, cleaning and general day-to-day activities. The next step would be carrying equipment between the camps and gaining experience at altitude as well as improving their climbing skills. Only then would they possibly get a lucky break with an expedition company to guide paying clients. The rate at which Sherpas work is something I've never seen before. They move around so quickly and are always on the go, quite often working until they're exhausted.

It took us about five hours to make it up through the icefall and onto the foot of the Western Cwm, where Camp One was situated. I was pleased to be feeling quite strong as we arrived at our tents, which had already been erected by our Sherpa team. Henry and Charles were sharing a tent and Becky and I would sleep in the next tent. We unpacked our roll mats and made ourselves comfortable. We had a gas burner inside the tent to melt snow for drinks and for cooking food. I was amazed at the amount of time it took for the water to boil, but this was due to the lower levels of oxygen. We made some hot chocolate and boiled up some ration packs. Darkness fell quite quickly so Becky and I both shot some video footage for our video diaries before it got too dark. It felt great to take off my boots, change into a clean base layer that I'd packed in my rucksack and jump into my sleeping bag.

I felt really pleased with the day's efforts, as I lay relaxing in the tent. I was also another step closer to the summit. My goal when I arrived in Nepal was to take it one step at a time. When I arrived at

Lukla, I just wanted to get to Base Camp, feeling as fit and fresh as possible. I had achieved that relatively easily, so the next step was to navigate the icefall and make it up to Camp One. I was never thinking about what lay ahead in days to come and would only focus on the next logical step up the mountain. Everest really was far too big to view as a whole and I knew that mentally, I had to break it down into bite-sized pieces. That concept had worked for me in the Atlantic so I knew it would work now.

I fell asleep quite quickly and didn't wake up until the morning. I actually felt very comfortable and cosy in my sleeping bag and would have been happy to have stayed there for a few more hours but we needed to get back down through the icefall before it started to warm up. We needed to make our descent as early as possible when the icefall is still partially frozen from the night before, at its most stable state.

We all descended in good time, making it back down to Base Camp for a late breakfast of porridge and eggs. Henry was happy with our progress through the icefall and planned for us to have one rest day and then head back up the icefall, this time passing Camp One and going straight up to Camp Two in one hit.

JK

On our rest day, Charles, Becky and I decided to hike up to the Base Camp of a surrounding mountain called Pumori. It's not climbed as often because it's extremely prone to avalanches but a trek to Base Camp would pose no danger to us. Pumori means 'Unmarried Daughter' in the Sherpa language and was actually named by the famous English explorer and climber, George Mallory.

We took some photos and returned back to Everest Base Camp. Charles was almost certain that lying around the whole day in a tent would not be as beneficial as a gentle walk and some active rest. He was right; I felt very strong that evening and was excited for the following day's climb up to Camp Two.

The next morning, we didn't do anything differently from last time and headed into the icefall at around 4.30am. This time, there were a few more climbers making their ascent. In the darkness, I could see their head torches up in the distance; they looked almost like little ants moving up the mountain together.

We made it to Camp One in good time and stopped briefly to eat some snacks and take some water on board. The terrain had now changed as we were up on the Western Cwm so it was a lot more stable and started to flatten out with a gentle incline up to Camp Two. One thing that really shocked me was just how hot it was getting in the afternoons. The sun would come up and reflect on the snow and ice, so not only was the sun shining down on me, it was also reflecting up from below me, causing the inside of my nose to burn.

Henry had heard from the Sherpas that there was a large crevasse that we would need to cross and then it was a fairly easy walk up to Camp Two. He wasn't wrong: I couldn't believe my eyes when I saw the length of this ladder. It must have spanned a gap of almost 30m. It took seven ladders lashed together to cross this crevasse. I watched as one Sherpa went across with a load on his back and even *he* was wobbling all over the place as the ladders were buckling and twisting from side to side. Charles and Becky were standing by my side and, for some mad reason, I said, "I'm happy to go across first." I was very nervous but knew that if I didn't panic, looked where I wanted to go and just took it step by step, I should be okay.

There was a little bank to walk down to the start of the ladder so I stepped down. I stopped and looked round to my right and there were about 20 Sherpas sitting resting with their heavy loads before continuing up to Camp Two. Every one of them was watching me intently. I looked at the other side and took my first few steps. It was quite straightforward to begin with and the ladder felt sturdy. As I started getting further out, the ladder started to twist from side to side, making it quite tricky to keep my balance. This was not a good combination when below my feet appeared to be an endless drop into darkness as it was so deep. I slowly carried on, taking one step at a time. I got to the halfway point and I heard Charles shout, "Well done James, you're over half way."

That's when I had the urge to just run across to get to the other side as quickly as I could but I knew that would be very dangerous, so I had to remain calm. As I started to get closer to the other side, my crampons were getting stuck in between the ladder sections. All of a sudden, I tried to move my right foot and, as I moved forward, it became stuck and caused me to lose my balance. Luckily, I stayed upright. My heart rate went through the roof and the adrenaline rushed through my veins, but I knew that I mustn't panic. I wriggled my foot and eventually managed to get the crampon free. I carried on moving, falling forwards and grabbing the ladder just as I made the other side.

I was only stuck for a few seconds but it felt like an eternity as I crossed one step at a time. I was so relieved when I looked back at the huge crevasse I had just crossed. It had really boosted my confidence to deal with the ladders. Charles was next to cross and managed it without any difficulty. Becky and Henry opted to walk around the crevasse but it would most likely add an hour of trekking onto their day, so Charles and I headed up to Camp Two. He had filmed me crossing the ladder so I was quite excited to play back the footage when we got there.

10

No shortcuts to the top

It was technically just a simple walk up to Camp Two but, by this stage, I was absolutely exhausted. I could see the yellow tents far off in the distance but they were a lot further away than they looked. Charles was walking slightly faster than me and, about an hour later, I was greeted by Lhakpa, who showed me where our camp was.

There were a lot of teams who had already established their camps for the night, so without Lhakpa showing me the way, it would have been tricky, as they all looked the same. We had a large, communal mess tent set up with a table in the middle and a bench down either side to sit on. There was also a kitchen tent where a cook would live and work. Around the mess tent were our tents for sleeping in.

I dumped my kit into one of them and sat in the mess tent with Charles, looking at the footage of me crossing the ladders. When Becky and Henry arrived, I heard a bell being rung, not dissimilar to a school bell, which was a sign that dinner was served. I couldn't believe it when the cook walked in with a plate of pizza that he'd cooked. With what minimal resources they had, as well as cooking on a gas stove, the quality and variety of food that was being cooked, even at Camp Two, was outstanding.

Soon after dinner, we all retreated to our tents. I was feeling tired but pleased that I had made it up to Camp Two without any problems. It had certainly been a long day coming up from Base Camp.

I got comfortable in my sleeping bag and chatted with Becky for a short while before falling asleep. The next thing I knew, I heard a voice calling, "James, James." I wondered what was going on at first and then realised it was Becky calling me. It was pitch black in the tent so I felt around until I found my head torch, which I had placed by my side as it was uncomfortable on my head while I was sleeping. I turned it on and looked at my watch. It was 2am; I asked Becky what was wrong.

"James, I'm a bit worried, I can't feel the left side of my body."

I sat up out of my bag and looked at her. She appeared to look okay.

"You're probably just cold, are you wearing enough?"

It was noticeably colder at Camp Two and I could really feel it. I'd say the temperature was falling to around -30° at night.

I did see that Becky didn't have any gloves on so I took mine off and put them on her. She held out her hand and I slipped one glove on, but she couldn't hold her left hand out straight when I was trying to put the other glove on. It was as if she had no strength in that hand at all. I looked at her face and all of a sudden, I noticed dribble coming out the side of her mouth. She could see I was looking at her in a slightly anxious way, so she tried to talk to me but was slurring and just grunting, unable to communicate properly. By this point, I was very worried, as this was more than just a case of being cold and she didn't feel that cold to the touch.

It was the middle of the night, freezing cold outside and pitch black but I needed to do something fast. Thankfully, Henry was in the next tent so I said to Becky that I was going to get Henry. She nodded in agreement, so I began to get kitted up to go outside. It wasn't a case of just unzipping the tent and walking outside, I had to put extra layers of down clothing on and put my boots on. It took about 10 minutes to get ready. I got out and carefully walked over to Henry's tent, making sure I didn't trip on any guylines coming off other tents as a lot of snowfall had covered them up. My headtorch was illuminating the area in front of me so I could just about see where I was going. I unzipped their tent, making sure my head torch didn't shine in their faces when I poked my head through and quietly called Henry. I was a little worried that he was going to go nuts for waking him up, as on occasion, he could be quite rude and abrupt. One climber who knew Henry joked that he always said, "Hello Henry" twice when he saw him, as he didn't know if he was going to get the grumpy Henry or the friendly Henry.

He was absolutely fine and asked what was wrong. When I described Becky's symptoms, he said he would come straight over and to go back to the tent. Becky was now talking coherently without any problem, which was a relief. Henry showed up a few minutes later with a bottle of oxygen and a mask. He told me to go and sleep in his tent with Charles and he would stay and monitor Becky in my tent. I moved over to the other tent with Charles.

"Henry was quite worried as the symptoms you described sounded very similar to a stroke," he told me as I clambered in to the tent. There wasn't a great deal that could be done due to the time and place where this was happening.

The next morning, Charles and I were up early and having breakfast in the mess tent when Becky walked in. She looked absolutely fine and said she wasn't sure what had happened in the night, but that she would be going back down to Base Camp with Henry. Charles and I were going up to Camp Three for an acclimatisation climb before descending back to Camp Two for another night. We left Becky and Henry having breakfast and headed out with Lhakpa up towards Camp Three. It was still quite a long walk up the Western Cwm until we got to the Lhotse face, which we would need to scale to get up to Camp Three, situated half way up.

The first hour was a very easy walk until we got to the foot of the Lhotse face. We were looking up at a wall of ice and snow about 800m high and at a 45 to 50 per cent incline. It was quite steep, but not technically difficult to scale. The Sherpas had fixed a series of ropes all the way up the face so it was just a matter of clipping in to the rope with my jumar and slowly ascending. Although we were out of the icefall, there were still very real dangers of avalanches from the surrounding slopes.

The noise and motion that an avalanche creates is hard to comprehend unless you're there. When you see the side of a mountain just give way and you hear a roar from the snow and ice hurtling down the mountain destroying anything in its path, it is quite unnerving. We were reminded of the dangers of avalanches only a few minutes later when we were just about to start climbing the Lhotse face. Lhakpa suddenly shouted, "Get down and cover your heads!" I could hear a sound from above and as I looked up, I could see bits of ice falling down that were gathering momentum and pulling larger chunks off, some the size of a television. They came whizzing past us like bullets and I could hear the whoosh from every chunk that passed me. My natural instinct was to pull my rucksack over my head to protect me and lean into the face. Had they hit anyone, these chunks of ice would have caused serious injury but luckily, no one was hurt.

The avalanche had been caused by someone hundreds of metres above us who had kicked some ice free by accident, starting a sequence of events that could have led to everyone below them being seriously injured. This was just the nature of being on Everest and the reality was that danger was all around us. Lhakpa joked that we'd had a close shave and we carried on climbing slowly. Every few steps were pretty tiring as we were now at almost 7,000m. I wondered what Camp Three was going to be like as the whole face of the mountain was on quite a severe slope.

A few hours later, we had arrived at some of the first tents that made up Camp Three. The Sherpa teams had dug them into the slope so they were pitched flat into the side of the mountain. We took a few minutes rest and then made our way back down. Descending wasn't difficult but we really had to be careful that we didn't rush as gravity was really trying to pull us down. Once we got to the base of the Lhotse face, we unclipped and casually walked back to Camp Two. Both Charles and I were buzzing as we'd just touched Camp Three with no real difficulties and were feeling good.

We had some dinner in the mess tent and then crashed out in our tents for the night. The next morning, we woke early again and had a good breakfast to see us back down the icefall. It didn't take long for us to be out of Camp Two and into the icefall again. I noticed that the route through it had changed quite significantly from the previous time we made our way up, only a few days before. There had obviously been a collapse in the ice causing the old route to be wiped out. A group of local Sherpas made up from various teams would fix a new route through the mess of jagged ice and hidden crevasses. Old, twisted ladders would occasionally protrude out of the ice that had most likely been caught in a collapse and that's where they ended up. This group of Sherpas called themselves the 'Ice Fall Doctors'. They were highly experienced Sherpas who would maintain the route through this dangerous section on a daily basis, assessing and testing if ladders were still safe or needed to be fixed.

Nobody would have been able to negotiate the icefall without these guys' expertise.

We made it back to Base Camp in good time, as we needed to be quick descending through the icefall. It was starting to get quite warm with the sun beating down on the ice and this is when the icefall is at its most dangerous. We got back to Base Camp and chatted with Henry for a bit. He was pleased that we'd had no problems at 7,000m. I put my kit in my tent and washed with some water that the cook had warmed up for me. It was lovely putting a clean T-shirt, socks and pants on to a clean body. I also had a shave and felt like a new person.

Becky was in her tent and came out to speak to me; she was pretty upset. Henry had told her that she was probably going home, as he wasn't happy with her climbing again. Obviously, I felt very sorry for her, as I knew how hard she had worked to secure a sponsor and had not given up when many others would have done. Henry told me that Becky had had some issues at altitude before which he hadn't known about. That was a game changer and he didn't want to take the risk of her going back up. He had consulted one of the doctors who was working at the Everest high altitude hospital, which is set up every year to deal with any medical issues and the advice was not to let Becky take the risk. It wasn't really any of my business what went wrong at Camp Two, or whether Becky should go back up, I just felt terrible for her. I tried to be friendly and supportive, although in the back of my mind, I knew I couldn't do or say anything that would take her disappointment away.

That night, Charles and I were the only ones in the mess tent at Base Camp as Tim and his clients were up at Camp Two. Becky walked in with tears in her eyes.

"I'm going home tomorrow and just wanted to say goodbye."

I walked out of the tent and put my arm around her to comfort her, as she was understandably upset. Later that evening, Henry walked in: "I know Becky is disappointed but I just couldn't take the risk with her if something similar happened higher up."

He then told us to stay at Base Camp for another day before we headed back up to Camp Three where we would spend one more night and then descend. If we didn't have any problems with that, we would be going all the way next time.

I had friends and family who were following my blog and they couldn't understand why we were going up and coming back down again as opposed to just going straight up. I had to explain that it was a process of acclimatisation. There are no shortcuts to the summit of Everest and each time I climbed to a higher camp, my body was exposed to lower levels of oxygen. So we would go up and come down, each time going up just a little bit higher, to the next camp.

During this process, the human body cleverly starts to build up more red blood cells to carry the oxygen around the body more efficiently. My body was acclimatising nicely as I could walk around Base Camp with no effort whatsoever; unlike the day I arrived when I had been absolutely exhausted. The rate at which we were ascending was critical and it was only now I realised why Henry was so adamant about not rushing up to Base Camp and always moving very slowly. I knew this from previous trips but it really was showing as we spent more time on the mountain.

The following morning, Charles and I got up to see Becky off; she was being picked up by helicopter. Helicopters were coming into Base Camp daily to deliver food and ferry out sick or injured climbers. A makeshift helicopter pad had been constructed out of stones and was positioned away from the camps. The pilots were incredibly skilled and generally never actually flew over the camps, or tried not to anyway. We could hear the roar as the helicopter flew up the valley and turned around to come back on itself, landing into the wind. The rotor wash was quite powerful as Charles and I stood just off the pad, taking photos. As soon as it landed, people were taking baskets of eggs and supplies out that had been brought up the mountain.

We hugged Becky and wished her good luck and, as fast as the helicopter came in, it was gone again. We walked back over to our camp.

"That's it James, it's just you and me now - let's get this done," Charles said.

He was right: although Henry was providing logistics for Tim and his clients, they didn't really have anything to do with us.

JK

We started to get ready for our next acclimatisation climb the following day. This acclimatisation phase would see Charles and I sleep at Camp Three, which was over 7,000m high, so we planned to sleep with supplementary oxygen. Henry spent some time with us, running through how to use the oxygen masks and the valve systems that control the flow of oxygen. They were very simple to use and weren't too invasive. A friend of Charles', called Kenton, had arrived at Base Camp a few days earlier. He was a friendly, likeable guy and I was actually borrowing a pair of his high altitude boots. I'd met Kenton before but only very briefly. It was going to be his ninth summit attempt, which he would be filming with a French climber/cameraman. Kenton was very good friends with Rob so he knew about my Atlantic Ocean row. He was extremely confident, but for someone who was arguably one of the best high altitude climbers to date, he was actually a surprisingly modest, approachable guy.

Charles and I were up at 4am ready to leave Base Camp at 4.30am. The first few hours flew by and we were both pretty strong and efficient at moving through the treacherous icefall by now. We made it up to Camp Two in a fairly average time. For some reason, I was feeling more fatigued than the first time up to Camp Two. I was getting a little bit of a cough which most people had by now as the air was so dry. Its nickname was the 'Khumbu cough' and it was quite nasty.

Kenton and his climbing partner were also at Camp Two and were heading for Camp Three the following morning. Charles mentioned that he was feeling strong and was wondering if Henry would send up a couple of Sherpas to go on from Camp Three to Camp Four and potentially the summit. Henry's advice was to just see how we felt. The original plan was to spend the night at Camp Three and come back down for a rest before the final push to the top.

I was slightly anxious, as I didn't feel as strong as I hoped I would. I was sharing a tent with Charles and we woke up slightly late, which put us on a bit of a back foot, and missed leaving with Kenton and his friend Sebastian. We needed to have a quick breakfast before we could go anywhere so we rushed down some porridge and got going. Charles appeared to be in a hurry and for some reason, I wasn't sure why, I was very slow. Charles went ahead and said he would wait for me when he got to the Lhotse face. To be fair, he did wait.

"James, for some reason you're struggling and you're very slow. Maybe you should go back."

I told him that I would rest for a bit and see how I felt. Charles carried on so I watched him start to climb up the start of the Lhotse face. We heard on the radio that Kenton and Sebastian had already made it to Camp Three.

I sat for a good 15 minutes thinking about what to do. All of a sudden, I had this strong urge to keep going. All I had to do was climb the last part. It was technically very easy, just physically demanding. I was one of the last climbers that day on the Lhotse face and was climbing on my own. I was incredibly slow but I knew that if I just kept going, I would get to the safety and luxury of my tent and sleeping bag. I was taking a mere 10 steps then stopping for a rest. I repeated that process for several hours and as I got closer to the tents, my adrenaline levels went up and I found a last wave of energy. I could see our tents but they were still about 20 minutes away.

I thought I was the last guy to make it up to camp that day as the sun had set and I was way behind schedule. As I stood resting after another set of 10 paces, I heard some footsteps. To my amazement, I turned around and was greeted by a Sherpa who was carrying a massive load on his back. It was almost the size of the Sherpa himself. He came up beside me, stood next to me and let out a gasp of breath.

"Almost there mate, are you okay?" he asked. I looked at him, feeling slightly embarrassed that I was so fatigued when all I had to carry was my rucksack which was extremely light in comparison to what he was carrying. I was leaning over, panting, but stood up.

"Yes I'm okay thanks, almost there." He spoke very good English and I couldn't believe what happened next. "No problem, man," he said, casually lighting a cigarette as he walked off, carrying this heavy load on his back. His effort was super human anyway with the load on his back but he was also smoking a cigarette like it was a walk in the park. The altitude just didn't appear to affect him in the slightest, he was moving twice as fast as me, if not more.

It was also because his physiology at altitude was so much more efficient than mine. A lot of the Sherpas lived all year round at 4,000m in some of the villages. Most of them have never been below 1,000m, which is Kathmandu's altitude, let alone seen an ocean. I wondered if they would be super human athletes if they came down to sea level but sadly, most of them would never get the opportunity to travel outside of Nepal. Some lucky ones do, such as those selected for Gurkha training.

After feeling rather embarrassed at how weak I was in comparison to this Sherpa, I carried on the slog up to camp. As I got closer, Sebastian, who'd arrived hours before me, very kindly came out and took my rucksack. We scrambled along the last 20m or so together. I crawled into the tent with Charles and I think he was quite surprised to see me. I was extremely relieved that I'd made it and pleased that I hadn't turned back. Charles made me a cup of tea and I quickly got into my sleeping bag. After a short time, I started to feel a little better and my heart rate had come down significantly. Charles called Henry on our two-way radio to let him know I was alright and that I had made it in, albeit a bit late.

Henry wanted to speak to me over the radio and he asked me if I was okay and why I was so slow. I told him I wasn't sure but I was feeling fine now. Kenton and Sebastian were in the tent next to us only a few feet away so we could hear them and they could hear us. They were resting up and going to sleep using oxygen. Henry told us on the radio that we ought to come down tomorrow, as the weather wasn't looking great. Charles was instantly unhappy about this and insisted that he wanted to stay and climb with Kenton and Sebastian. Henry wanted Charles to accompany me back down so I felt responsible for Charles being asked to come down. I felt awkward, but I hadn't actually done anything wrong. We were supposed to be going back down anyway. I think Charles was transfixed on the summit as this was his second attempt and he was feeling strong.

For about 10 minutes, there was a full-blown argument on the radio between Henry and Charles. I apologised to Charles if it was my slow progress that was denying him the opportunity to go for the summit now as opposed to coming down. He calmed down later and was absolutely fine about it. Charles was a very driven man who owned three MacDonald's restaurants and had invested in numerous properties. He was a very financially astute businessman who worked extremely hard. He was also involved in buying and selling art, something I understood very little about.

At the time of the Everest climb, Charles was also buying another house back in the UK and the deal was just going through. I took the satellite phone I'd used on the row out to Everest, as I knew I wouldn't always be able to get reception on a mobile. I would occasionally call home and send messages with it. I also let Charles use it to call home but he mostly called the estate agent who was working on his new house. I didn't mind as we got on quite well; he was very supportive and I felt very comfortable around him. I could tell he was a vastly experienced business man and had a lot of life experience. I thought it was perhaps just meant to be that I ended up climbing the world's highest mountain with Charles.

The following morning, we woke up and started melting ice for a cup of tea. Kenton popped his head into our tent as he and Sebastian were off to Camp Four. We wished them well as they would be standing on the summit in 24 hours' time, all being well. We got out of our sleeping bags and kitted up ready to make the descent back down to Camp Two.

I now had plenty of energy and felt quite strong, a far cry from how I'd felt the previous day. We made it back down the Lhotse face very quickly, almost keeping up with some of the Sherpas who were also coming down. I was actually slightly ahead of Charles and he made a comment that I was obviously feeling better today. It was odd how I'd felt so weak the day before. Charles said to me that night, "That's the problem with altitude, one minute you can be fine and the next minute you can be dead." It was a sobering thought.

We headed back down to Base Camp the following day, which was fairly uneventful as we were more than accustomed to moving through it now.

"Have you heard what happened at Camp Three last night?" asked Henry on our return. We had no idea.

"The bad weather that was forecast hit the camp hard and wiped out half the tents." Everest can be a hostile place and it was worrying how quickly things could change. It can be perfect conditions at one camp and up at the next camp, it can be blowing at over 100mph.

The wind is what stops Everest being climbed all year round and the main climbing season is during the months of April, May and early June. This is the monsoon in Asia, which pushes the jet stream north, opening up a small window of opportunity to summit. This, of course, can change quickly and many climbers have been blown off the mountain in the past when the forecast has been wrong and a sudden change in the jet stream has occurred. Henry had a forecast sent to him from the Met office in the UK, which indicated that the wind was going to pick up significantly around the 7,000m mark, but above and below would just be moderately windy. The forecast was incredibly accurate, demonstrating how jet stream forecasting is a vital part of high altitude climbing. Luckily, no one was injured in the high winds, just tents destroyed, which could be replaced.

Henry knew Charles wanted to try and get up with Kenton but it wasn't meant to be and Kenton was far stronger than Charles and I would ever be. Some people have a natural ability too and doctors still don't know what defines that ability over someone who can't acclimatise. It's not always a reflection of how fit someone is; even extremely fit athletes can struggle at high altitude. There were two loud-mouthed Americans to whom I'd been speaking in the icefall only a few days earlier. They were boasting about their marathon times and how they were in the best shape of their lives. They probably *were* extremely fit back home, but this was a different environment altogether and, by pure chance, I saw one of them being taken back down through the icefall looking extremely sick. He recognised me and said he was going home because he was sick and couldn't acclimatise. It was only a matter of days since I'd seen him dashing up the through the Western Cwm as if he was in a race.

Everest was proving to be a real leveller: it didn't matter how much money you had or what your background was, everyone was exposed to the dangers and possibility of altitude sickness. Even climbers and Sherpas with years of experience were getting sick and being brought down on stretchers. I quickly learnt that one should never judge a book by its cover because the people who were doing well were quite often the quiet ones who had just plodded along, letting the more testosterone-driven guys crack on. They were often the ones who eventually slowed up or succumbed to sickness.

Charles and I took some much-needed rest for a few days as Henry suggested, while we waited for a good weather window. We heard on the radio at Base Camp that Kenton and Sebastian had successfully summited and were now on their way down. They were one of the first teams to summit in 2011 and were only a few days behind the Sherpas who had just finished fixing the ropes to the summit. Within 24 hours, they had descended from Camp Four all the way to Base Camp, which is a massive day in itself. Charles and I congratulated them and the next day, they were on a helicopter out of Base Camp, back down to the relative luxury of Kathmandu.

11

On top of the world

The next few days passed quite slowly and the nerves were building, as we knew what was coming. I washed my clothes and had everything packed away that I wasn't planning to take with me. I made sure I had all the flags I needed to lift at the summit packed neatly into my rucksack. I certainly didn't want to forget those.

The morning came for Charles and I to leave for the summit and Henry also got up early to see us off. We made it to Camp Two later that afternoon, and I was feeling fine. I made sure that I had plenty to eat that evening, but a few hours later, I had terrible stomach cramps. There was a toilet at Camp Two, which was a small tent that gave a modicum of privacy. It was extremely cold, so every time I went to the loo, I'd end up being freezing cold. I was quite anxious about what to do as I had excruciating stomach pain. I knew I was losing fluids due to extreme diarrhoea, so I made a conscious effort to stay hydrated and kept sipping water with Dioralyte in it, which was absolutely disgusting.

I had to get up four times in the night so I didn't get a great night's sleep at all. I wasn't sure what caused it but there was no point feeling sorry for myself. I'd soon have to make the decision to carry on or head back down. I really didn't want to go back down but it would be almost impossible to climb if I kept having to unzip the back of my down suit and squat. It would also be incredibly embarrassing.

I didn't feel too bad at breakfast the next day and the pain had subsided which was good news. I decided to go to the loo one last time and then I would leave with Charles for Camp Three. I was praying that I wouldn't shit myself halfway up the Lhotse face, so before I left, I packed my boxer shorts full of toilet roll, just in case I *did* have an accident!

Luckily, after an hour or so of climbing, I'd completely forgotten about my stomach and felt absolutely fine. I'd had a lucky escape really, as I'd obviously eaten something that disagreed with me and that could have potentially brought my climb to a premature end. The more time I spent on Everest, the more I realised there was a massive amount of luck involved. It was luck that would ultimately shape the outcome of the climb.

About six hours later, we arrived at Camp Three where we would get our final night's sleep before our summit push. We had our oxygen masks with us and there were canisters of oxygen in the tents to use while we slept. There were different flow rates that controlled the amount of oxygen delivered per minute through the mask. The idea was just to have a trickle feed coming in through the mask. This would improve our sleep and recovery and also conserve the oxygen, which was costly.

Charles spoke to Henry on the radio that night and he informed us that Dorje and Lhakpa would be coming up from Camp Two in the morning to climb with us for the rest of the way. I couldn't quite get comfortable in my bag and then I realised I still had a thick wad of tissue stuffed down my pants. Thankfully, my stomach was still fine, so I pulled the tissue out and put it in a rubbish bag. All of our rubbish was taken off the mountain and I made a conscious effort not to leave any behind. I believed I needed as much luck as possible so I didn't want to tempt fate by polluting the mountain (a bit of a spiritual outlook I suppose). Charles saw me putting a large amount of toilet paper in the tent's bin bag.

"Can you pass me some of that before you throw it away please," asked Charles, not knowing where it had been. I passed him some fresh tissues from my bag instead.

The next morning, our guides Lhakpa and Dorje were with us at 7am. Charles and I were up and almost ready to go. We just needed to tidy the tent up as it was going to be used by Tim and his clients a few days later. We wouldn't be staying at Camp Three on the way back down as the plan was to descend from Camp Four to Camp Two after our summit push.

We checked our oxygen levels, adjusted the flow rate and started to move out of the camp. It was quite simple climbing, as we just needed to carry on up the Lhotse face for another couple of hundred metres. We clipped our jumar devices into the fixed rope and pulled ourselves up. There were a few other climbers making their way up to Camp Four as well, although there was more than enough mountain to go around. Charles was just in front of me by about five minutes. We were climbing slowly; despite the oxygen, it was still tough going on the lungs. Ten steps, rest, 10 steps, rest: this was the pattern I used for most of the way up to Camp Four.

We eventually made it to the top of the Lhotse face and would now traverse across the face to an area known as the 'Yellow Band'. The traverse wasn't too tricky as there was a good trail that had been established and kicked in by previous Sherpas and climbers. Once we made it up onto the Yellow Band, it was a little tricky at times. It was a section of mostly exposed rock that we needed to scale in order to make it up to the next section before Camp Four. Some years, Everest can be quite dry with very little snowfall and settled snow on the ground. This can make certain areas like the Yellow Band quite tricky because it's actually easier to stand and climb on snow and ice that the crampons are designed to grip against. On some occasions, I would slip and lose my footing when I was standing on rock so I was constantly looking for patches of snow and ice to stand on as I pulled myself up.

I started to slow up a little at this point and Charles, climbing with Lhakpa, pulled away from me slightly. After a lot of panting and feeling sorry for myself, I eventually made it up on to the Geneva Spur. This was a straightforward section that spurs round to provide a route to the South Col, otherwise known as Camp Four. There is a fixed line running around the spur so it is fairly safe and flattens out slightly. When I saw the start of the Geneva Spur and realised that there was only a slight incline, I thought I might be able to catch up with Charles and Lhakpa but the altitude and thin air quickly reminded me who was boss as I tried to hurry along the trail.

"Slow down, we have plenty of time," Dorje shouted. I wasn't slow, it was just a mental thing I guess. Eventually I made it onto the South Col, tired and fatigued. I still had a little way to go before I found the safety of our camp that had been established by the expedition Sherpas. The South Col is renowned for being a particularly harsh place, often ravaged by winds that can exceed 200mph. This does leave the area fairly free of significant snow accumulation.

Along with the high winds, one of the biggest dangers now was altitude sickness. We were just above 8,000m, a point where the amount of oxygen is insufficient to sustain human life and referred to by climbers as 'The Death Zone'. At these altitudes, the atmospheric pressure is significantly lower, about a third of sea level pressure, resulting in less oxygen to breathe. This can be a significant threat and has taken the life of many climbers. Camp Four is also a pretty unpleasant place as it's incredibly difficult to sleep and quite often the digestive system slows down or, in some cases, completely stops. At this altitude, the body in most cases prefers to use stored energy sources (fat) rather than digest food.

Camp Four was set up slightly differently to the rest of the camps. There were just two large eight-man tents, which would be our home for the next 24 hours. Before I got into the tent, I was bursting for a wee. I needed to be pretty careful as it was around -35°C outside so I couldn't leave myself exposed for too long. I needed to be quick! I'd been making a conscious effort to drink as much as I could, as the colour of my urine was a good indicator of how dehydrated I was. I was trying to drink enough water for my urine to be clear and, on this day, I'd drunk what I thought was a lot of water. I was bizarrely excited to see if my urine would be clear or not. I quickly found a place away from the tents and was disappointed to see that it was the darkest yellow I've ever seen. I felt fine, but knew I really needed to drink more.

Now Charles and I were at Camp Four, we had a strategy for our final summit push. We arrived into Camp Four at around 2.30pm and would rest up until 10pm. We would then leave for our summit push and climb through the night, hopefully arriving on the summit in the early morning as the sun was coming up, then descend back down to Camp Four in the daylight.

With this in mind, I wanted to get as much rest as possible and tried to eat and drink as much as I could. Lhakpa and Dorje had their own tent next to us and Charles and I shared. I managed to get a ration pack of beans and sausages down me. They were the same type of ration packs that I'd been eating on the row and ordinarily, one pack wouldn't even touch the sides. Now I was absolutely full and couldn't manage any more. We had some Pringles in the tent, which were quite easy to eat. At this altitude, everything was difficult, just a simple task like putting my boots on left me completely out of breath.

The trick appeared to be no sudden movements and to move as slowly as possible. I managed to get some sleep and woke up at about 8pm. Charles was awake and I wasn't sure if he had managed to get any sleep or not. I certainly couldn't sleep again as I was too apprehensive. Charles was very supportive as he'd been here before and told me what to expect. He said there was nothing coming up that I couldn't manage, considering how far I'd already come.

At 9.30pm, Lhakpa unzipped our tent and poked his head through. "Be ready in half an hour, guys," he said. I was as ready as I was ever going to be. I no longer felt tired, I was actually starting to feel hyped up and I could feel the adrenaline coursing through me, a similar feeling to what I'd experienced at the start of a motorcycle race, when I'm sitting staring at the start lights, revving the engine and slipping the clutch to make a fast getaway when the lights change.

We set off very slowly and I didn't have a problem at all with the pace; I was feeling comfortable. It was a stunning evening, not one cloud in the sky and the moon was shining bright, so we hardly needed our head torches to illuminate the ground in front of us. Gradually, the incline started to increase as we moved further up. There weren't many people going for the summit that evening, so it was extremely quiet on the mountain. A few teams were in front of us and we were the last team making our way up. We could see the head torches high above us in the distance, not a dissimilar sight to looking up in the icefall early in the mornings.

It wasn't too difficult at this stage as we all had a nice rhythm and the supplementary oxygen, albeit a trickle feed, but it was really helping.

The hours just drifted away and when no one was talking, which was most of the time as that used precious oxygen, it was an amazing silence with just the crunch of snow under our boots. Looking up at the night sky was something I will never forget. I thought the night skies were good in the middle of the Atlantic Ocean and they were, but this was something else. Of course there was no light pollution so the sky was crystal clear. Thousands of stars littered the sky and shooting stars would whizz across the horizon. Every time I saw a shooting star, I would make a wish; they were the same every time. I just wanted to stand on the summit and return safely.

I could feel the weight of responsibility on my shoulders from all my sponsors and I really didn't want to let them down. I was starting to feel fatigued now so I asked Dorje how long we had been climbing for. He confirmed we'd been going for over six hours and would soon be at the balcony where we would rest for a few minutes. This was a flat area where we stopped and swapped out our oxygen canisters for fresh ones. I wasn't sure if my previous canister had run out because I felt a real difference when Dorje connected the new one. A few minutes later, as we were about to continue, I had a sudden urge to wee but when I told Lhakpa, he said I shouldn't undo my down suit as I wouldn't be able to warm up again. He was right. It was extremely cold, around -40°C, so I decided to try and forget about it. After 10 minutes or so, the urge had completely disappeared.

We were now climbing up the south face of Everest towards the south summit. It was a lot steeper now so progress had slowed up a fair bit. I went back to the rhythm of 10 steps, rest, 10 steps, rest, and continued to slog my way up the mountain. The sky was starting to brighten up as I looked to the east and the sun was gradually lighting up the magnificent scenery all around me. Another hour passed in the blink of an eye and we were approaching the south summit. The sun had come up and was casting a gigantic shadow of Everest on the horizon. It was a sight that words just can't describe, a true once-in-a-lifetime view.

As I stepped up on top of the south summit, the true summit came into view. Everest can be an extremely demoralising place; it just keeps going and going. It's almost impossible to grasp the scale of it without actually being on the mountain. As I was making my way up the south summit, Dorje was shouting, "Good work, almost there." I knew I still had the Hillary Step to go but had only seen it in pictures before. I was running on pure adrenaline at this point and didn't really have any emotions or thoughts, I was just putting one foot in front of the other. As I looked up, I could see the Hillary Step in the distance and other climbers making their way up to the summit. They weren't that far ahead of me and I could see Charles moving slowly along with Lhakpa. We needed to climb down a ledge of snow and ice to traverse along a ridgeline to the base of the Hillary Step.

By now, some climbers who had summited were on the way back and were coming past me. Some were friendly and shook my hand and others just passed without a word. Most of them were wearing goggles, so along with oxygen masks, we all looked like fighter pilots and couldn't really make out the person underneath. Dorje and I carefully manoeuvred our way along to the base of the Hillary Step, where we waited for a couple of climbers to descend. The ridgeline running along to the Hillary Step was incredibly exposed, so although we were clipped in to a safety line, we still needed to be exceedingly scrupulous.

The Hillary Step was a wall of rock and ice, around 40ft high. There were ropes that had been fixed by the Sherpa teams but they don't take the old ropes down from previous seasons. This could sometimes cause confusion: if a climber were to clip an ascending device onto an old rope and it snapped, it would most likely have a fatal outcome. Dorje showed me which rope to use that had been fixed that year.

To make it slightly easier, the rope was colour coded so it was clear which one was newest. Due to the lack of oxygen, it can sometimes be quite a challenge figuring out what rope is what, as the brain's ability to function is massively reduced at such altitude.

The Hillary Step has been the cause of much controversy over the years as it's typically a real bottleneck for climbers all trying to push for the summit. I was extremely lucky that there was no one else around apart from Charles and Lhapka who had already hauled themselves over it. Without any pressure, I clipped into the red and white rope that Dorje pointed out and began to climb. Strangely, I wasn't out of breath at all and managed to get up and over without any real difficulty. I went up before Dorje so I waited at the top for him. I surveyed the ground in front of me to see the route up to the summit and as quickly as I could turn my head to look back, Dorje was standing right there. His strength at altitude was just mind-boggling, scaling the Hillary Step in a matter of a few seconds and a couple of large lunges.

It was quite a surreal feeling as I advanced up the Hillary Step. To think I was climbing in the same footsteps as Edmund Hillary and Tenzing Norgay. I also wouldn't be surprised if George Mallory and Andrew Irvine trod in those very steps, but that's still the subject of much debate.

It was now a very straightforward walk up to the summit. Again, a trail had been kicked in and there was a rope to clip into. It took a little while to see the summit. I can only describe the last hundred metres like walking around a long, gradual corner and expecting to see something any minute, but you just keep walking and walking. Eventually, the summit came into view and it was an incredible feeling. I was staggering along, breathing at an uncontrollable rate, with the most amazing feeling of relief that I had done it. Little did I know at the time that I was in fact only half way and things were about to go seriously wrong for me.

Charles and Lhakpa came past us as they were making their way down. At this point, we were only metres from the summit. Charles stopped and shook my hand, shouting under his oxygen mask, "Well done James, you've done it!" I was breathing hard at this point and moving slowly so Dorje put his arm around mine and quickly walked me over to the summit where I immediately sat down, relieved and exhausted. I managed to catch my breath as the oxygen was still flowing into the mask despite all the ice that had frozen around my beard.

I then found myself in what appeared to be like a pre-programmed state, going through the motions of taking my sponsor flags out of my bag and getting Dorje to take the photos. I needed those photos and prayed that the camera didn't fail me. Unfortunately, the wind had picked up so the flags were blowing all over the place. Despite needing to take 10 separate photos with various branded sponsor flags, it didn't take long.

It was only then that I really stopped and stared at the breathtaking view and it sunk in that I was standing on top of the world. I'd made it to the summit of Everest. It was 8.30am on 16th May, 2011, and it was just me and Dorje standing proudly on the roof of the world, with not another soul to be found. It was a rare experience to be standing on the summit of Everest with no one else there.

I stared out to the south, looking down into the valleys of Nepal and further on with India in the distance. The horizon was over 150 miles away and I could just make out the curvature of the earth. Despite the sun shining down on us, the sky above was very dark, almost like we were looking out into space. I turned and looked to the north and could see clouds covering the entire Tibetan plateau; mountain tops protruding through the clouds in the distance.

The summit area was a lot bigger than I'd imagined and was

covered in prayer flags that Sherpas and some climbers had put there. The locals, being mostly Buddhist, believe that the wind will carry their dreams and prayers. It was quite common for climbers to carry things to the top to either take a photo with or to leave in memory of someone. Some climbers even take the ashes of loved ones who have passed away and scatter them at the summit.

Charles had a photo of his daughter that he threw off the summit. I never understood why he threw it off; she was my age and absolutely gorgeous! One chap apparently set a record for carrying a bike to the summit of Everest. I thought this was slightly strange but a good effort; I don't believe he rode it down. Most pictures or mementoes that are left there in memory of someone are soon blown away by the ferocious winds that batter the summit for most of the year.

I didn't personally leave anything on the mountain but I asked Dorje if it was considered acceptable to take a small piece of summit rock home as a souvenir. I wasn't sure if it would be frowned upon, spiritually, but he said it was fine. Dorje told me to wait while he got me some rock from the very top of the summit. He came back with a massive grin on his face and two massive chunks of rock in his hand.

"Dorje, I don't want to take half the mountain back," I proclaimed. He just laughed and put them in the top pocket of my rucksack.

We had been on the summit for about 15 minutes and the excitement that I initially felt had subsided; I was cold and very tired. I became very nervous as the realisation suddenly hit me that I was in fact only halfway and I hadn't made it at all. I still needed to get back down and if anything went wrong, there was nothing anyone could do. The whole time I spent on the summit I knew what I was doing but it was all very surreal and I couldn't get moving to make my descent any sooner.

12

The reality of Everest

Initially I was okay and was taking slow but consistent steps back down towards the Hillary Step. Dorje was hurrying me along until we were at the top of the Hillary Step looking down. It looked a lot steeper now I had to go down it rather than looking up at it. I used my figure of eight device to abseil down the rope. For some reason, I was finding going down far more punishing than going up. It was the gravity that was constantly pulling at me and the effort I made to hold myself back was tiring.

It didn't take long before I was exhausted and, after taking two or three steps, I had to stop. Dorje wasn't happy at all and kept shouting at me. It was frustrating, as I wanted to move without stopping. However I was completely out of breath and was panting so hard, it was hurting my chest. It was like I'd just run a 100m sprint as fast as I humanly could, after only taking a few steps. Something was seriously wrong and I had no idea what was going on.

We stopped briefly and changed out my oxygen canister, which improved things slightly. I hauled myself up over a little ridge to get myself back on the south face and started making my way down. I would now start to lose altitude quickly as I was descending straight down. To play it safe, I was abseiling down some of the steeper parts while trying to make sure I didn't lose my foothold. I was woefully slow which was worrying, considering I was quite strong on the way up and now I was coming down into thicker air.

"This is shit, you're going to die! Do you want to end up like that Japanese guy?" Dorje shouted at me. I could see the worry in his face as he said it, which stressed me out even more. I had no idea what was happening to my body and why I just couldn't breathe. I also had no idea what he meant by his reference to a Japanese guy, but he continued to say it over and over again.

A little later, I saw an object in the snow just off the route. I thought it was some empty oxygen canisters at first. I slowly worked my way closer, step by agonising step. I then realised that it wasn't empty oxygen canisters, it was a climber, lying lifeless, frozen solid in the ground. It was a Japanese man - now I knew why Dorje kept referring to him. It turned out he had suffered a heart attack and died instantly a few days before our ascent. His team was unable to get him down at the time so descended without him. They did retrieve and repatriate his body a few weeks later. I hadn't spotted him on the way up as it was dark and his body was just off the route.

I will never forget what he looked like, as he lay flat on the ground with his arms outstretched, almost like he was reaching out for help. I could tell he was frozen solid by the way he was positioned in the snow and his eyes were shut as if he was sleeping. It made me feel desperately sad that he would never get to see his family again and they had lost someone who was probably a son, father and brother.

It was the kick up the arse I needed, realising that if I didn't get a move on, that may also be me lying frozen in the snow. I was so tired that I was falling asleep standing upright. If it wasn't for Dorje shouting at me and hitting me, I would have fallen asleep and never woken up again. This just couldn't happen - I *had* to get back. Despite having to rest every few steps, I knew that if I just kept repeating the pattern over and over again and focused on moving forwards, I would make it back to the safety of Camp Four where there was more oxygen and I could rest. The concept of continuing to do something until I either got what I wanted or where I wanted had never failed me yet and now I really needed it. Something was seriously wrong but it wasn't the time or place to worry about it, I simply had to keep moving.

I eventually made it back down to the balcony where Dorje was waiting for me. He told me to keep going as he was restacking some empty oxygen canisters that were going to be collected. I carried on in front of him and continued to make my way down. I was by no means out of danger but I knew that I was getting much closer to Camp Four. At this point, everyone else who'd made it to the summit was back down in their camps, it was Dorje and I who were still descending.

I was exhausted but that same feeling of adrenaline I had when I was nearing the summit started to come back as I could just about make out the yellow of the tents in the distance. I stopped for a few minutes to take a sip on some water and to catch my breath. It was a futile effort as I was just as tired after only taking a few steps. All of a sudden, my right leg slipped out from underneath me and I fell back onto the snow and ice. I slid down the slope for what felt like a long way and then my safety line that was clipped into the fixed rope came to an abrupt stop, jerking me back. I was extremely fortunate: had I not have been clipped in I would have fallen a lot further.

It all happened so quickly that I had no idea how it happened. After realising I was safe and wasn't going to fall any further, I breathed a sigh of relief, looked down at my feet and saw that my right crampon had fallen off and that's why I'd slipped over. I was perplexed as to how it came off without me noticing. I carefully lowered myself down to retrieve the crampon, which was about 20m below me and was fortunately stuck in a pile of snow. I reattached it, making sure it was tight and double-checked my other one.

Dorje was still up at the balcony so was quite a way behind me. I carried on making my way slowly down and, to my delight, the yellow tents in the distance were getting bigger. By this point it was starting to flatten out onto the South Col so the walking conditions became a little easier.

It was a massive relief making it back to the safety of our camp. As soon as I arrived, Lhakpa came out to see me. He opened my tent and I just collapsed inside the doorway. Charles was just relaxing in his sleeping bag.

"Well done James, we just climbed Everest, we can head home now."

I was utterly exhausted on a level that I'd never experienced before, way beyond anything I'd felt while rowing the Atlantic. Lhakpa helped me take my boots off before I got into the tent and I crawled into my bag.

To my amazement, I couldn't actually sleep. My eyes were wide open, staring at the roof of the tent. The last 24 hours had been a complete blur. Charles and I were chatting about how lucky we were that we had summited and were now homeward bound. We still weren't out of danger until we were back at Base Camp but we were at least one step closer. I eventually drifted off to sleep but woke up in a panic a few hours later, panting for breath. I checked the gauge on top of the oxygen canister and I was out of oxygen. I couldn't see another bottle in the tent so I called for Lhakpa, and in so doing, I woke Charles up and he asked me what was wrong. He said I could use his oxygen for a few minutes, as he was feeling fairly good.

Lhakpa came in with another bottle and I swapped the canister out. I took a few deep breaths with the flow rate right up and then turned it back down to just a trickle feed. I fell back to sleep and didn't wake up until the following morning. I was feeling much better so was quite relieved and eager to have some food and get moving again. We had some tea and biscuits, which wasn't a great breakfast, but we had limited supplies with us. We knew there was an abundance of food at Camp Two and that was where we were heading.

We got kitted up fairly quickly and chatted with Dorje and Lhakpa who were going to stay at the South Col for a bit longer, just to organise some things for Tim and his clients who were arriving the following day. We started walking slowly down the trail off the South Col and round to the Geneva Spur. After only 15 minutes, I started to feel exhausted and I was breathing much more heavily than I should have been, not dissimilar to how I felt descending from the summit. I started to slow down and was stopping frequently; Charles was getting quite agitated and annoyed at my slow progress. He stopped with me when I was stopping but eventually said, "James, this is dangerous mate, we still have a long way to go and you just can't stop like this. If you can't keep moving, you're going to die and I can't wait for you. It's as simple as that."

I knew what he was saying was true: my brain was functioning but my body just wasn't responding. I had no idea what was wrong but I just couldn't get any rhythm going and was starting to really worry. Dorje and Lhakpa caught us up quite quickly and told Charles to carry on and they would see me down. They kept asking what was wrong, why was I stopping, why was I so tired. I just didn't know.

I managed to descend through the Geneva Spur and through the Yellow Band but it was taking twice as long as it should have done. Lhakpa had now gone on to catch up with Charles. Dorje was not happy with me in the least, shouting and swearing at me every time I stopped to catch my breath. I was now approaching Camp Three where I would stop for a short while to eat and drink. I climbed slowly down and was quite relieved that I had made it to this point, albeit painfully slowly.

Camp Three was occupied by Tim and a few of his clients. Some of them were still coming up the Lhotse face. I sat with Tim for about half an hour and he kindly made up some orange tang, which was like orange squash. It was very refreshing and my parched mouth and throat quickly absorbed the fluid. I ate a Mars bar and chatted to Tim for a bit. I was still incredibly tired and asked Dorje if I could stay at Camp Three and get back to Camp Two the following day. Tim was very quick to say that it wouldn't be possible as there was no space; his teams were going to be occupying the camp and I should descend, no matter what. I knew if I could make it to Camp Two, I'd surely feel better as I would have descended over 2,000m, which would make a massive difference.

I wished Tim good luck with his summit push, although he was looking strong and probably wouldn't have any problems. Dorje and I got cracking and started to head back down the Lhotse face. For the first 10 minutes, I was moving much better than I had been and thought that maybe the thicker air was finally starting to make a difference. No sooner did I think that, my body just stopped again. I could only take a few steps at a time before having to stop as it felt like my lungs and heart were about to explode. There were more anchor points on the Lhotse face so I had to stop at each point to unclip and re-clip. I had two safety lines so I was always clipped into a fix rope. A slip on the Lhotse face would almost certainly have been fatal. By now, Dorje had given up shouting at me and was just following and watching over me. I did feel sorry for him as the stopping and starting would have been tough for him as he was carrying quite a heavy load.

On the way down, we passed some of Tim's clients who were on their way to Camp Three. Some of them looked as tired as me, and things were only just beginning for them. I managed to get off the Lhotse

Face and on to the flatter Western Cwm but was totally exhausted. I needed to sit and rest before I could move on. By now, I hardly had the energy to stand up, let alone walk. In the distance I saw Lhakpa who was clearly coming back from Camp Two to help Dorje get me back.

Dorje's behaviour had changed towards me; he could see that something was seriously wrong. My eyes were glazed over and I struggled to even string a sentence together. Lhakpa told me to sit down and hold up both hands, then he and Dorje tried to drag me along. I didn't like it and, although I was beyond exhausted, I knew I had to stay on my feet. I got up again and with Dorje and Lhakpa either side of me, we walked at a snail's pace back down towards Camp Two. Both my arms were around each of them taking a little bit of my weight.

As we approached Camp Two, I could see people looking at me. I still had an oxygen mask on, which was not a common sight at Camp Two. The local Sherpas from other teams started to come out to see if I was okay and to ask if they could help. I could hear them asking where I had come from and Dorje spoke in English, informing them I was coming back from the summit. One American guide came out and asked if I was all right. I remember looking at him and saying that I was okay. Our tent was established at the bottom of Camp Two so we walked all the way through the camp with everyone stopping to look at me as I was nursed back to the tents.

A few climbers congratulated me on my summit and I felt proud, but at the same time I had a feeling of shame that I was using oxygen and being helped back to my camp. I couldn't understand why I was struggling so much when I had been very strong and should have been getting my energy back as I descended, not finding that it was deteriorating. Much to my relief, we made it back to the tents and I was greeted by Charles, who was looking quite fresh, casually reading a book in the tent. I crawled in and Lhakpa kindly helped me remove my boots. He then pulled out an energy gel and squeezed it into my mouth. I drank some tea and reflected in my mind back on the last 48 hours, which had been a surreal blur.

Whenever I lay in the tent, whether at Base Camp or on the South Col, I'd always felt safe and relaxed. However, in the last two days, I had been massively out of my comfort zone. At about 5pm, I leant back in to the tent to lie down, and the next thing I knew, I was waking up at 7am the following morning. I was still shattered and wasn't really looking forward to the trek down through the icefall. As if Henry was reading my mind, he called on the radio and told us to take a rest day and remain at Camp Two. I was extremely relieved, as I still needed to rest, although Charles was frustrated so I didn't let him know that I was secretly very pleased.

I spent most of the day sleeping and relaxing in the tent. I did get up to stretch my legs by walking around the camp. I sent a few text messages and called my parents to let them know I was okay. By the evening, I was feeling much better and looking forward to heading down to Base Camp the following morning. Charles and I chatted in the tent that night about all the things we were going to do and eat when we got back to Kathmandu. I was getting really excited.

We got up early the following day and had breakfast. Charles and I headed off down through the Western Cwm, while Dorje and Lhakpa were going to catch us up later. For the first hour, I was fine and walking along at quite a good pace with Charles. I'd had plenty to eat and drink so my body was fuelled and certainly should have been in a better state than it was. I asked Charles if we could slow up a bit and he said that was fine. I kept slowing up as I was becoming increasingly fatigued until I had to stop altogether.

"James, what's going on?" asked Charles.

"Come on, I want to get down and I'm getting cold now, we need to keep moving."

I felt like I was back up on the South Face at over 8,000m, gasping for every breath. Charles told me to sit down and stop moving while he took my pulse.

"Jesus, your heart rate is through the roof! You shouldn't be breathing this hard - we are much lower now. Something is wrong," he said worriedly.

I absolutely knew something was wrong; my entire decent from the summit had been agonisingly slow and laborious.

Charles called Henry on the radio and told him we had a problem. Henry calmly told us not to worry because the 'boys' (Dorje and Lhakpa) would be with us soon. I was still able to walk but I could only manage 10 steps at a time. We still had the icefall to descend and that wasn't a place where you wanted to be stopping. Only a few days before, there had been a serac collapse, killing a climber.

Dorje and Lhakpa did arrive a short while later.

"What the hell is wrong with you now?" Dorje asked, in a very abrasive manner. I had massive respect for him and I truly believed that without him, I may have been a frozen corpse on the mountain, but I wasn't going to continue letting him speak to me in that manner. I spoke firmly and calmly, looking him straight in the eye.

"Dorje, do not speak to me like that, I have a problem and something is wrong. I don't know why I can't breathe but I want to get down just as much as you do. If you want to go on, that's fine. Do you understand?"

He considered my words, "No problem, just keep moving."

They were carrying some oxygen canisters down and Lhakpa suggested that I use it. Instantly I felt a bit better and was able to move slowly without stopping. Charles continued on through the icefall on his own as he was feeling strong and just wanted to get off the mountain. We made our way through the icefall and across the rope ladders. I was embarrassed to be using oxygen but it was making a positive difference and I needed to get down. It was mostly Sherpas making their way through the icefall as most climbers had either summited and were at Base Camp or were on their summit attempt thousands of metres above us.

My sunglasses were steaming up when I was wearing the mask so Dorje lent me his. As we came to the bottom of the icefall some time later, I took the mask off as the oxygen had run out and it was impairing my breathing anyway. Base Camp was extremely quiet and I didn't see anyone until I'd navigated my way around the boulders and chunks of rock back to our camp. The first person I saw was Karmi, who worked as a Sherpa years ago but now managed the Sherpas who worked for Henry. He was a kind, calm man who was always smiling. I really liked him and he made me feel at ease. He shook my hand and gave me a hug, then disappeared to the storage tent and came out with a Mars bar for me. I woofed it down and sat in the mess tent drinking copious amounts of lemon tea, which tasted delicious.

"James, come here!" Henry's voice came bellowing out of his tent. I was actually really nervous as I thought he was going to give me a massive dressing down for being so slow and using oxygen on the descent. I dumped my rucksack in my tent and walked over. Henry had his own large, five-man dome tent that had a fold-up bed with a duvet, big pillows and a big gas heater in the middle of the floor. This was the Operations Room where he conducted all the logistics on the mountain. Vastly experienced, Henry had put many people on the summit and also saved many lives with his experience on Everest.

I walked down to his tent and took my boots off outside. I entered the tent and Henry was standing there with a sat phone to his ear and the biggest grin on his face. "Well done, I've got someone on the phone for you." I had no idea who it was and was slightly taken aback. It was Rob on the other end, who was back in Canada.

"I knew you would do it Ketch, you are very strong. I'm so proud to know you," he gushed. It was wonderful talking to him; he was so supportive and kind. I certainly didn't feel strong but had a euphoric kind of feeling at that moment in time. I passed the phone back to Henry who ended the call.

"I have something for you," said Henry. I wondered what it could be. It was a bottle of Fanta. Henry knew I had a bit of a soft spot for soft drinks. I opened it then and there and took a long swig; it was so refreshing and just what I needed. It was amazing how the simplest of things could become a luxury.

Henry didn't mention anything about why I was so slow and had struggled so much on the way down, which I was quite surprised about. I said I was sorry for being so slow and weak descending. He told me not to worry about it, as I had just climbed the world's highest mountain. He suggested that I just rest up and start eating and drinking as much as I could. I went and sat with Charles in the mess tent and one of the cooks made me a large bowl of noodles, which went down a treat.

I then went to relax in my tent and fell asleep. That evening, I was starting to feel like I was getting my energy back but I was still having problems breathing and became breathless every time I moved around. I spent a couple of hours in the communications tent writing a blog, informing everybody that I was safely back at Base Camp and describing the last week's activities. I was getting excited at the prospect of heading back to Kathmandu and travelling home.

JK

The next morning, Charles and I were chatting over breakfast, and he mentioned that he wanted to leave today. I was still anxious about the fact I was still struggling to breathe, so I wanted to stay on for another day's rest. I was sure I wasn't suffering with any altitude-related sickness, as I didn't have any headaches, dizziness or sickness.

I actually felt very alert; it was just the breathing that was a problem.

The moment Charles mentioned that he wanted to leave Base Camp, Henry happened to walk in and asked if we would stay another day, as he wanted to walk with us but couldn't leave until the following day. Henry's work was almost done; all of Tim's clients, including himself, had successfully summited and were on their way back down. I instantly said that was fine by me and Charles reluctantly agreed too. I mentioned to Henry that I was thinking about going to see the doctor at the Everest Base Camp Hospital.

"Well, if you want to waste $200 to be given some Paracetomol, then be my guest," he replied gruffly. I was quite taken aback, but thought maybe he was right and I just needed to man up a bit.

I also had some frost nip on my fingers. Frost nip isn't quite as bad as frostbite; it's where the surface of the skin has been exposed to cold temperatures. As a result, the skin forms a large blister and swells up. Years ago, it was considered quite cool and a bit of a war wound to have some frost bite and a few fingertips missing. Nowadays, it's completely different: with the advances in kit, there are no excuses why somebody should get frostbite. It's now considered to be poor personal admin if climbers are succumbing to severe frostbite, unless of course they happen to be involved in some kind of accident or situation where they become stranded on the mountain.

I packed my kit away and decided what I was going to take with me and what I was going to leave for the yaks to bring down. Kenton had kindly lent me some high altitude boots as mine were a little too big. Unfortunately, where I tripped and fell on my way back to Camp Four, my crampon from the other boot caught on the gaiters and ripped them quite badly. I did mention it to Henry but he said not to worry about it. Apparently they were a very old set, but I did offer to pay for them nevertheless.

The next day, we were up early and got ready for the walk from Base

Camp back down to Pangbouche. Henry now had a change of plan and couldn't leave until later so he told us to go ahead without him. Charles wasn't impressed, as the whole reason we waited another day was to walk with Henry. We set off and luckily Charles walked at a gentle place for me to keep up. I was still struggling to breathe but I was able to push on without stopping.

We stopped in Pheriche for a quick drink and a slice of cake before continuing on to Pangbouche. Just over an hour or so later, we arrived back down in Pangbouche to the luxury of the lodge. That evening, I was in my room relaxing when there was a knock at the door. It was Ang Nuru who I'd met back in October when I was trekking with Rob. It was a really good feeling being able to tell him I had summited. He instantly noticed my finger that was badly blistered due to frost nip. He fetched some warm water and I soaked it as he advised. He then wrapped a bandage around my finger. We chatted for a short time before he had to leave.

I didn't have a particularly good night's sleep as I had an excruciating pain around my coccyx area. I couldn't lie on my back, so had to lie on my side or front and I really struggled to get comfortable. I wasn't sure what was wrong but thought that perhaps I'd damaged that area when I fell coming back down to Camp Four and it was only starting to show now.

The following morning, I got up for breakfast, despite still feeling pretty rubbish. My body still wasn't right and I wasn't looking forward to the day's trek that lay ahead of me. Charles was feeling fine, as he had pretty much fully recovered by now. Henry stayed in a small village just above Pangbouche and was planning to meet us at the lodge for breakfast. When he arrived, we had porridge and toast, with lemon tea. We ended up chatting for about an hour or so before deciding we should get a move on. I was sitting at the table in a huge amount of discomfort but didn't mention it. I was trying not to cough and was breathing deeply.

Henry noticed I was struggling so he suggested that I hire a porter to carry my rucksack. I really didn't want to do this and felt uncomfortable with the idea. I think he could tell.

"Listen, you've just climbed the world's highest mountain and you're sick. There is no shame in having someone carry your bag, you have nothing to prove," he insisted.

I reluctantly agreed and a porter arrived a few minutes later. We made slow progress as Henry walked quite slowly but that was fine by me. It certainly made a difference not having a rucksack on my back but I was by no means feeling strong, it just made it a little easier getting up some of the slopes.

We stopped in Tengboche for coffee and cake. We were sitting outside, eating our cake, when a friendly trekker started talking to us.

"You guys look like you have been out here for a while," he said. We laughed and told him we had been there for six weeks. He asked us what we had been doing and we told him we had been on an expedition. I'm personally not one for gloating so we didn't mention that we summited about a week ago but when he asked, if we "got to the top," in his words, we did say yes. It was quite funny as he started getting really excited and wanted to take our pictures and get our signatures for his diary. He appeared to be a genuinely friendly person, so we chatted with him for a short while before moving on.

We had a long descent down the Tengboche hill, which was quite straightforward, but with every one downhill, there would be an uphill. The next few hours were spent slowly making our way up the other side of the valley. We eventually passed through Khumjung, which is famous for being the home to the school Edmund Hillary set up many years ago. By this point, we had been trekking for the best part of 10 hours and we still had a little way to go. I was exhausted by now and even Charles was feeling a little tired.

Now that we were back in an area with good mobile coverage, my phone started ringing. I answered it and it was my dad, just seeing how I was getting on. I had spoken to him that morning when we set off and he couldn't believe we were still walking. I told him that all was fine, we were just moving very slowly. Our destination was Syangboche Airstrip, which sits just above Namche at almost 4,000m.

It was starting to get dark so we put our head torches on and carried on. There was something about walking in the dark with head torches that I quite enjoyed. A short while later, we arrived at Syangboche Airstrip. There isn't a great deal there, just a lodge and that's about it. It's an unpaved airstrip and for most of the time, it's used for supply drops by helicopters; occasionally, small aeroplanes would land but not that often. We went straight to the lodge where we would stay the night and get picked up by aircraft the following morning to be taken to Lukla.

That night would be our last night in the Khumbu Valley so we all had a beer that evening. I was feeling shattered and I'd had a porter to carry my bag for me. I gave him a good tip for his efforts although it was probably the easiest day he had ever had as a porter, since my bag was very light in comparison to what he would usually carry.

We were up at 6am the following day as the plane was due to arrive at 7am. We were out on the airstrip at 6.40am and a few minutes later, the small single engine plane touched down. I've flown a fair bit over the years but there is something about these small planes that fascinates me. We jumped in and strapped ourselves in tight; it would only take around eight or nine minutes to make the flight to Lukla; it takes around six hours or so to walk.

The pilot manoeuvred the plane into position for take-off and, without any warning, he applied full throttle and we were thrown back into our seats. I was surprised at the power and speed at which we were accelerating. The airstrip was effectively a large field that had a dusty strip cleared of stones and debris. The plane was still violently shaking as it hurtled down the strip, getting closer and closer to the side of the mountain. There was no room for error and, had we had an engine failure, there was no escape route. We would have just plummeted straight off the side of the mountain into the valley.

Just as we were getting closer to the end of the strip, the plane lifted off and we left our stomachs in our seats. We climbed at quite an impressive incline and then turned sharply to the right to avoid the mountain that was now in front of us. The skill of the pilot was simply astonishing. The flight was over so quickly but I will never forget those magnificent views. We touched down in Lukla where we would change planes to a bigger twin-engine Otter. We had to wait a few hours before we could get a flight as there was some cloud cover that rolled in which put a temporary stop to the flying. We had breakfast at the same lodge we ate at on our first day in the Khumbu, about five weeks earlier. Thankfully, the clouds lifted and the planes quickly began flying again. We were on the next flight out so made our way over to the small airport terminal building to go through security and board the plane.

After a short while, the plane shot off down the runway and into the air. I sat on the right hand side again so I could see the Himalayas and survey the mighty peak that is Everest, reflecting on the past week, which had been one of the hardest of my life. It was a very surreal feeling looking back at Everest's summit in the distance and reminiscing what it was like to be standing there.

We touched down in Kathmandu about an hour later and the first thing that hit me was the temperature. It was very hot and couldn't have been any further from the weather that I'd been subjected to over the past few weeks. Charles and I chatted weeks ago in Camp Two about wanting to stay in the Yak and Yeti Hotel, which is one of the top hotels in Kathmandu. Henry didn't want to stay there but he got the driver to drop us both off. It was early afternoon when we arrived so we checked into our rooms.

The first thing I did was find clean clothes and took a long shower. It was my first shower in almost six weeks as I'd been washing with baby wipes and bowls of hot water. This had been sufficient but I'd missed the luxury of a hot, powerful shower. I stood under that shower for almost half an hour, washing myself again and again; it felt divine. I then headed out to the same barber I'd visited the last time I was in Kathmandu for a decent shave and a haircut. My beard had grown pretty long and my hair was an absolute mop.

"Bloody hell James, I didn't recognise you, you look 10 years younger!" said Charles when he saw me. I certainly did look a little smarter.

We had one very important job to do and that was to head over to the North Face shop to sign the Everest Summiteers wall. We walked in and discreetly told the shop assistant that we had just summited and asked if we could sign the wall. She fetched a black marker pen and handed it to Charles. He quickly signed his name, but there were quite a few signatures, so I wanted to choose a space carefully. Suddenly, I spotted Rob's name and knew instantly that I wanted to sign my name next to his. I took the pen and very slowly signed my name, thinking back to the time that Rob and I were standing in that very same spot. "Your name will be on here soon," he'd said to me.

After we signed our names, we grabbed some lunch and picked up a few things to take back for family and friends. I was still in a lot of pain in my coccyx region and found it very painful sitting down, so when I got back to the hotel, I decided that I wanted to see a doctor. The hotels were very good at arranging this sort of thing and about an hour later, there was a knock at my bedroom door.

I explained to the doctor that I'd just returned from Everest and was still having problems breathing. I also told him that I was in a great deal of pain and couldn't sit down properly. I was flying home to the UK the next day and, to be fair, there wasn't much he could do, but he was very helpful and friendly. He listened to my chest and said that as I was flying home the next day, the best thing I could do was to get home and go straight to my doctor. "As for the pain, take these," he said, passing me a few tablets and telling me to take one before I got on the plane. I had to pay around £50 for his time and the tablets but it put my mind at ease, as I was still quite anxious about my breathing.

It was my last night in Kathmandu so Charles and I went out for a meal; we did invite Henry but he was busy. After the meal, we went back to the hotel, which had a casino so we decided to check it out. I had no clue what I was doing but Charles appeared to have a vague idea so I just followed his lead. It was actually really good fun and at one point, we were both winning. Inevitably, we lost our money some hours later but we had a fantastic evening and, for a short period of time, I forgot about the discomfort I was in. We got back to our rooms at about 2.30am and crashed out.

My flight was departing at midday so as I left, I shook Charles' hand before jumping in a taxi. I waved to him out of the window as we pulled away up the road. He was flying home the following day. It was an incredibly strange feeling as I left Charles and drove off. In some ways, I felt sad it was all over, as I had become quite close to Charles, despite him being old enough to be my dad. I was dropped off at the airport and made my way through check-in and security.

As I was queuing up to get on the flight, I was minding my own business when a gentleman pushed right in front of me. I thought it was quite rude and was going to ask him what he was doing, but for some reason, I didn't. When I got to the person who was taking my ticket before I boarded, he asked me to wait. He started counting on a spreadsheet and then looked at me and said, "Ah, it's your lucky day, you'll be in business class." It was a real result and I mentally thanked the guy who'd pushed in front of me, otherwise I don't think I would have been upgraded. It was simply a case of right time, right place.

It was only a short flight to Delhi where I was transiting and, apart from bigger seats, business class wasn't that different to economy, but I was still very grateful. When we touched down in Delhi, I walked over to the check-in desk for my next flight back to London. The assistant behind the counter was an Indian woman in her mid 20s who was very friendly. When it was my turn to check in, she smiled at me and said, "Wow, you look tired, where have you been?" My eyes were bloodshot for some reason and my face was still very burnt. She also commented on my finger, which was partially frostbitten and now black. I told her that I was on my way home from Everest.

I joked that an upgrade would be just what the doctor ordered.

"I will try, sir," she said, shaking her head. I didn't think anything of it until I saw her again at the departure gate.

"Sir, I have upgraded you from economy to premium economy." I was quite taken aback so decided to hug her in front of all her colleagues to say thanks.

"Oh sir, it's okay, I hope you have a good flight," she said in a lovely, soft Indian accent. I think I had embarrassed her. I found my seat and sat down. I was next to a woman in her mid 30s who had a very small, newborn baby on her lap. She smiled and acknowledged me but didn't instigate any conversation.

I remembered that I needed to take the tablet the doctor had given me but I didn't have any water. I just put it in my mouth and swallowed hard and down it went. About 20 minutes later, the discomfort and pain I had from sitting down had completely gone and I was in quite a day-dreamy, relaxed state. I fell asleep for most of the flight until a few hours before our arrival. The woman next to me asked if I minded if she breast-fed her child. I thought it was very polite of her to ask and quickly told her that was fine. We got chatting while her baby was on her lap, being fed.

Suddenly, I noticed a white spray fly past my face and onto my sweatshirt. I looked down and it was her breast milk that had squirted on me. I've never seen anyone's face go so red.

"Oh my god, I'm so sorry, I'm so sorry!" she said frantically. I reassured her that it was totally fine and not to worry. I thought it was the best ice-breaker for a conversation you could ever get. She turned out to be a really friendly person who was travelling home to see her parents.

We landed at Heathrow a short while later and I was excited to see my parents who were coming to pick me up. I collected my luggage; a couple of large bags full of kit, then dumped them on the trolley. I was out of breath just pushing the trolley and my chest felt extremely tight, like someone was sitting on me. I saw my parents and walked over to them. My mum stood and looked at me.

"Oh my god, you look like a druggy."

"Thanks mum, it's good to see you too," I replied. I'd lost a lot of weight and my face was tired, sunburnt and haggard. We decided to go home and get straight to the doctor.

Above: Looking down on the village of Namche Bazaar.

Below: Lama Geshe of Pangboche blessing me before the climb.

Above: In the Khumbu icefall.

Right: Becky flying out of Everest Base Camp.

Below: Looking up at the Lhotse Face (Photo: Rob Casserley).

Above: The Australian shopkeeper who knew of Basingstoke.

Below: Michelle and I at The Twelve Apostles in Victoria, Australia.

Above: Taking control of the rickshaw on the streets of Delhi, causing more traffic chaos.

Below: On the road in Arizona.

Above: Chatting to schoolchildren in Bangalore.

Below: My very gracious host in India who kindly gave me a safe place to stay after being held at gunpoint.

Above: Texan dentist who put a stop to my agonising toothache.

Below: Bob and myself on the couch of BBC Newsround on my return.

Above: About to begin the 90-mile straight on the Nullarbor Plain.

Below: Crossing the finishing line. This meant I was the only person to have completed a round the world cycle, rowed the Atlantic and summited Everest.

13

Trial run

We managed to get a doctor's appointment and arrived a few hours later. He looked at me while I explained my problem and without any hesitation, he suggested I go to the hospital right away. Dad dropped mum and I off at the hospital and we sat in the waiting room. The first doctor looked at me and noticed my black finger.

"So where have you just come back from?" he asked. I told him where I had been and what my symptoms were.

"Okay, the first thing I want to do is X-ray your chest and then we can take a look at your coccyx but for now, I want to get to the bottom of this breathing issue," he said insistently.

I went off for an X-ray and then the doctor came in.

"Mr Ketchell, no wonder you have been fighting for breath so much, you have a severe lung infection. You must have really struggled in Nepal."

In a strange way, I was quite relieved, as there was now a valid explanation as to why I had been finding it so tough and feeling so weak.

"Okay, that's great, let's pick up the antibiotics and I'll be on my way," I naively exclaimed. The doctor explained that it wasn't as simple as that. It was quite serious and I'd need to stay in hospital so they could be sure that the infection cleared up. I was quite taken aback but by this stage, I was just happy to be home and was feeling very tired. A nurse escorted me to a bed where I would end up staying for five days.

Later that day, I was approached by a doctor who didn't have anything to do with my case, but took the time to come and find me. He stood by my bedside.

"I just wanted to shake your hand, I understand you have just climbed Everest," he said. We chatted for a bit and he asked me what it was like. Over the course of the next few days, I think four different doctors made the effort to come and congratulate me. It was at that point it really started to sink in that I had just climbed the world's highest mountain.

I was still in quite a bit of pain and couldn't really lie flat as my tailbone was killing me. I told one of the doctors who said he would send someone over to take a look. Initially, they sent me for an X-ray but that didn't show anything out of the ordinary. A few hours later, a female doctor came over and stood by my bed. She was incredibly attractive and just stood there looking at me while putting some latex gloves on. I wondered what on earth she was doing or better still, going to do.

"You have pain coming from your coccyx, lower back area, yes?" she asked. I told her what my symptoms were and in a perfunctory fashion she said: "Right, roll onto your side, pull your boxer shorts down and I'll take a look." Now I knew why she was putting the latex gloves on. She firmly pressed her fingers into my coccyx and was looking at my behind.

My face was bright red and I was incredibly embarrassed while this doctor was rummaging around with my backside. After an interminable few seconds, she said: "Ah, I've found the problem. You have a nasty boil that is causing you pain. I'll burst it and clean the area and it should feel a lot better." I joked with her and apologised about the fact that she had to see this.

"Trust me, this is nothing compared to some of the things I have done over the years," she quipped. She was very pleasant and professional and I hoped I might see her around the ward, but no such luck.

It was strange lying in hospital again. It was a feeling of déjà vu and there was one thought that I just couldn't get out of my mind. I thought it would be a great idea to cycle around the world. The idea kept going round and round in my head. I was thinking of the bike that I would use, the route I would take and how much it was going to cost me. After my motorcycle accident some years ago, I was never able to run particularly well and found that cycling really worked for me. I also knew a few people who had cycled around the world and had read a few books about it. Something just felt very right about cycling the globe.

A few days later, I was feeling a lot better so I was released from hospital, armed with a large bag of tablets. The weeks passed very quickly and most of my time was spent catching up with friends. I needed to find a job fast as my finances were dwindling. It's funny how things happen for a reason; I was starting to look for a job to tide me over and I had a call from one of my sponsors, Ian, from a technology company called ARM. Ian was the Vice President of Marketing and had been very supportive of my previous expeditions and of the talks I was giving in schools.

Ian asked me if I wanted to have a coffee and catch-up in Basingstoke so we met a few days later. Ian very kindly arranged for me to contract for six months in the marketing department, just helping out. I was extremely lucky as it was a very good company to be involved with. The six months passed pretty quickly. Most days I would commute to the office in Maidenhead and they even flew me to California on two occasions to speak at a few conferences. Ian also lined up a talk at his children's school, which was very well received.

I started to fall into speaking almost by accident. I was being asked to speak at various schools and Scout groups. I really enjoyed doing it and I was no stranger to public speaking as I had given quite a few talks after the row. My confidence on stage was growing and I was starting to get paid for the talks, which was a nice way of supplementing my income.

I was quickly learning that the life of a full-time adventurer trying to break into the speaking circuit was not all that glamorous. Most days were filled with emotions that left me either as high as a kite, speaking to hundreds of people, or incredibly depressed, with very little going on. Some friends and family were asking me when I was going to get a 'real' job and stop playing. This really upset me but at the same time, I could see their point. I was earning very little money but was happy doing what I loved. I was fortunate to have the support of some great people around me. Mike Rawlins, who I'd met at the networking meeting, was helping me out with some of my sponsorship opportunities for the world cycle and I was also speaking to Richard Cribb who had now left National Grid and was setting up his own firm, Ofsure.

I finally met up with Richard and I needed to thank him as he had worked hard to raise some fairly significant sponsorship for me. It was great meeting up at last. He was a really friendly, motivated man and I could tell he was genuinely really pleased that everything had worked out well for me. He asked me what I was up to now and I told him about my plans to cycle around the world. He thought it was a brilliant idea and asked what he could do to help, apart from the obvious financial support. Richard had a vast array of contacts from over 30 years of working in the corporate world.

I mentioned to him in passing that I was planning to cycle across America in the summer of 2012 as a warm-up for the world cycle. I wasn't sure if I'd be going solo or if I'd have a support vehicle with me, as renting or buying a vehicle and driving it across the US would be costly and I was on a bit of a tight budget. Richard had a very senior contact at the Tata Group who happened to own Jaguar-Land Rover. He said he would see if he could arrange for them to lend me a Land Rover. My dad was particularly keen to come out and drive across the States with me, so I thought that would work perfectly if Richard was able to secure it.

A few weeks later and after several emails had been exchanged, I had been given a Land Rover to use for my US cycle. I did think that perhaps I'd be better going on my own as having a support vehicle wouldn't really replicate what it would be like cycling around the world unsupported, but my dad really wanted to come along, so I thought I'd be foolish not to use the Land Rover. I was fit and training hard but I also liked the idea of having a support vehicle as a backup as I hadn't cycled big distances like this back to back.

I also needed to secure some funding for the trip. I had a small amount of my own money that I would use but it was not enough. At the time, I was chatting with a technology company called SecurEnvoy about potentially sponsoring me. I actually knew the owners of the company from my days working in IT sales. They were very supportive and the cycle would also provide them with an opportunity to test their technology. Thankfully, they agreed to fund the cycle so I booked the flights and put the wheels in motion, so to speak. The only time my dad could make the trip was between August and September, which wasn't the best time to cycle across the southern states of America, due to the extreme heat, but there was no other option.

I decided to take the 'Adventure Cycling Association' route across the States. It was around 2,800 miles depending on route options from San Diego in California, to St. Augustine in Florida. The route would take me up over the mountains of southern California and drop me down into the desert. I knew this would be tough as the temperatures would be well over 40°C.

The route would then take me through Arizona into New Mexico where I would cross the continental divide. This is actually a drainage divide on a continent, so any water to the west of the continental divide would flow out to the Pacific Ocean and anything to the east would flow into a drainage basin that would lead to the Atlantic Ocean, or a separate drainage basin that's not connected to an ocean.

After the continental divide, I'd head into Texas, down to the southern states of Louisiana, Alabama, Mississippi and Florida. The route would provide a bit of everything in terms of terrain: mountain passes of almost 10,000ft and flat, long, baking hot desert roads. The terrain would be a good test for the world cycle where I was going to come across every environment possible.

Around the time I was due to fly out to San Diego, I was in conversation with Vicki, who worked for a large American company called Qualcomm. They were potentially very keen to sponsor my world cycle, so I managed to set up a meeting with Vicki when I was in San Diego. On 27th August, 2012, my dad and I flew out to San Diego. We had a few days to sort things out and met up with Vicki. It turned out she was really into her triathlons and a good athlete in her own right. She really pushed things at her end to try and make the sponsorship deal happen. Unfortunately, she wasn't the decision-maker and the person who was decided not to take me on. I personally believe that, had the idea been hers, then it would almost certainly have happened, but the corporate world is fraught with egos.

By this time, I was used to dealing with large corporates and negotiating sponsorship deals. I had learnt not to take rejection personally and realised that, most of the time, it was due to not dealing with the right person. There is a much greater chance of closing a sponsorship deal if the opportunity is pitched to the top of the corporate chain, i.e. CEO level, and then filtered down, as opposed to trying to go up the chain.

A few days after our arrival, I set off from Pacific Beach. I had a few people join me for a couple of miles and one of them was Vicki and her friend who was also a triathlete. It was really useful as they helped me navigate through the crazy San Diego traffic. After an hour, they turned back and I carried on.

The first few days were pretty tough. I wasn't in as good condition as I thought I was, actually far from it, and the heat wasn't helping either. It was about 45°C as I made my way through the deserts and into Arizona. I would have really struggled without the support vehicle and at that point, I realised that I'd made the right decision to use it. It was actually a brand new vehicle with only one mile on the clock when we collected it from LA International Airport.

About a week later, I was cycling through El Paso in Texas. I was averaging just over 100 miles a day and was now starting to feel a bit stronger and acclimatising to the heat. I was cycling on my own, as my dad was about 25 miles ahead of me in the support vehicle. I saw a female cyclist on her own so I caught her up. She was quite taken aback when I told her that I was cycling across America. Her name was Shannon, a very pleasant individual with lots of enthusiasm and very chatty. I told her my name and thought nothing of it. I think I was meant to meet her that day as she made contact with me via my website a few days later. Almost six months to the day after I'd met her, I flew out to El Paso to undertake a speaking tour that she had organised with the The University of Texas at El Paso and a few local schools in the area.

I carried on cycling through Texas, which was very undulating in parts and also quite remote in some areas. One evening in Del Rio, after checking into a motel, dad and I were walking over to a diner when I spotted a massive Winnebago-style truck that had Scout branding all down the side. I decided to take a photo and tweeted, "Good to see Scouts in the US." I thought nothing more of it and it must have been pure coincidence, but the very next morning I had an email from a women called Fi from the Scouts Association, asking me if I would be interested in becoming an official Scouting Ambassador. The role would involve visits to Scout groups to give talks and generally attend events, actively promoting Scouting in a positive way. It was strange because I was basically already doing this. I'd been asked to speak at several Scout groups in the past and was being approached by leaders on a more regular basis. I had been a Sea Scout when I was younger, although not for long, and I really like the ethos of Scouting and everything it stands for.

I was specifically asked to be the Hampshire Scouting Ambassador, which really appealed to me as there are over 22,000 Scouts in Hampshire alone and seeing as I've lived in Hampshire all of my life, I thought it was perfect for me. I emailed Fi back and arranged to meet up with her on my return.

It didn't take long before I was out of Texas and into Louisiana, although not before giving a talk at one of my sponsors and ex-employer's ARM offices in Austin. The terrain started to change quite considerably once I started to make my way through Louisiana. It was very flat and humid with a lot of marshland and swamps, sometimes just off the side of the roads. I kept seeing warning signs for alligators but rather disappointingly, I didn't see any.

By now, I was strong on the bike and had dropped almost 10kgs in body weight, allowing me to push some bigger days. I have to admit, having the support vehicle did make things a lot easier. It only took a few days to get through Alabama, Mississippi and into Florida, and on 22nd September 2012, I arrived on the old wooden pier at St. Augustine where the journey ended. I had cycled across America: just over 2,800 miles in 22 days. We loaded the Land Rover up with the bike and drove down to Miami where we flew back to the UK.

14

Another farewell

The months passed quickly with various talks and sponsorship meetings and, before I knew it, Christmas was approaching. I'd been in contact with Fi from the Scouts about my role as an ambassador and arranged for her to come along to a talk I was giving. Ironically, it was an event that I'd agreed to speak at to help two local Scouts fundraise for a trip.

When I met Fi, we instantly clicked. I was surprised that she was 25, as she looked no older than about 19. She was on the Board of Trustees for the Scout Association, which is a very senior position for someone of her age. Fi is a lovely, selfless person with a massive heart. Not only is she a Scout leader and trustee, she also volunteers for a charity that supports children with disabilities and manages a support group once a week.

I carried on training and pursuing sponsorship leads but it never got any easier. One company called me in response to my email saying that they wanted to become the major sponsor and pay for everything. I obviously thought my luck had changed until I received an anonymous call, saying it was a joke and they were sorry for leading me on but they thought it would be funny. This made me feel pretty low and I temporarily questioned what I was doing with my life, pursuing adventures and just about scraping a living through my speaking events.

A few years prior to this, I'd briefly met an extremely successful entrepreneur who owns one of the world's largest groups of companies and he was telling me his story of success, and how he nearly lost everything.

"James, I could either lie down, cry like a baby and give up, or I could fight like a warrior to turn my business around. If things still didn't work out, at least I could hold my head high and be proud that I never gave up."

He continued: "I decided to fight like a warrior and luckily things worked out. So remember James, when you think you're working hard, I can guarantee there will be someone out there who's working twice as hard as you, so never forget that!"

I hadn't forgotten those words and they came back to me now. Instead of feeling sorry for myself, I thought about fighting like a warrior, although fighting like a warrior for *me* would actually just involve sending out and following up on another round of emails to potential sponsors. My luck changed almost overnight and I had a reply from a former sponsor. It was the owner of Pentland Group and he was interested in aligning Berghaus to the cycle project.

We arranged a conference call and the only time he could make was the day I was flying to Europe to give a talk. I was able to take the call in the airport departure lounge about 30 minutes before boarding the plane. He happened to be at his holiday home in Florida, orchestrating his multi-billion pound empire. He was a very direct, straight to the point type of person but I liked that, as I knew where I stood. If he said he would sponsor me, I knew it would happen. Thankfully, he agreed to sponsor the cycle as Berghaus was introducing a new line of cycle clothing that they wanted me to promote and test. As I finished the call, I was being ushered onto the plane by the airline staff. I was so happy: it was the break I'd been looking for. A week later, I also heard back from another of my previous sponsors, Ian at ARM, who agreed to come on board as a sponsor. A mere week had passed since I was feeling pretty sorry for myself and, in that time, I had secured two sponsors and was now buzzing with excitement.

Christmas came and went quickly and before I knew it, it was almost February. The Scouts decided to launch my new Hampshire Scouting Ambassador role by organising a bike ride around Hampshire with a group of Scouts, and visiting Scout groups along the way. The route was a 50-mile loop around Hampshire and was a thoroughly enjoyable experience. The support I received throughout the whole day was absolutely amazing, with so many people turning out to ride with me. To this day, I am extremely proud to be an ambassador to so many amazing Scouts.

A few weeks later, I was getting into my car after a Scouting awards evening where I'd been speaking and my phone vibrated, notifying me that I had a new email. Before I pulled away, I thought I'd take a look at it. It was from a guy called Richard who owned a local IT company called Centrix. He told me that my name had come up twice in one week in conversation so he thought he would introduce himself and offer me some sponsorship, if I was interested. This was the first time that anyone had come to *me* offering to sponsor me, without months of pestering, so I was quite shocked. I emailed him back that evening but didn't hear anything for a few days, so thought I'd give him a call.

Richard hadn't received my email for some reason but said I should come to his office for a chat. I met with him and two other guys, Dave and Ian, Richard's business partners who all co-owned the company. They were very laid back and asked lots of questions, mainly about my previous Atlantic row and then we got chatting about the world cycle and how they could help me. They said they would certainly do something for me and would get back to me. True to their word, they did, and Richard sent me an email confirming they would give me half the funding I'd asked for (they didn't get where they were without negotiating). I was happy with that: a week ago, I didn't even know they existed and now, they had just transferred a four-figure sum into my bank account.

It was getting closer to my departure date of 30th June 2013 and I was being asked a lot about the bike I was using. I did have the budget to buy a brand new bike and I looked at a few but something didn't feel quite right. I really liked my bike that I'd used to cycle across America. It was actually a second-hand bike that I'd paid £300 for about six months prior to the US cycle. I was filming a promo video for a project I was working on and didn't have a bike at the time. A friend of mine, Tim, who was helping me with some video production, introduced me to East Street Cycles in Farnham, where I ended up buying the bike.

I really liked the idea of cycling around the world on a second-hand bike. Too many people get wrapped up in thinking that they have to have the best, biggest and most expensive of everything to go away and do something cool. I wanted to try and demonstrate this wasn't the case, so I was going to cycle around the world on my second-hand 'Trek' cyclocross bike. A cyclocross bike generally looks like a road bike with dropped handlebars to the untrained eye but there are a few differences. The brakes are different from a road bike and the geometry tends to be slightly different.

Although I wasn't going for a speed record, my plan was to adhere to the Guinness World Records' criteria for cycling around the world. This meant that I had to cycle a minimum of 18,000 miles in a west or easterly direction, with no zigzagging and the ride must cross the equator twice. As long as these criteria were met, I was free to go anywhere and through any country I wanted.

I'd spent a lot of time looking at routes and speaking to other people who had cycled around the world and there did appear to be one popular route. It started in London and headed down through Eastern Europe to Turkey and then through Iran and Pakistan, then on to India. Most people who cycled this route flew from Calcutta to Bangkok, cycling down to Singapore and then flew to Perth, where they would head over to the east coast of Australia and fly down to New Zealand. From there, there is a long flight across the Pacific into the US to cycle over to the east coast, generally Florida. The final flight is across the Atlantic Ocean, finishing by cycling up through Europe and back to London.

This is the route I decided would be best for me, although my movements in India would still need finalising. Richard from Ofsure had decided to sponsor me and his main line of business is outsourcing IT to India, so he was planning to fly out to meet me there. I then planned to take a week off as Richard had arranged a speaking tour with some corporate clients and at a few local schools.

One thing I needed to figure out was how I was going to carry my kit on the bike and what I was going to take. My goal was to average 100 miles a day but ideally, I needed to be doing slightly more than that, in order to allow for a few rest days. The more kit I carried, the more weight I would have to push and that would certainly slow me down. I decided to take a bit of a risk and travel with a minimalistic setup and the bare essentials, not even using panniers on the bike. Instead, I would use specially designed frame bags and a large saddlebag. I would run my lights and charge my phone from a dynamo hub I had built into a new set of wheels that would be able to handle the wear and tear they would inevitably encounter on a global cycle.

A few months before I was due to leave, I tested the specially designed bags I'd ordered from the US and the general setup, by cycling from John O'Groats in Scotland to Land's End in England. It was a distance of just over 900 miles. I cycled with a good friend of mine, Ian, who was a strong cyclist. We planned to camp at night so I took everything that I was going to take around the world with me to try and replicate the exact setup and weight of the bike.

I flew up to Glasgow where I met Ian and we picked up a train to take us the rest of the way. The first thing that hit me was the weight of the bike with all the kit I was carrying. I had my bivi tent, sleeping bag, roll mat, a few spare clothes and my notebook laptop that I would take around the world, so I could still write my blogs.

We stopped off in a little village for breakfast and both had a full English, which went down well. About an hour after eating it, I started to feel very weak and tired. I was noticeably slowing down and I didn't know what was wrong. Ian kept asking me if I was all right. I felt light-headed and incredibly weak. We finally made our first camp for the night where we slept. I hoped that I would feel better in the morning. I managed to get a fairly good night's sleep and was up at about 6am.

The sun was shining and it was looking like it was going to be a good day, but after half-an-hour on the bike, I was feeling terrible again: sick, light-headed and with no energy whatsoever. At this point, I realised that it wasn't a case of just being a bit fatigued, I was actually quite ill. We made it to Inverness where I paid for us both to check into a B&B in the hope that a good sleep in a bed might make a difference. It didn't and the following day, I was very ill. After chatting to Ian for some time about it, I decided sadly that I would have to get the train home and leave Ian to finish the ride, as I didn't want to hold him up.

We headed down to the station where I caught the train back to London and said goodbye to Ian. I felt guilty for leaving him but I was slowing him down and was quite sick. I also felt incredibly embarrassed that I was supposed to be cycling around the world in only a few months time and I couldn't even manage to cycle for a few consecutive days. I got home and went to the doctor, who confirmed that I had a nasty case of food poisoning. The one good thing I did get out of the few days was knowing that the bike setup appeared to work quite well and the custom frame bags were just enough to carry the essential items.

About a week later, I had fully recovered and was out training almost every day. Things were going well and I was feeling confident for the impending cycle. I'd nearly raised all the funds I thought I was going to need and had managed to organise bills and get things set up for my absence from the UK for the next six months. I had about four weeks to go before I was due to leave and I hadn't been out for a few drinks with my close friends for quite some time. I decided to head to Guildford for a night out with some of my good friends, Andy and Romeo.

It was a fun night and we ended up in a nice little bar. Andy and I were chatting to two women who were attractive but turned out to be quite boring. Romeo was chatting to an old school friend so we both headed back over to him to see what was going on. Andy and I were steaming drunk at this point and Romeo was stone cold sober. When we stumbled over, Romeo introduced us to his friend and a few others in the group, including a tall, dark-haired girl who introduced herself as Genevieve. She was absolutely stunning and I thought she needed to know that, so I told her. We chatted for some time until Romeo said that he wanted to go home; Genevieve and I exchanged numbers.

The next day, I got a message from Genevieve asking if I usually slap women's bums and tell them how stunning they are within five minutes of meeting them. I had no recollection of it at all but said I would make it up to her over dinner. We went on a few dates and we got on very well. I became very fond of her, which I knew was probably not a good idea, due to the fact I was about to cycle around the world for six months. Most of the time we spent together was really enjoyable and we had a good connection.

About two weeks before I was due to leave, we went out for the day and started chatting about the next six months.

"James, you're an amazing guy but you have no money and are about to disappear for six months and nothing will change when you get back. You're basically completely and utterly useless as a boyfriend," she exclaimed.

I was quite shocked but laughed it off at the time. In truth, it really hurt my feelings, but I tried not to dwell on it as I had lots of other things to sort out before my departure.

I had a message on Twitter from a lady called Pru Gayton, who lived locally and had heard me speak at a fundraising event. She was a copywriter and was offering to help me out with writing blogs and general comms support while I was away. Her offer of help was unconditional, simply because she thought my talk had been inspiring and motivational, both traits that she respected and admired. This was a very kind gesture and was very helpful as I had no one helping me with marketing for the project, so her offer couldn't have come at a better time. We decided to meet up at our local Nando's and chat things through. I was running all over the place on the day we had arranged to meet, picking up last minute bits and pieces and seeing people.

I was tempted to cancel the meeting but I was so pleased I didn't. Pru was a lovely person, really bubbly and full of enthusiasm. I instantly warmed to her and had a gut feeling that she was meant to come into my life. I asked her if she wanted to come to the start of the cycle but she couldn't make it due to an impending operation on her ankle. Before I left, I popped round to her house and showed her how to edit and create blogs on my website. I was very grateful for Pru's support.

Before I could get going, there was one more job I had to see through and that was to be the guest speaker at a fundraising evening for two scouts who were trying to raise funds to go on a trip. I had actually spoken at the venue before for the very same reason, to raise money for two scouts who had planned an overseas trip. One of their parents had contacted me months ago asking if I would do it. I didn't want to let them down so I said I would, despite it being the night before I was due to cycle around the world.

They were selling tickets to a dinner and I was the guest speaker. They told me I could bring along a guest but I didn't want to ask Genevieve as we hadn't spoken and I didn't think I was going to see or hear from her again, so I invited Richard from Centrix. We had been chatting a fair bit and he was a very keen cyclist too. The evening went well and by the end of the night, they had raised a few thousand pounds. I, rather stupidly, didn't get home until gone midnight, and most people couldn't believe that I'd agreed to give the talk the night before I departed.

I woke up at 7am and slowly got up. By now, I was starting to get a little bit nervous and the butterflies in my stomach were making themselves known. I was due to leave Greenwich Park at midday and had arranged for my parents to give me a lift up to London. My start point would be just outside the Royal Observatory. I really liked the idea of starting in Greenwich and on the meridian line, where time starts. At the top of the hill next to the Observatory is the General James Wolfe Statue that overlooks the city of London and Canary

Wharf with the most amazing views. That was the meeting point for the start. I strapped the bike onto the roof rack and loaded the car up with promotional leaflets about the project. It was a tight squeeze driving up to London with my mum, dad, brother and his girlfriend, plus me in the car. We were aiming to be at the start for about 10.30am to do some filming.

I had arranged for some friends to cycle with me on the first day down to Dover and the Scouts were planning a big send off from the park. There was a particularly large amount of traffic on the road that morning, for some reason, and we didn't arrive until 11am. As we were driving along Chelsea Embankment, I was looking out of the window over to the river and was wondering if I'd ever hear from Genevieve again. Although my gut feeling was to leave it, I just thought I'd drop her a quick text message to say hi, but I didn't get a reply.

We managed to drive into the park and I quickly unloaded the bike and cycled up to the start. There were quite a few people waiting for me, including a large group of Scouts and numerous friends and family. The Scouts had been fantastic and they introduced a 'Captain Ketch Ambassador Challenge Badge', which had been Fi's brainchild. It was a badge that was open to all ages of the Scouting community. A series of challenges would be set, such as fixing a puncture, sending me a tweet of support, or cooking a meal from a country that I had been to or was going to cycle through. The challenges varied in difficulty, depending on the age. When the challenges had been completed, they would earn their badge. To have my own Scouting badge really was an honour. I was determined to do the Scouts proud, as well as everyone else who was following me.

The nerves were replaced with a feeling of excitement and adrenaline. The crowds were building, and there were a lot of people who were generally out and about, asking what the bikes and film crew were doing. A friend of mine, Tim, who was an excellent video producer/ director and who had helped me with promo material, came up to capture the start. He was with another mutual friend, Richard, who at the time was running a company, who had designed and built my website for me. Richard was Tim's sound guy and helped out with the interviews and filming of the event.

Anyone who didn't know me would have probably thought I was some kind of celebrity, signing autographs for the Scouts and doing photo shoots for the media. It was a bit of a whirlwind experience and I was overwhelmed with the kindness and support I received. I was standing chatting to a few people and I noticed my friend Romeo standing in front of me.

"I have someone here for you," he said. I wondered what on earth he was talking about until he stood to the side and I saw Genevieve standing there, looking at me, with a big smile on her face. Although she had upset me, I was so pleased to see her. I didn't know what to say for a split second, which is unlike me. Apparently my face lit up with a smile from ear to ear when I saw her and I put my arms around her and thanked her for coming.

I was being ushered around a bit as there were various people who wanted to speak to me before I left and time was going very quickly. It was already midday so I needed to get a move on. The last photo taken was of Richard from Ofsure, my main sponsor and his two children, Charlie and Millie and then it was time to go. Altogether, there were about 15 cyclists who joined me, most of whom I knew but a few who I'd not met before. It was a great atmosphere. We lined up at the start line after I'd said all my goodbyes and the crowd counted us down. We all slowly made our way down the road with everybody clapping and cheering. It was certainly a much bigger send-off than I'd imagined.

At first it was quite a slow ride out of the city and thankfully, I wasn't leading the ride so I could chat with everyone who had taken the time to ride with me. The ferry across the channel wasn't until 10pm so there was plenty of time. As someone else had planned the route to Dover, I didn't really think too much about the mileage but it turned out to be a bit further than I thought. Ordinarily it would be no problem at all but when riding in a group, it can be tricky staying together if there is a mix of rider abilities, which there was on the first day.

We briefly cycled on the A2, which wasn't ideal as the traffic is very fast-flowing, similar to a motorway. Thankfully we weren't on it for long and managed to come off to some quieter roads, although by this point, the group had split and we had already lost a couple of people. It was an absolutely lovely day, with the sun shining down on us, but it wasn't long before one of the group got a puncture. A couple of lads who were mechanics at East Street Cycles were riding with the group and quickly sprang into action. With the puncture fixed, we were soon back into a rhythm and were making good progress again.

The group split up, with three faster riders going ahead, as they had to get a train back to London from Dover and were on a tight time schedule. They were fairly strong riders so I knew they would be fine to do their own thing. After all the buzz of the start and excitement that was rushing through me all morning, I started to feel incredibly drained, both physically and mentally. Thankfully, no one noticed that I was struggling a bit to keep up. We stopped a little while later and I grabbed a coffee and a Red Bull, which soon picked me up.

I joked with one of my friends, "I'm amazed I haven't had a puncture yet." Five minutes later, we were still riding side by side and with a hiss, my front tyre instantly deflated, causing me to wobble all over the place until I came to a halt. We both chuckled, "You spoke too soon," he said. I stopped and fixed the puncture with everyone joking about how long it was taking me. By now, we had covered around 60 miles and had just shy of 30 miles left. My parents were planning to meet me before I got on the ferry and had a few things to give me. We decided to meet them at Folkestone train station where a couple of the other guys would jump on the train and head home.

A few hours later, we arrived at the station where my family was waiting. I swapped my cycling shoes and pedals over to a mountain bike set-up, as it was easier to walk on them as opposed to road racing shoes. We chatted and had some cake that my mum had made and then I said goodbye. It felt quite strange, knowing that I wouldn't see them for six months.

It was now just myself, Ian and Jonnie who were cycling down to the ferry terminal. It was only a short ride but it was an incredibly hilly one over to the Dover ferry terminal. When we arrived, I said goodbye to Ian who was going to get a B&B locally. Jonnie was a good friend of mine who was going to cycle for the first three days with me over to Eindhoven and pick up a flight home from there. I'd met Jonnie a few years earlier when I rowed across the Atlantic. He was also rowing across the Atlantic with a friend. We stayed in contact and caught up every now and then at rowing reunions. He was a pretty tough guy in his own right, a serving Royal Marines Commando and a giant of a man, standing at well over six feet tall. Jonnie was a very modest guy and a real pleasure to be around, so I was pleased that he was joining me for the beginning of my journey.

We checked in for our ferry crossing with about an hour to spare so we sat down and grabbed a coffee in the terminal. I checked my phone to see an abundance of messages, tweets and missed calls. So many people had turned up to support me at the start, I felt like I needed to thank them all, so I pretty much spent the hour before boarding on the phone, thanking everyone for such a fantastic send-off.

Our ferry was taking us to Calais and Jonnie happened to ask me what the plan was in terms of finding a place to stay when we got there. In the madness of the last few days, I hadn't even thought about where we were going to stay. I needed to go through some of my kit and charge up some electrical items so I decided that we should just find a cheap hotel for the first night in France. It was a bit late to be booking one about five minutes before boarding the ferry. I decided to 'phone a friend', Chris, who had come to the start and asked him to jump on Google and find a place in Calais for us to stay. He thought it was hilarious that I was calling him to book a hotel for me just as I was about to board the ferry. I gave him my card details and he kindly booked a place.

Jonnie and I locked our bikes up in the hold downstairs where all the motorcycles were parked. It was only a quick one-hour hop across the channel so we just sat ourselves down on some comfy chairs. I was absolutely exhausted and felt completely drained. I pulled out my laptop and decided to write a quick blog while I was on the ferry, as I could use the Wi-Fi signal to post it. When the ferry docked in Calais, we grabbed our bikes and rode off the ramp. Even though we were only just across the channel and England was only 20 miles away, it instantly felt different.

15

Speeding through Europe

The first obvious big difference was the change in road layout and we would now be cycling on the right as opposed to the left. Just looking at the different road signs felt very weird. It was only now I really felt like I was at the start of an adventure of epic proportions. We cycled out of the docks and a few minutes later we found the motel. I wasn't sure if the gentleman on reception would be able to speak English but he was as English as Jonnie and I. We asked if we could take our bikes into the room which he had no problem with, then I grabbed a quick shower and crashed out. I felt relief and happiness as I lay on the bed, shattered, looking up at the ceiling, pondering the last 24 hours. I was quite overwhelmed and incredibly grateful for all the support I had received.

The next morning, we were up at 6am and feeling much fresher. We took advantage of the breakfast, consuming as much as we could, then set off in high spirits. The area was as flat as a pancake, and we had a lovely tailwind blowing us along as we headed east. We passed through Dunkirk and into Belgium where we stopped in Bruges for lunch. The culture difference and the positive way that cycling is accepted in Europe was instantly recognisable from the minute we were on the roads. No car drivers would beep their horns and they were very patient, always passing with plenty of space: a far cry from some of the lunatics in England on our first day to Dover. Despite doing nothing wrong and being in a cycle lane, one driver had made a conscious effort to tell us what he thought of us using the foulest language I'd ever heard.

My first day in Europe finished close to the border of the Netherlands in Zelzate, 103 miles after leaving Calais that morning. It was a very easy day really, with great tailwinds and lovely, warm weather. As Jonnie was only cycling for a few days, he didn't bother with any camping equipment so we just found another cheap place to stay. The next morning, we made an early start for Eindhoven. We had to be there for 5pm as I was due to give a talk to a small IT company that was a business associate of one of my sponsors.

After cycling 98 miles, we ended up arriving half-an-hour late as I'd succumbed to a couple of punctures. They were very happy to see us when we arrived and had laid on beers and food, which was a very kind thing to do, and very well received by Jonnie and I. I popped into the office toilet to change out of my cycling kit into some clothing that Berghaus had kindly sponsored, which would be my clean kit when I wasn't on the bike.

They showed us into a small room and I plugged my laptop into a projector and gave a quick talk. It was all very easy stuff and nothing I hadn't done hundreds of times before. We stayed for a few hours and then headed off to a hotel the company had very kindly booked for us. It was Jonnie's last night as he was going to fly home the following day after finding a bike shop to pack the bike up.

We had a couple of beers in the evening, which went down a treat, while gorging on massive bowls of pasta. In the morning, we went our separate ways, after taking a final picture together. I also gave Jonnie some kit that I'd decided I didn't need, to save me carrying it around the world.

That day was a very easy day of cycling for me as I was heading up to Utrecht, which was only about 50 miles away. I promised a friend of mine, who I'd met in Nepal the previous year, that I would visit her. Her name was Femke and she had a lovely little flat in the centre of Utrecht where she worked as a doctor. She was an immensely intelligent woman who loved travelling whenever she had the chance, so we got on quite well.

That evening, Femke very kindly treated me to a steak and we sat out in a restaurant by one of the many canals that run through the city. It was a lovely atmosphere, with lots of happy people cycling around, enjoying the sun and sitting drinking beer. I thoroughly enjoyed the cycling in the Netherlands. They are well geared up for it, and more people cycle than walk. Utrecht was similar in looks and feel to Amsterdam but much smaller with fewer tourists and not so commercial. Everyone could speak almost perfect English.

I slept on her sofa that evening, which was a lot more comfortable than I thought it would be. In the morning, Femke cycled with me for a few miles as the hospital she worked at was on my route. I was heading for Dusseldorf in Germany, about 120 miles away. Over the course of the next few days, I would need to make up for only cycling 50 miles up to Utrecht, as my goal was to average 100 miles a day.

The route down to Dusseldorf was absolutely lovely, passing through little villages that probably looked the same as they had 60 years ago. I followed a river all the way down to Arnhem where I spotted a great ice cream shop just on the outskirts, so I had to stop to satisfy my weakness: chocolate ice cream. Two Dutch tourists who were cycling also stopped to take advantage of the ice cream and chatted with me. They were riding with what looked to be a pretty heavy setup, loaded panniers front and rear. It turned out that they were on a trip for a few days. They asked me what I was doing and assumed I was on a day trip with the little kit I was carrying, compared to the amount they were lugging around. When I told them I was going round the world, they couldn't believe it.

"You must be out of your God damn mind," the wife exclaimed. I laughed and chatted with them for a short while before heading off.

It started to get more industrial and built up as I approached the outskirts of Dusseldorf. There were a lot more places to take wrong turns and potentially get lost. I was navigating with my iPhone using Google maps, which was working really well. Thankfully, I had a European data package on my phone contract so I wasn't being charged extortionate amounts of money. Over the next few days, I would be heading south through Germany as I made my way to Munich where I was due to give another talk on behalf of a sponsor.

As I was now cycling through industrial, urban areas, it wasn't that simple to find a nice quiet spot to camp for the night, which I'd planned to do. I did notice that the cost of budget motels was very reasonable, some as low as 30 euros a night. Over the next few days, I passed through Limberg, Heidelberg and Ulm, all of which appeared to be very pleasant. I hadn't had much interaction with other people apart from chatting to people in passing, either at a garage where I was buying food or checking into a place where I was going to stay.

I was cruising along when, all of a sudden, a woman on a fairly high-end road bike came past me on my left. She didn't come past that quickly so we caught each other's eye and ended up riding together, chatting for about half-an-hour. She was on her way to work, as a police officer. She was 27, blonde and absolutely stunning. She thought it was quite cool that I was cycling around the world;

I enjoyed chatting to her. We pulled up at some red lights side by side and she unclipped her shoe and put her foot down. As I came to a halt, I also went to unclip my shoe from the pedal but for some reason, it was a bit stiff and wasn't coming out. It was like slow motion as I felt myself falling to the side, thankfully to my right and not in to her. I knew I was going to go down and I hit the ground like a rookie who has never worn cleated pedals before. I could feel my face go crimson from embarrassment. She asked me if I was okay as I picked myself up. I felt pretty stupid but these things happen, albeit slightly awkward in front of someone else.

The terrain started to become a bit more undulating as I was heading south toward Munich from Ulm. I was cycling up a hill, which was exceptionally steep and it was also very hot. I'd stupidly run out of water and was extremely tired and thirsty. For some reason, I started to think that perhaps I should walk up this hill. Let me explain that I've never walked up a hill with my bike in my life and it's just a silly cyclist thing that one should never get off a bike and push it up a hill, unless you really have no choice. My lips were parched and I was panting for breath as I grinded the cranks and rather stubbornly made my way up the hill.

To my amazement, when I reached the top and turned the corner, there was a fruit stall that was being run by two girls who, I would say, were in their early 20s. I stopped to buy some fruit and water and it was just what I needed. They were very keen to ask me questions about my bike and to find out where I was going. When I told them what I was doing, they were very surprised and wouldn't let me pay for any of the fruit. They were two extremely pleasant young ladies. I cycled off refreshed, and thought to myself how funny life is - you really never know what's around the corner and nine times out of 10, when you're about to give up with whatever you're doing, there will be something good waiting for you.

I needed to inform the company I was visiting that I was getting close to Munich. I thought I was going to their office on the outskirts and closer to the direction I was coming from. I gave my contact a call to let him know where I was and what my arrival time would be; based on the miles I had remaining. By this point, I was quite tired as I had covered over 100 miles and had to fix several punctures along the way. This chap Robert went on to tell me that they were not at the office but in central Munich apparently waiting for me. I looked at the map and realised that they were in fact 30 miles away as opposed to the eight miles I thought they were. I was really hungry and running out of energy and had planned to hold out until I arrived at their office, but another 30 miles would mean having to stop briefly to have something to eat. I stopped at a garage and grabbed a salami sandwich and a Coke, then quickly made my way into the centre of Munich.

Robert had texted me the address of a hotel to meet him at so I headed straight there. I arrived a couple of hours later, slightly anxious, but Robert was a really nice, laid-back guy. He was waiting outside the hotel standing by his BMW touring motorcycle, dressed in biker kit. "Ah, greetings Mr James, you would have been much quicker on this," said Robert, pointing at his bike. "Let's go and have some beers now that you're here." I quickly dumped my bike in the hotel he had kindly arranged for me to stay in, jumped in the shower and headed out with him. We took a short walk over to a large communal square where there were thousands of people relaxing, drinking beer and eating. I thought I was meeting these people to give a talk to them but they preferred having beers and just chatting informally. I was quite pleased about it, as I was very tired and hungry.

I met the rest of the team that Robert had working for him, who were all really great guys. I decided not to have a beer and stuck to Coke, as I knew I would feel it in the morning if I did. We sat and chatted for a few hours, with questions mostly about my cycle and past expeditions. Their German sense of humour was just fantastic. Some of the things they were asking me were so direct, it was just brilliant.

I managed to talk a couple of the guys into cycling with me for a few hours the following day. The sensible ones at the table passed on the opportunity but Robert and another guy called Daniel decided to join me. I did wonder if they would be able to make it or not as they had both been drinking a fair bit. The next morning, I got up and had breakfast. We had arranged to meet at 8am and it was 7.50am. I was just pushing my bike out through the hotel doors and, as I looked up, I saw Robert and Daniel standing with their bikes, smiling at me. I thought that was a bloody good effort, as I honestly didn't think they were going to turn up.

I knew that cycling with them would be nice and easy but I was surprised to find that they were going quite a bit faster than I'd expected. We cycled out of Munich along a river called the Isar. It was a wonderful cycling route and the sun was glistening off the water as we made our way along a tow-path that ran parallel with the river. There wasn't anyone else around apart for the odd dog walker. Some of the path was washed away quite badly, leaving potholes so big that they could swallow a car. Rather stupidly, I wasn't really concentrating on where I was cycling and happened to be looking at the river when Daniel, who was riding in front of me, swerved sharply to avoid an area of the path that had been completely washed away. He narrowly missed it but I went flying into it with my front wheel falling away from me into the hole. I then proceeded to fly straight over the handlebars onto the tow-path with the bike landing on top of me. It was the first time I'd properly fallen off my bike since the start (not unclipping my pedals at the traffic lights didn't really count).

We were heading north east and my next major city was Prague. We had covered about 30 miles since leaving the hotel in the morning. I was feeling fine but noticed that Daniel was sweating quite a bit. I thought that they might turn around and head back but they kept going: 40 miles passed, then 50 miles. We approached a lovely little town where we stopped for lunch, and they both said they would go back from there. There was an option for them to get a train back to Munich but they said they would prefer to cycle.

I really was impressed at their efforts after the previous night's drinking, and they were brilliant company. We grabbed a table outside in a street café. I destroyed a large margherita pizza followed by a huge bowl of chocolate ice cream. They very kindly paid for my lunch and we said our goodbyes. I found the German hospitality to be outstanding. That night, I made it up to the small town of Cham, which was very close to the border of the Czech Republic.

The following day, I had my first encounter with the law on my trip. I was about to cross the border into the Czech Republic when I was pulled over by the police. They were in an unmarked blue BMW estate car. They came up beside me waving a 'police' sign out of the window. I pulled over and they asked me where I was going. I told them I was cycling around the world and they just looked at each other blankly. They then asked me if I was crossing the border into the Czech Republic. When I said I was, they weren't really interested in talking to me and just told me to use an adjacent road to the one I was on, to cross the border. I think it was just a routine check as they saw me looking at my phone while I was cycling. I was actually just checking I was on the right road.

I'd been riding in the Czech Republic for a few hours and needed to grab some food. I came across a small village supermarket so decided to try and pick something up. I was particularly hungry so grabbed a fair bit of food and I planned to sit outside on a bench to eat it. I got to the checkout and pulled out some euros. The woman on the checkout desk looked at me and shook her head, saying, "Oh no, oh no!" I then realised they didn't take euros; I'd forgotten that the Czech Republic have their own currency which is the Czech koruna. I felt pretty stupid, as they didn't take cards either, so I was going to have to put everything back and try and find somewhere else to pick up food.

As I turned around from the counter, about to put everything back, the person behind me in the queue started talking in Czech to the checkout woman.

"She is saying you don't need to put the food back, she will do that for you," she spoke very good English.

"If you wait for me to pay for these, I'll help you." I thought she would show me where a cash machine was or direct me to another supermarket. I waited just outside the entrance and she came out and started chatting to me. She was asking me where I was going and we had a great conversation for a few minutes. She said there weren't any cash machines around and no other supermarkets that would accept cards. She insisted that she bought my lunch for me. I said I would give her my euros but she wouldn't take them, no matter how much I insisted. I was very grateful for yet another kind gesture from a total stranger.

I continued on to Prague, feeling fresh and strong after my lunch. About four hours later, I was on the outskirts of the city. It didn't take long before I remembered why I needed to take care when riding through built-up areas and especially cities with trams. I was cycling down a street where I could see tram tracks running parallel to my road so I knew I had to pay attention. Without warning, a tram came out of a side street right across in front of me. There were no road markings suggesting that I needed to give way and I only just came to a stop a few feet from it as it rushed past. Had I been there only a few seconds earlier, I would have ploughed into the side of it. It was a really close call and one I didn't want to have again. I decided that I would walk into the city centre, pushing my bike, as there were so many trams hurtling around the roads.

I needed to find a place to stay, as I didn't fancy sleeping rough or trying to camp in the city. I used my phone to go on to laterooms. com and found a five star hotel for £25. I thought there must have been a mistake, checked the details again and decided to make the booking online. It was only a few minutes from where I was sitting so I headed over to the hotel. I half expected them to turn me away but I was surprised by how welcoming they were. They even offered to put my bike in a locked room so it was safe. There was a gigantic bath in the bathroom so I sat and chilled in it for what seemed like hours.

The next day, I set off for the Polish border but decided to stop short in a small town called Trutnov. By now, I had covered just over 1,000 miles and had been fairly lucky in terms of staying safe, avoiding cars and generally anything that could potentially cause me harm, but I was wondering if my luck was starting to run out. I was cycling down a hill at about 40mph with some parked cars on my right. I made sure that I wasn't too close to them, or at least I thought I wasn't too close to them. All of a sudden, the door of a parked car flew open and missed my handlebars by a couple of centimetres. If I had made contact with the door, it would have almost certainly ended my world cycle at the speed I was travelling. Thankfully, I didn't hit it, so I just took the experience as a lesson and a reminder not to cycle too close to parked cars.

The following day, I crossed into Poland where I would be visiting a couple of shopping centres over the course of a few days. The plan was to visit one in Wroclaw, Gliwice and Krakow, cycling from one to the other, and at each one, I would be met by the local press to give interviews. There were also groups of young people from local orphanages to whom bikes had been donated from charitable bicycle shops. It was all organised by one of my sponsors, Balmain Asset Management, who managed the shopping centres. The whole experience was fantastic and I was blown away by the support I was getting. I had a Polish translator for all of my interviews and the local mayor even came along to one of the shopping centres to present me with a cycling jersey from a local team. Krakow was the last centre I visited and I was joined by a local cycling club, who cycled with me to the motel where I was staying for the night.

The following day, I wanted to cross in to Ukraine so made my way. It was just over 100 miles to the border and then another 40 miles to the city of Lviv. I made it to the border at around 6pm. As I approached, a guard was trying to talk to me but I carried on cycling, as I couldn't understand him. There were lorries parked up everywhere and cars queuing in long lines. I arrived at the Ukraine border check post and was instantly stopped by a female guard. She told me that I was at the wrong checkpoint as this was for vehicles only.

I instantly knew I'd made a mistake and I should have crossed at a border about 40 miles south and I really didn't want to cycle back. She knew I was coming because the guard who I had initially seen and couldn't understand was trying to tell me that I couldn't cross there. I told her, trying to wing it, that the other guard said I could go through and she said with a stern voice of authority, "No he did not!" She went on to tell me that the only way I could cross the border was to get into a car or bus and be in the vehicle when I went through Passport Control. She stopped a car with two guys in it and asked if I could sit in the back with them. They didn't speak English but told the guard that I could. We put my bike in the boot of the old Volvo that they were driving which was falling apart. I had to give my passport to the driver, which I wasn't happy about, but I had no choice.

I quickly realised it was so that he could present them all to Passport Control. I thanked the guard for sorting everything out for me and sat in the car. The two guys were chatting away in the front, probably laughing at me in the back, but I couldn't understand a thing. They put some loud kind of dance, rave music on which was very repetitive and sparked up a couple of cigarettes. They didn't wind their windows down so the car quickly filled up with smoke. I wound my window down to get some fresh air so I could breathe without choking. The windows on the car were all blacked out with a tacky kind of window wrap that was peeling off at the edges. It was quite a surreal feeling, as I had no control over the situation at all. I was sitting in the back of what could easily have been a drug dealer's car with the two of them in the front, chatting away in another language and one of them clutching my passport in his hand. I felt very uncomfortable.

The queue of cars wasn't moving very fast at all and it took over an hour to get to Passport Control. The driver handed the passports to the guy in the office and he gave the two guys in the front their passports back immediately but kept mine. He then asked me to get out of the car. Thankfully, he spoke enough English to get by and, after asking me a few questions and checking my passport, he stamped it and allowed me through. The guys parked the car up and helped me take my bike out of the boot. They both shook my hand and then said, "good luck" in English. I wondered why they hadn't bothered speaking to me if they could speak English. I gave the driver 10 euros that I had in my pocket to say thank you. I wondered if he would accept it; he quickly snatched it out of my hand.

I got back on my bike and carried on cycling towards Lviv. I was pretty tired by this point so I found a place to camp just off the road, before it started to get too built-up, out of sight from anyone. The roads in Ukraine were absolutely terrible. I'd cycled down dirt tracks that were better than some of their main roads, there were massive potholes everywhere. The next couple of days passed in quite an uneventful manner. I did however meet a couple of Polish guys who spoke great English and were cycling to Odessa on the Black Sea. They were heavily loaded up with kit but cycling well, considering how much they were carrying. It was always nice meeting other cyclists on the road and chatting. I cycled with them for a couple of hours before I needed to turn off.

There was no border control going into Romania and the improvement in the roads was phenomenal. They were super smooth, which would make a massive difference. I also started to get quite lucky with the wind, as there was a strong northerly wind pushing me south at a fairly quick rate. The terrain wasn't mountainous or hilly but it was certainly undulating, however with the tailwind, I was making very light work of the miles. On my first day in Romania, I managed just over 200 miles from the town of Suceava to Buzau. It took 12 hours, which wasn't a bad day's work at all and would only leave me 60 miles the following day, into Bucharest, where I was planning to take two days off. I was way ahead of schedule and hadn't had a rest day since the start.

I'd been chatting to Genevieve over the past week and she wanted to come out and see me for a few days. I explained that the only time she could do this would be in Bucharest as I'd be taking two days off to rest so I would be able to spend some time with her before flying to India and South East Asia, where it would be virtually impossible to meet. I was pleased she wanted to see me but anxious that it might be a massive distraction from the task in hand. She decided to fly out, so we found a hotel for us both to stay in. I arrived in Bucharest and spent the next couple of days resting and chilling out with Genevieve. We explored the city, which was a nice break from cycling and I really enjoyed her company.

Towards the end of the weekend, her behaviour became quite

unpredictable: one minute she was really warm and friendly and the next minute she would be quite cold and distant. I found this confusing and mentally quite hard to cope with. The day came for her to fly back so I arranged for a taxi to take us to the airport. I waved her off as she walked through security and stood there wondering if she would turn around to look at me but she didn't. I jumped in a taxi and headed back to the hotel where I'd collect my bike and get moving again. On the way back, the taxi driver was telling me about all the different girlfriends he had and was asking if I wanted to go to a strip club with him. I declined but thanked him for his offer. He was the sleaziest, little rat-faced guy I had ever seen in my life.

I felt emotionally drained and far from recovered; the last thing I wanted to do was to get back on a bike and start cycling again. This little break had caused me to fall off the rails mentally and I was really struggling to get motivated again. I looked at all the wonderful messages I'd been getting since I left which really helped me. I genuinely felt quite low and remembered something that my dad had told me before I left. "Most people could cycle round the world when they are in the right frame of mind and everything is going well. It's when things are not going so well that makes the difference. As long as you keep getting on your bike, that's all you have to do. No matter how you feel – keep moving." It was so true.

It only took a day to get into Bulgaria from Bucharest, which was very pleasant cycling. Just before I crossed the border into Bulgaria, I came across a young girl cycling along on a very old bike that must have weighed a ton. She was a French girl from Paris who was only 20 and had been cycling around Europe for the past three months. We got chatting and stopped for lunch. It was a shock to me to find that her diet was literally red wine and cigarettes and the odd bottle of water. We had lunch at a petrol station, which had a cafeteria. I ate a sandwich and a few other bits, while she only had a couple of biscuits and chain-smoked five cigarettes. She had no phone and no way of knowing how far she had travelled. When I told her that she had just cycled over 60 miles with me, she decided that she was going to pitch a tent at the side of the road in some fields. I helped her with her kit for a few minutes and then said goodbye. I carried on to the town of Veliko Tarnovo and had covered a respectable 115 miles, where I found a cheap motel and crashed out for the night.

The next day, I covered 120 miles to the town of Svilengrad, just on the Turkish border. It proved to be one of the hardest days of the trip with temperatures exceeding 40°C, mixed with some brutally steep hills. About 20 miles out of Svilengrad, I caught up with a young lad who was cycling along on a mountain bike. I thought he was a local as he was very scruffy, in jeans and carrying a small rucksack on his back. He shouted for me to stop when I passed him so I slowed down and let him catch me up. He spoke good English and was from Holland, travelling around Europe. I instantly identified that he was young and very confident. There was something about him that I just didn't like but I couldn't put my finger on it. He was only 18 though, so I had respect for him, doing what he was doing at that age.

He told me he was hitchhiking around but had only started cycling because he had acquired a bike. I asked him how he acquired a bike and he said, "Well, I saw this kid put the bike down to go into a shop and he stupidly didn't lock it up so I took it, his loss really." For a few seconds I didn't know what to say so I said nothing. I could see he was probably regretting his confession.

I can't stand thieves, especially bike thieves, and I wanted to get away from this person before I said or did something I would regret. There wasn't really anything I could do; I had no idea where he stole it from or who he stole it from so I decided to leave him and cycled on. He knew I wasn't happy and the atmosphere turned very awkward all of a sudden. He'd made my blood boil and I was so angry, but I managed to stay calm. It was funny how my gut feeling turned out to be spot on.

The next day, I made my way into Turkey and thankfully, the border crossing and Passport Control wasn't anything like my experience of getting in to Ukraine, only that I didn't have enough money to pay for the visa that I needed to enter the country. I was able to pop into the service station by the Passport Control Office to withdraw extra cash. I decided to stay in Çorlu on my first day in Turkey, which would leave me with an easy day into Istanbul where I could find a bike shop and get my bike packed up.

Before I left Greenwich, I had been in contact with a specialist visa company that was arranging an Iranian visa for me, as my original plan was to cycle through Iran and Pakistan to get into India. A few months before I departed, I was told that, despite having the visa, I may still face problems on the border trying to get in. I decided to fly from Istanbul to Delhi and cut out Iran and Pakistan, making up the miles somewhere else. My parents were quite pleased and relieved when I told them my decision.

I arrived into Istanbul at around lunchtime, 28 days after leaving Greenwich Park, and that was the end of my European leg. It had gone incredibly quickly. I still needed to find a bike shop so I located one near the airport. The shop I found must have been there for years; it had a mix of old bikes and new ones lined up inside and outside. There was an old chap who I think was the owner sitting on a stool outside the shop, putting a new bike together. I parked my bike up and explained that I was looking for a bike box to pack my bike into. He spoke good English and asked where I'd come from and said it was no problem at all. One of his assistants came out with a brand new bike still in its box and took the bike out of it. "Here you go," he said, "a brand new bike box for you." It was just what I needed.

I went into the shop and changed out of my cycling kit and into a pair of shorts and a T-shirt. There was another young lad working for them who didn't speak English but who kept smiling at me and asking me questions, through the translation of the shop owner. They were a very friendly bunch of guys and couldn't have done any more for me. Once the bike was packed up, they called a taxi to take me to the airport. I passed some money for the box to the owner and he said it was far too much and that he only needed half that. I took a couple of photos of them standing proudly outside their shop and then headed off to the airport, with the bike box sticking half way out of the boot.

I walked into the airport and looked at the flight departures board. I hadn't booked one or even looked at the flight timings but amazingly, there was a flight with Turkish Airlines to Delhi in four hours time, which was perfect, so I booked a ticket and was soon on my way to India.

16

Tough times in India

It was a great feeling, sitting back on the plane, having just cycled through Europe. I'd met so many lovely people and had been on the receiving end of much kindness. I was sitting next to an Indian man who worked in Istanbul and was travelling back to Delhi for the weekend to see his family. When I told him my name, he said, "I worked with a guy called John Ketchell." I couldn't believe my ears. He was talking about my dad. It turned out they had worked together on a project many years ago. It's such a small world - what are the chances of getting on a plane and the person I'm sitting next to recognising my name as he'd worked with my dad? Incredible.

We chatted for most of the flight about India and what to expect, and exchanged contact details. When we landed, we both went through immigration and through to baggage reclaim together. I was getting anxious as I waited for over an hour before my bike was delivered to baggage reclaim. I said goodbye to the guy I'd met on the flight and found the driver who was waiting for me as I was going to stay the night with a friend called Kalpana. I arrived at Kalpana's house and instantly crashed out in the spare room where the last 24 hours caught up with me. I didn't wake up until the next morning and was feeling refreshed, fit and motivated. I walked outside the house and instantly broke out into a sweat. It was so incredibly humid and, by the time I had finished taking my bike out of the box and built it, I looked like I'd just taken a shower with my clothes on.

I had one planned rest day with Kalpana, who also had another friend staying with her, so we decided to head into Delhi to have a look around and grab some food in a local restaurant that she said I should try. Having travelled to Delhi before, I knew how chaotic the streets would be but it still makes me smile every time I go back to India. You've never seen such organised chaos in your life. Most of the streets are littered with thousands of people going about their daily business and the sounds of horns going off is constant, 24 hours a day. The streets of Delhi never sleep and there is always something going on.

After we had dinner in a lovely, local restaurant, we decided to visit the famous Red Fort, so we jumped in an auto-rickshaw. There was a tiny little Indian chap standing on the pedals, grinding them round and round to propel us forward. There were so many people in the streets, we weren't going anywhere fast. I was sitting in the back watching this chap power us through the streets and thought about how much fun it looked. I wanted to try it, so when we had stopped I leant forward and asked the guy if I could have a go.

"Are you crazy, sir?" he asked.

"Yes I am!"

He jumped in the back and I stood on the pedals and started to pedal us round the streets.

Kalpana was in the auto-rickshaw in front of me; she looked round and did a double take as she couldn't believe I was cycling the thing. It was probably the only time the owner had ever been taken for a ride in his own auto-rickshaw by a paying passenger. It was attracting a lot of attention; people were stopping to take pictures and even the police who were directing traffic were laughing and waving at me. One Indian woman was trying to pass her baby to pose for photos with me but I didn't feel comfortable doing that so I smiled at her instead. After 10 minutes, I swapped back over with the driver and let him navigate the busy streets. I was quite surprised that it wasn't as difficult as I thought it would be to move the rickshaw around with people in the back.

The next day, I left Delhi and headed to the city of Agra, which was just over 100 miles away. I was slightly nervous about cycling in India but it wasn't that bad once I'd got used to the traffic. I'd managed to get my hands on an Indian SIM card for my phone so I was able to use Google maps, which made things a little easier getting out of Delhi. When I eventually made it to Agra, I was completely shattered but wanted to make a quick trip to the Taj Mahal to marvel at the famous wonder of the world. It didn't disappoint and was a truly magical place.

I was starting to get a bit more comfortable on the roads and getting used to the cultural differences. Food was tricky on the road as service stations were few and far between and the types of food available were very different to typical Western food. The one thing that was very easy to get everywhere was bottled water and soft drinks. There were stalls on the side of the road selling meat and sometimes rice but I'd been vehemently told not to eat from them, as it would almost certainly make me very sick. Over the course of a few days, I made my way through Rajasthan. It was now getting a lot more remote with most people farming the local land. I thought it would be perfectly safe to camp off to the side of the road, now that I was out of the main cities and urban areas.

One night, I'd been cycling all day and had covered about 140 miles so I decided to find a place to camp just off the side of the road. Most of the terrain was very dry and sandy and I came across an area that I thought would be suitable. I pulled over and carried the bike over a small sand dune and sat down. I cleared a little area and pulled out my roll mat and sleeping bag. It was still pretty hot so I didn't need my bivi tent, so I left that packed away on my saddle bag. I lay there staring up at the stars. It was a beautifully clear night with not a cloud in the sky, and the moon was shining brightly. I lay there for about an hour, just pondering various things, wondering what my friends and family were up to at home. There was no one around and I wasn't using my head torch so I didn't expect to see anyone. I was in the middle of nowhere.

All of a sudden, I heard some voices far off in the distance but I didn't think a great deal of it to begin with. It wasn't until I noticed they were getting louder that I realised they must be getting closer too. I looked up and saw two lights coming from torches that were heading towards me. The voices were getting louder and louder, closing in on me. How on earth they knew I was there was just beyond me; I didn't move and stayed perfectly still, wondering if they would walk straight past. However, a few minutes later they came over the little sand dune and spotted me. They shone their torches in my face and started shouting. I had no idea what they were shouting but I realised very quickly that something wasn't right and they were clearly not happy with me being there.

I started to pack my kit away but the atmosphere quickly changed and they became very aggressive, shouting at the tops of their voices as if they were shouting for back up. At that point, I became quite scared, as I had no idea who these people were, what they were saying and what they were going to do. I was completely powerless, being unable to communicate with them. They were dancing around and one of them started waving a gun in the air and the other had a large stick in his hand, which he was raising at me as if he was going to hit me. Their shouting was getting louder and louder and I could hear other people shouting as well.

By now, I had gone into fight or flight mode and knew that I needed to move very quickly. I left my roll mat and sleeping bag on the floor, grabbed my bike and jumped down the sand dune onto the road. It didn't take a genius to figure out that these people were seriously unhappy and had a problem with me being there. As I jumped down the sand dune, I slipped and fell head over heels, rolling down the hill. Luckily I didn't hurt myself, although I wouldn't have felt it anyway as I had so much adrenaline coursing through my body. I got the bike on to the road and pedalled as hard as my legs would let me.

It was pitch black but thankfully my dynamo light kicked in and illuminated the road in front of me. The shouting stopped but I was still very worried. There was no escaping these people if they wanted to come after me, as there was only one road and I was on it. It was 50 miles to the next town and I'd already covered 140 miles that day. I had so much adrenaline running through me that the next 20 miles flew by in what felt like the blink of an eye. My mind was spinning at a thousand miles an hour, imagining all the different scenarios. I was only a few hundred miles from the Pakistan border, so had I just tried to camp on land controlled by the Taliban who were hiding out in India? The more I thought about that, the more I realised that couldn't have been the case, but I was half expecting some kind of 4 x 4 vehicle to come flying up from behind and bundle me into the back.

As the miles passed, I began to think that I should be okay. The two guys who had threatened me were actually quite old and ordinarily, would both be no physical threat to me whatsoever. However, there were no police out here and from what I'd heard from the village police themselves, had I got into a scuffle with the locals, I'm pretty sure I would be the one who would come off worse. That was something I certainly didn't want, especially as one of them was armed.

I carried on cycling and gradually my heart rate slowed and the adrenaline started to subside; I began to feel pretty tired. I noticed a lot of bright lights in the distance and lots of trucks parked up. It was a truck stop and I could see there was food and drink being sold, so I cycled over. I asked the man standing behind the counter if he spoke English and he said yes. I've never been so pleased to hear someone speak English and I recounted what had happened. He had no idea who, or why these people would do this but he said I could sleep in his garden for the night where I would be safe.

His son made me some rice and I bought a couple of bottles of Coke. They pulled out a sun lounger, which I could sleep on in the garden, while I sat and chatted with the man who owned the truck stop. I now felt at ease and just put the whole experience behind me, but it shook me up a fair bit. I locked my bike to a tree and fell asleep, despite all the noise of trucks coming and going through the night. I woke up in the morning to find I'd been bitten alive by mosquitoes.

Over the next few days, I carried on grinding out the miles without any real issue until I came into one small town. I was trying to find a hotel so I was riding quite slowly when I saw a police officer directing traffic. I asked him for directions and he just pointed down a street at the same time as grunting something that I couldn't understand. I assumed that was the way I needed to go, so I headed off down the street, carefully navigating my way through the absolute chaos of people and tuk tuks that were whizzing around everywhere. Out the corner of my eye, I saw a tuk tuk come flying out of a side street and he crashed straight into me, knocking me off and sending my bike flying. I was sure I'd broken my arm as I was in absolute agony. I looked down at my bike and the front wheel was very badly bent. The driver of the tuk tuk looked at me rolling around on the floor in pain and then just casually drove off.

A bystander helped me up and picked up my bike for me, while I wiped the dirt off myself. The bike was unrideable. Fixing it was now a priority. I pushed it to the hotel that I was looking for and checked myself into a room. They charged me double the price that it should have been but I'd had such a rubbish day, I didn't bother questioning it, as it was still very cheap. There were no bike shops able to fix the wheel so I had to weigh up my options and decide what I was going to do.

I was 300 miles from Jaipur and I knew I could get the bike repaired there, so I spoke to the hotel owner who arranged for a driver to take me back to Jaipur to get the bike fixed. It took 10 hours to make the journey and cost me a total of 5,000 rupees, which was around £50, which I thought was amazingly cheap. I arrived back into Jaipur and immediately got the bike repaired. Luckily, I found a shop that had the expertise to rebuild the front wheel for me.

I was due to meet Richard from Ofsure in a couple of weeks' time to go on a speaking tour of India for a week. This trip was budgeted into my schedule and I'd planned for the break all along. I got a call from Richard while I was in Jaipur telling me that the trip had been moved forward and he would be flying out in exactly one week. This wasn't enough time for me to cover all the miles I wanted to in India and I really wanted to cycle a lap of Sri Lanka before leaving this part of the world.

I decided that I would cut some of my India leg short and fly to Sri Lanka. I'd planned to go to Sri Lanka anyway, I was just going to arrive ahead of schedule, as our speaking engagements had been moved forward in Bangalore. I booked a ticket to Sri Lanka and made my way to the airport. That evening, when I arrived, I realised it had a completely different feel to northern India and was much more tropical. It took me a week to cycle around the whole island, which was just over 700 miles and it was thoroughly enjoyable (apart from a day where I succumbed to heat stroke on the east of the island). Everyone who I came into contact with was very friendly.

It was my last day in Sri Lanka and I was staying in Hikkaduwa at a lovely little place called Coral Sands. I was due to fly out late that evening but thought I would go for a quick cycle before packing the bike up as the roads and scenery were outstandingly beautiful. I was cycling along and an older guy on a moped came up behind me and asked if I would pull over, as he wanted to chat with me. He was wearing a cycling jersey and wearing a motorbike helmet. At first, I thought he might be trying to sell me something but I could tell very quickly that he was a nice guy and genuinely interested in cycling. I chatted to him for a while and he asked me what I was up to. I told him I was due to fly back to India that night but was just enjoying Sri Lanka before I left. He asked if he could cycle with me so we spent a couple of companionable hours cycling together.

His name was Jayalath and he was an ex-Sri Lankan Army Warrant Officer, an ex-road racing champion and just a wonderfully warm, friendly person. I cycled back to his house and met his wife and daughter who were intrigued to see me. We ate some bananas and carried on cycling, eventually getting back to the hotel. He kindly offered to give me a lift to the airport, which I took him up on. Before I left, I gave him one of my spare cycling tops, which I hadn't worn yet. He seemed very pleased with it.

Later that evening, I flew to Bangalore where I was going to visit a school for a day called the Sri Aurobindo School. It was through a contact of Kalpana's that she had lined up for me while I was in Delhi. They picked me up from the airport and drove me back to their school. It was a lovely school, run by such enthusiastic people who made me feel so very welcome. One of my goals as I cycled around the world was to try and speak in a school in every country I passed through, encouraging young people to pursue their own dreams and goals, whatever they may be. My talk at Sri Aurobindo was very well received. It also happened to be Indian Independence Day, which is a big annual occasion in India, as they gained independence from the British Empire on 15th August 1947.

To commemorate the occasion, the school had laid on an afternoon of dancing and prize-giving ceremonies. I was invited to sit at the head table with the headmistress and her staff. It was a wonderful experience that I'll never forget and a fascinating insight into the traditions of the country.

The next day, I met up with Richard from Ofsure in a hotel in Bangalore. We had a packed schedule of visits, ranging from large corporate organisations to small village schools. During the first two days in Bangalore, we visited a company called Tata Consultancy Services (TCS). I gave a talk in their auditorium to an audience of around 500 people. It was a fantastic venue and all the staff were incredibly friendly, all queuing to speak with me afterwards.

That evening Richard took me to an Indo-Chinese restaurant called Mainland China. We had wonderful food and a few beers, after Richard had paid the bill he said to the waiter, "Do you realise this guy is cycling around the world?" The waiter looked amazed and he went to get the manager. The manager came over and asked me my name, then disappeared and came back with a bottle of Champagne and all the staff came over for a few photos. I am sure to this day he checked my website before taking the bottle out of the fridge – what a great night we had.

The next day, Richard and I visited a school that Richard had been involved with sponsoring called the Anjana Vidya Kendra School which is run by a man called Dr. Channa Raju, an aerospace scientist. His passion and drive for learning and supporting his pupils was hugely infectious. I cycled into the school with some of the pupils and gave a short talk to them.

The following day, we flew to Chennai where we met one of Richard's business colleagues, Shankar. We visited an eye clinic, where Shankar volunteers his time, and another school. It was only a short visit and before we knew it, we were boarding another plane bound for Cochin where we would be speaking in one last school before I continued with my world cycle. In Cochin I was made so welcome. I was given a room at a hotel by Michael, one of the owners of the CGH Earth group, an eco-friendly hotel chain. At the hotel, Jose and Shagzil, both from the 'Happy Bikers' club arranged for my bike to have a complete overhaul. While that was happening a local TV company came to the hotel to interview me. The broadcast went out the following day. Once the bike was finished I cycled to the school with members of 'Happy Bikers' where I gave my final talk. They were a great bunch of guys and Jose lined me up with a place to stay in Bangkok, which would be the start of my next leg. That evening we were invited to the house of Ravi, another business colleague of Richard's. To have home cooked Indian cuisine is just great. Ravi's wife did us proud, again illustrating the friendly and generous nature of Indian people.

My time in India passed by in a flash: some of the memories were not so good, like being chased and hit by an auto-rickshaw, but the rest of the time was amazing. I often talk to people about India, and if they have been before, they often either love it or hate it. I personally find the country fascinating for many reasons but for me it's the people that make it. After my talks in Cochin, I flew to Bangkok, where I would start the South East Asia leg of my cycle.

17

The beauty of South East Asia

The person whose name I'd been given as a contact to stay with for the first night was a guy called Thomas, an Indian living and working in Bangkok with his family. I arrived into Bangkok and managed to pick up a SIM card and dropped Thomas a message. He gave me his address and I got a taxi over to his apartment. It was a beautiful penthouse overlooking the Bangkok skyline. I arrived in the afternoon and my plan was to hit the road the following day. I was pretty tired, so he showed me to my room where I crashed out. That evening, we went out to dinner with his wife to a local restaurant. When we got back to the apartment, we sat out on the balcony staring at the skyline and listening to the noise of the city.

Thomas very kindly agreed to sponsor me $1,000 for my cycle. We had just been chatting about the finances behind cycling around the world and I was explaining that the challenges of getting to the start line are far greater than actually cycling 100 miles every day. I was in no way asking him for money, but he said he'd see what he could do to help out.

"I've had a quick chat with the CEO and we want to help you out," he told me later.

"If we transfer $1,000 to you now and another $1,000 next month, would that be okay?" Obviously, that was fantastic and a very kind gesture.

The next morning, I was up early and back on the road. It was quite an exciting feeling, cycling through the streets of Bangkok. I had explored the city before, around eight years ago with my best friend, and we'd had a lot of fun, from what I can remember. This time, I was just passing through, but it brought back a lot of great memories from that particular holiday. It was the smell in the streets that I'll never forget and the souped-up Tuk Tuks with alloy wheels and big bore exhausts, with guys flying around like boy racers. Thankfully, none of them hit me, as my arm was still in pain from being hit in India.

It took a good few hours to negotiate my way out of the city, thanks to Google maps. It was still extremely humid and I was sweating profusely as I rode. Luckily, it was all very flat so the cycling was easy. I was surprised at just how Westernised everything was; there were Seven Eleven garages everywhere, fast food chain restaurants and rest stops all the way along the roads. I was cycling on a main road called the AH2, which runs south all the way to the Malaysian border. The roads were not as chaotic as in India but there were still locals riding mopeds the wrong way up the roads and pick-up trucks swaying around precariously with their entire family sitting in the back. This was something you would be instantly arrested for back in the UK, but it was completely normal here. Even the music coming from the radios of passing cars was pretty much exactly the same as back home.

I'd not had any problems with the heat in Europe or India but it was so humid here, I was having to stop pretty much every hour to rehydrate and rest. I was getting through almost a litre of water per hour and as fast as I could drink it, I could feel it seeping out through my skin. Thankfully, there was no shortage of places to stop and everything was so cheap. I managed to cover 115 miles on my first day in Thailand and found a place to stay in Cha Am Beach. That evening, I grabbed a shower in the motel and took a quick walk along the beachfront, looking up at the beautiful stars and out on to the Gulf of Thailand, where the moon's reflection was glistening off the water. I felt really comfortable cycling in Thailand and had a good feeling about this 1,200-mile leg to Singapore.

The following day, I decided to cut my cycle slightly short as I had a mountain of emails to reply to and needed to make some phone calls, so I stopped after 80 miles in Khiri Khan to get some food. I happened to stumble across a place to stay for 200 Thai baht, which was not even £5, so I was happy with that. The highlight of the day was meeting three Malaysian guys who were cycling up from Singapore to Bangkok, the exact reverse of what I was doing. They were a little older than me but were like really excited kids when I told them I was going around the world. They couldn't believe how little I was carrying and we chatted for almost an hour about the route to Singapore and all the things I should try and look out for on my way.

The following day, I pushed a slightly bigger day to Chumphon Beach and covered just short of 130 miles. I was going to look for a place to try and camp by a beach as I fancied sleeping by the sea but I had a text message in the day from a sponsor saying they wanted to Skype with me when I had finished cycling for the day, so I needed to find somewhere with Internet access. I called the sponsor and explained that there were no Internet cafés on the side of the road and to get Internet access, I'd need to check into a hotel and my budget was rapidly dwindling. They agreed to pay for a hotel as they wanted me to Skype in to an awards evening that they were having and thought it would be quite cool to be speaking to me live from Thailand while I was cycling around the world.

I found a hotel on Google maps that would do the trick and decided to make my way there. I was just following the map but something didn't appear to be right when the roads I was cycling down were getting smaller and smaller. Then I found myself standing where the hotel should have been but it was just an area of trees and residential huts. I managed to stop a local guy on a moped and, with the little English that he could understand, he told me where the hotel was. I asked him if he could ride his moped there and I would follow him. It was only a couple of miles so he very kindly agreed. I was in a hurry to get there so I was cycling as hard as I could. He was riding at around 25 miles per hour and I was keeping up with him on the flat. It was a bit like a three-mile time trial where I was sprinting to keep up with this guy on the moped.

Eventually, we came out of a small road and onto a main road where I could then see the lights of buildings and we stopped outside the hotel.

"Wow, you're very strong, fast cyclist," he said in his broken English. I chuckled and thanked him for showing me where the hotel was and tried to give him some money for his time, but he wouldn't take it. There was a security guard on the gate who spoke good English so I asked him to translate that the money was to thank him and to buy himself a beer. He smiled and only took half the money I offered him.

It was quite a nice hotel and was part of a golf and spa resort. I checked in and went to my room, where I connected to the Internet and just about made the Skype call in time. I couldn't see the audience but I could hear them. There were apparently 300 people in the room who could see my sunburnt face on a big screen in front of them, while someone was asking me questions. After the Skype call, I went and had some food and noticed a pool that looked amazing, so I asked one of the members of staff if it was still open as it was about 9.30pm and pretty quiet. She said that technically it was shut, "but I guess it wouldn't hurt anyone if you swam in it". I thanked her and went for a relaxing swim to chill out.

Over the next couple of days, I covered just over 250 miles, through Surat, and was looking for a place to stay in Trang. The previous evening, I had camped out and had been bitten alive again, despite using mosquito spray. Just off the side of the road, I saw a couple of small shack-type buildings and a sign that suggested they were guest houses. I went in to have a look and was greeted by a very friendly man who could have been a double of Mr Mayaki from the film *Karate Kid*. He spoke great English and invited me straight in for food and said that I could stay there, no problem. I instantly felt comfortable in his home and his wife made me some delicious seafood dishes.

'Mr Mayaki' had a large TV in the dining area that was connected to the Internet so I showed him my website and YouTube videos - he couldn't believe that I had climbed Everest and also rowed the Atlantic.

"I can't believe someone who has climbed Everest is in my house," he kept saying. I laughed with him and changed the topic of conversation, asking him questions about himself. He called himself Dr Chase; he was no longer a medical professional and spent most of his time trading stocks and shares online. After dinner, he showed me to my room where I crashed out. When I woke up in the morning, I had some breakfast and tried to settle my bill. Dr Chase and his wife wouldn't let me pay for a thing, which was so kind of them.

I was only just over 100 miles from the Thai/Malaysian border so I planned to get into Malaysia that evening. I wasn't sure if the border was open 24 hours a day, so I tried to cover the miles as quickly as I could but I had a few punctures and I was struggling with the humidity. I didn't arrive at the border until 7pm. It wasn't the main border and was situated in the middle of a forest with steep hills either side of the valley that the road traversed through. As I cycled up towards the border, I noticed there were quite a lot of stalls selling food and clothes, but they were packing everything away. I stopped at the gates that were locked and looked into the office. All the lights were on but no one was around.

Throughout the day, I'd been speaking on my mobile to Dr Chase who was trying to find out what time the border shut but he couldn't find out any more information on the Internet. He asked me to call him when I got to the border so I gave him a quick call to tell him that I'd just missed it. There was nobody in sight so I was just going to sleep on a bench and wait for the morning. He told me not to do that but I didn't see that I had much choice. A few minutes later, he called to tell me that he had spoken to one of the National Park managers as the border was in a National Park. Apparently, I could stay with them in one of their huts for the night. He said that someone would be coming up to the gates to meet me on a moped, and I was to follow them back to their building where I could stay with them. It turned out that Dr Chase's daughter had made a couple of phone calls to someone she happened to know who worked there and they agreed to let me stay.

Soon after I spoke to Dr Chase, right on cue, a guy arrived on a moped, so I followed him back to a compound in the forest where I was greeted by the man in charge. He asked to look at my passport, which I showed him and then he asked if I wanted something to eat. I was pretty hungry at this point so I took him up on the offer. There were five guys sitting on a patio off the main building, which must have been their office, and they were all chatting in Thai and looking at my bike.

After I finished eating, I was shown to a small lodge tucked away down a trail in the forest. I asked what they did and they were basically Forestry Commission workers, looking after and monitoring the forest and the wildlife that inhabited it. It was like being in the middle of a rainforest with all the noises that one would expect from all the different creatures living there. One of the guys who showed me to the small lodge told me not to go out and wander around and to lock my door. For some reason, that made me feel a bit anxious. It was pitch black outside. I stood by the door, looked around and then went inside. There was a shower in the bathroom with hot running water so I grabbed a refreshing shower, and went to bed.

As I tried to fall asleep I couldn't help thinking about the different sequences of events that had led up to me being in a cabin in the middle of a forest. I felt like I was on a real adventure. Every day something different was happening and I was meeting people quite unexpectedly, like Dr Chase, who helped me in some way, shape or form.

When I awoke the next morning I put my cycling kit on, which was in desperate need of a wash, and cycled up to the main building where I arrived the previous night. I found the guy who I'd spoken to before bird watching with a large telescope. He was very excited as there were apparently some very rare birds nesting in the trees.

I handed back the keys to the chap and thanked him for letting me stay. He wished me good luck and I cycled up to the border gate, where I was stamped out of Thailand and changed up some money.

JK

It was only a 200m walk through what I can only imagine was the neutral zone and I was at the Malaysian border where they stamped my passport and granted me access. It was a beautiful morning. The roads were damp where it had rained in the night, which had cooled things down a bit, birds were chirping in the trees and the view into the valleys was breathtaking.

The border was at the top of a hill so I descended down the other side through a series of switchbacks and into Malaysia. As I was coasting down the road, I passed some fairly serious looking cyclists who were coming up the hill. I passed them quite quickly so just waved as opposed to stopping and chatting. After about an hour, the terrain flattened out and I cycled into the town of Perlis where I stopped in a Domino's Pizza for some lunch. Soon after, I was cycling along, when a group of cyclists came up beside me at the traffic lights while I was waiting for them to change to green. They were riding fairly high-end road bikes and one of them asked where I was going. I told them I'd just crossed the border from Thailand and was aiming to get to Butterworth. They told me they were going that way too, so I followed them and we got chatting. They all spoke excellent English, as did most people I came across in Malaysia.

They were cycling quite fast and I wasn't sure if they were trying to lose me at first but then they slowed down a little as they had an older guy in the group who couldn't keep up with them. I thought if I was going to tag on to these guys, I should make an effort to introduce myself, so I cycled up and down the group chatting with them. They were all very friendly and welcoming and were asking me loads of questions about my bike and the kit I was carrying, they knew their stuff. It was fantastic cycling with them as it meant I didn't have to worry about navigating and could just enjoy the view. They asked if I wanted to take a scenic route along the coast, which I thought would be a fantastic idea.

The coastline was amazing: beautiful, blue ocean with beaches covered in golden sand for miles and miles. There was also a fantastic tailwind blowing us along at over 25mph. After a few hours, we stopped for lunch by a ferry, which was going to take us across a short stretch of water.

A short while later, we said goodbye to a couple of the guys who were going a different way; it was now starting to get dark and none of them had lights which I was quite surprised about. My dynamo light was lighting the way for most of us. One of the cyclists I'd been chatting to for some time suggested I stay at a new budget hotel. His name was Karhor and we both rode back to the hotel and I checked in. Karhor had all of the Malaysian Garmin maps and was convinced he could get them on my Garmin Edge 800.

Karhor very kindly came back to the hotel in the evening where I planned to meet him. We were going to find somewhere to grab some food and try to transfer the maps. He took me to a local market that had street stands with lots of different selections of meat and fish. He assured me that it was all clean and that I would be perfectly fine to eat any of it, so I didn't hold back.

We couldn't get the maps to work but it didn't matter as I now had my iPhone up and running with a local SIM card, which was giving me data so I could use Google maps. I exchanged contact details with Karhor and said farewell. It was one of the most unexpected, but best days of the trip so far.

The following day, the terrain started to get a little more undulating as I started to get closer to Kuala Lumpur, 200 miles away. I decided to stay in the city of Ipoh as it was 120 miles from Kuala Lumpur and would leave me with an ideal cycling distance the next day. I woke up early after a good night's sleep in a hostel so got straight out on the road. The sky was looking very menacing with huge, dark clouds looming over the horizon, getting closer and closer. I could tell I was in for a soaking, although it was so hot and humid that the rain was welcomingly refreshing. I was no stranger to torrential rain but when these clouds came over, it was like a scene out of an Armageddon film. It was the middle of the day and the clouds were dark and dense, it almost went black. It was as if someone just turned a switch and the heavens opened.

At first, it was quite good fun and then as the rain got harder and harder, it was so painful that it was like being shot in the face by a BB gun. I needed to find somewhere to take shelter but there was nowhere suitable. To make matters worse, there was a huge bang as a clap of thunder roared from the clouds above me. A few seconds later, a bolt of lightning came down about 20m away from me and I could feel the hairs on the back of my neck stand on end. Then the thunder followed, probably the loudest clap of thunder I have heard in my life.

I was now quite worried as I really didn't want to get struck by lightning. I was completely exposed, riding slowly up the side of a hill, which was lined with trees. In the distance, I saw a bus stop with people taking shelter so I aimed for that as fast as I could. Another bolt of lightning came down, this time much closer and I really did feel the charge and power of it reverberate through my entire body. I didn't want to find out where the next lightning bolt was going to strike so I stood up on the pedals and pumped them as hard as I could to get to the bus shelter. Thankfully, I arrived before I was struck by lightning and joined the other group of people who were standing there, marvelling at the power of Mother Nature.

I thought it would be a good opportunity to get my camera out and shoot some video footage. Everyone who was in the bus shelter was looking at me like I was some kind of lunatic, soaked through, talking into a camera like an excited little boy. After half-an-hour, the storm disappeared as quickly as it came and blue sky started making its way through the clouds. The passing rain had certainly cleared the air and cooled things down quite considerably so I carried on my way. The lightning was still around but it had moved through so it was safe to carry on. As soon as the sun came out, the wet roads started steaming and within 15 minutes, they had completely dried out.

A few hours later, I was on the outskirts of Kuala Lumpur when the traffic became heavier. I needed to have my wits about me as I was cycling on much bigger, busier roads. I knew exactly where I was going to stay so I navigated my way through the streets with my iPhone, eventually arriving at about 6pm and 125 miles from where I had started.

That night, I spoke to a good friend of mine called Chris, who happened to be in Singapore on business and we planned to meet up. He was in a hotel and said that I could share the room and use the facilities to save on cost. I did some route planning and, from what I could see, it was around 230 miles from my current location to Singapore. I remember chatting to Chris on the phone and him saying, "That would be a bloody good effort to do that in one hit." He wasn't directly challenging me to do it (I don't think) but I wanted to see if I could do it and I was really looking forward to catching up with him.

I found a Subway that night and consumed two foot-long steak and cheese baguettes with a chocolate cookie and a Coke to wash it all down. By this point, I was around 78kg in weight, which is light for me. Cycling unsupported meant that I quite often had to just eat what I could get my hands on easily and what was fairly cheap.

I set off the following morning at around 8am, after a good night's sleep, and slowly made my way through the city and out the other side. After an hour, I'd lost sight of the famous Petronas Twin Towers behind me. I deliberately cycled a little slower than normal, trying to conserve energy and eating as much as I could. The first 100 miles passed quite quickly, in around eight hours, which included some breaks. From around the 100-mile mark to the 140-mile point, I felt very fatigued and wondered if I should just try and find a place to stop, but when I thought of stopping, I kept thinking of arriving and seeing the look on Chris's face when I told him that I'd cycled through the night. Plus, I wanted to see my Asia leg off in style so what better way to do it?

The feeling of tiredness left me after 150 miles and it was replaced with excitement and adrenaline. I was actually cycling through the night and was on target to cover the distance and arrive in the morning, if I just kept going. The closer I got to Singapore (even if it was only one mile closer), the more determined I became to get there. The bike was riding really well, no squeaks or creaks and my dynamo light was illuminating the road ahead. I was eating up the miles and feeling great. I was now determined to make it to Singapore.

It was around the 180-mile mark when I ran over a pothole and got a pinch puncture so I had to quickly swap the tube out. A guy on a moped who was riding by stopped to see if I was all right. I told him I was fine but thanked him for stopping. He hung around for a few minutes and then rode his moped alongside me while I was cycling. He asked me if I wanted to go for a drink with him. Considering it was 2am and I was most likely stinking, I thought that was quite weird. I didn't want to offend the guy so told him I didn't have time and was running behind schedule, hence why I was riding through the night.

From 3am to 4.30am, I didn't see a soul on the road and, by this time, I had covered over 200 miles and was feeling good. I thought the city of Johor was only 20 or so miles away so I was expecting to see some lights in the sky or at least the yellow glow of a city, but there was nothing, still pitch black. At around 230 miles, the area started to become a bit more built-up and I could tell I was on the outskirts of a city but was still miles away from Singapore, although I did start seeing road signs with Singapore on them, so I knew for sure I was on the right road.

At about 5am, the roads started to get busier with people leaving early for work and the sky was starting to brighten as the sun was gradually coming up over the horizon. Eventually, I made it into the city of Johor and could see a sign for the bridge that would take me into Singapore. By this point, I had covered nearly 250 miles so my calculation of around 230 miles was certainly out. It started to get really busy so I just stayed in the lanes with all the mopeds and scooters. I was almost travelling as fast as them anyway. In the distance, I could see the tall skyscrapers of Singapore. I just needed to go through Immigration and I was there. I wasn't sure what lane to get in when I crossed the bridge and couldn't see any signs for pedestrians or cyclists, just cars and motorcycles, so I stayed in the motorcycle lane. My gut feeling told me that I wasn't in quite the right place but I decided to just go with the flow. I arrived at a toll and paid my money to go across the bridge. I then ended up in a queue of hundreds of motorcycles taking it in turns to go through a checkpoint where they were showing their passports.

When I got to the barrier, a representative approached me and told me that I had come through the wrong way but it didn't matter. He opened the barrier for me and asked me to step aside, which I did. I gave him my passport and he escorted me over to an office where I sat down with an Immigration Officer. She was very friendly and was asking questions about where I had been. We chatted for about five minutes and then she handed me back my passport, after stamping it and said, "Right, I'd better not keep you, on your way then." It was around 8am and I'd made it into Singapore.

I now needed to head over to the hotel where Chris was staying, which happened to be on the other side of the island, by the airport. My phone rang and it was him, seeing where I was. I told him I was in Singapore and on my way over to the hotel. He sounded quite shocked that I had actually cycled over 250 miles to get there. He had to go to work so told the staff on reception that I was arriving. Singapore was fantastic: everything was so neat and tidy and even the grass on the sidewalks was immaculately kept, not dissimilar to what you'd find on a golf course. There was something about Singapore I instantly liked.

I cycled past the hotel Chris was staying at by accident and ended up by a little beach, so I sat on a bench, looking out at the sea and the aircraft coming in to land, as I was just under the main flight path. Following my day dreaming, I went to the hotel and checked in to the room where I jumped straight into the shower. It felt amazing. Chris had some really expensive Hugo Boss shower gel and I didn't think he'd mind if I used some, so I spent about 20 minutes cleaning off the sweat and grime that had embedded in to my skin and hair. I dried myself and lay on the bed. I thought I'd have a few hours' sleep and then get up and find a bike shop to pack the bike up, as I planned to fly to Perth, Australia, the following day.

I had cycled 262.9 miles so I was feeling quite wired and couldn't sleep at first, but eventually I dozed off. I woke up at midday after about five hours' sleep, and felt surprisingly refreshed. I grabbed some food in the hotel then headed out to find a bike shop. I found a fantastic little place, run by an older guy who cleaned and packed my bike into a box after he replaced a gear cable that had started to fray. While I was waiting, I caught up with a fellow adventurer called Jon, who had driven from London to Singapore in a 4x4 pick-up truck and was about to start the drive back to London. We had been communicating via email over the past few weeks and thought it would be great if we could meet up, albeit briefly.

Jon had given me his contact number so I sent him a text message to let him know that I had some spare time while my bike was being packed up. He said he was only a few minutes away and would come down to meet me. He was giant of a man, standing at around six foot five. He was really friendly, so we sat in a bar, grabbed a Coke and just chatted about the experiences that we'd both had to date on our travels. I was due to be going out that evening with Chris and his work colleagues so I invited Jon along too but he couldn't make it. After about an hour of chatting, we shot some video diary footage, took a couple of photos and went our separate ways. The bike shop owner had done a great job at cleaning and packing my bike up, taking the liberty of putting a sticker of his bike shop on the bike. I didn't mind and was starting to build quite a collection of stickers on the bike. Every shop I stopped at wanted to put one on.

I managed to wave down a taxi and made my way back to the hotel. Chris was now due back from work so I sat and waited for him. It was fantastic catching up with him. He was a good friend and a very accomplished individual in his own right, having previously rowed across the Atlantic Ocean with his brother, Matt, a few years prior, and he also served as a Landing Craftsman with the Royal Marines. Chris was a very modest guy and someone who was generally fun to be around, especially while having a few beers.

Chris had mentioned to his boss that I'd pushed a 260-mile day from Kuala Lumpur the previous day. He was apparently so impressed that he invited me out for dinner with them, all expenses paid. I didn't really have anything suitable to wear so I borrowed some jeans and a shirt from Chris and we headed out to downtown Singapore. It was absolutely amazing and not dissimilar to being in London, with all the high-rise buildings and shopping malls. It was very Westernised and certainly an international city in the truest sense of the word, with so many different nationalities living there.

We ended up in quite an upmarket, trendy restaurant. Everyone seemed to be very well dressed, drinking Champagne and cocktails. We sat down and ordered our food. Since Chris and his boss ordered the most expensive steak on the menu, I took that as a green light to go ahead and order it as well. It was a blessing in disguise as I wanted to order it but I wouldn't have done if everyone else had just ordered a burger. It was divine, cooked rare, just how I like it, with fries and salad. It didn't touch the sides and went down in a few minutes, as I was ravenous. After dinner, we went to another bar and had a few drinks. Chris' boss and some other colleagues suggested we check out a different part of town so I went along with the plans.

We jumped in a taxi and headed to another bar, which was quite a glamorous place at the top of a high-rise building. I didn't want to drink too much as I was heading to the airport at 8am the following day, but it was hard to resist the temptation. The one thing that kept making the world cycle so interesting was the uncertainty of what the next day would bring and what situations I would find myself in. I knew I was going to meet Chris but I had no idea I was going to be taken out to one of Singapore's elite clubs, rubbing shoulders with the island's high flyers. It was a funny contrast to what I'd been doing 24 hours earlier, cycling through the night in my stinking cycling kit that was in desperate need of a washing machine.

Chris' boss and colleagues decided to leave but Chris and I thought we would stay a little longer. The next thing I remember was waking up in the morning with absolutely no recollection of what had happened. My head was killing me and I felt incredibly drowsy. Chris was late for work so he got dressed and stumbled out the door after saying goodbye. I was in a right mess and couldn't figure out if our drinks had been spiked or if it was just the volume of alcohol catching up with me. I needed to get a grip and sort myself out, so I dragged myself into the bathroom and took a cold shower.

I spoke to my friend, Matt, who was living in Perth and who happened to be Chris' brother. He had said I could stay with him when I flew in so I needed to let him know my arrival time. After struggling to find a taxi that would take my bike in its box, I arrived at Singapore Airport and proceeded through Immigration and security. I made a couple of calls in the departure lounge, and then boarded the plane.

THE ULTIMATE TRIATHLON

18

Adventures Down Under

Eight hours later, I arrived in Perth, Western Australia. I was queuing up at Passport Control and I noticed everyone in front of me was being, from what I could gather, interrogated by Immigration Officers. I wondered what they would say to me when I stepped forward. I like to try and carry myself with confidence so I moved forward, looked at the Immigration Officer who happened to be a female and said hi.

"Hi, so what brings you to Australia?"she said with a smile.

"I'm cycling around the world," I replied.

"Wow, that's amazing man, good luck," she then stamped my passport and let me through without asking any further questions.

I walked outside and was quite taken aback at how cold it was in the evening, certainly too chilly for just shorts and a T-shirt and it was the first week of September. Matt wasn't able to pick me up so he had arranged for a friend to collect me, who happened to work at the airport and was finishing her shift at the same time that I was due to land. We went back to Matt's house where I was going to stay for a day, rest, pick up any last minute kit and start to make my way out to what I thought was going to be one of the hardest legs, crossing Australia from west to east.

Matt had a friend staying with him who was into skydiving; he asked me what my route would be out of Perth. He went on to tell me I was going to cycle right past the drop zone where he did all his skydiving jumps. He asked me if I wanted to do a jump and, never having jumped out of a plane before, I thought it sounded like a great opportunity. The next morning, I said goodbye to Matt and his partner and thanked them for kindly letting me stay and get myself sorted. It was about 60 miles out to the drop zone and it was very hilly but it was amazing to be cycling. The temperature in the day was just right, warm but not too hot. When I arrived at the airfield, which was in a little town called York, it was pretty much in the middle of nowhere, although the vast majority of Australia is uninhabited.

Part of me was thinking that perhaps this was not such a good idea. If I got injured, it would be an embarrassing end to my world cycle. Something inside me made me feel it would be all right, and it was quite an amazing opportunity, which I probably wouldn't get again, at least not in Australia anyway. The guy that had asked if I wanted to jump was called Rob. He was British, living and working in Australia and was very keen to hear about my world cycle and secretly wished he could be doing it himself. Rob introduced me to the guy I was going to jump with, an American skydiver with over 10,000 jumps under his belt, so I was feeling pretty safe.

It was all quite informal, perhaps because I was with Rob, but I remember the instructor telling me that there really is nothing to it. He showed me how we would approach the door and how we would exit, along with a few other bits, but that really was it. Rob and his friend were going to come up with us and we planned to jump at the same time. We all sat in the back of what they called the 'caravan', which was the plane we would jump out of. It didn't have seats as such, just padded benches to sit on. We all jumped in and started the climb up to 13,000ft, which took about 20 minutes. I thought I might feel a bit nervous but I didn't at all; I was actually really looking forward to it.

The light in the back of the cabin went green and we started to shuffle our way to the door. Rob and his friend climbed out and were holding on to the side of the plane, standing on a ledge. My instructor checked my goggles and we moved into position. I was leaning over the door and he counted "three, two, one, go." I could suddenly hear this 'whoosh' as the air was whistling past my face and, for a split second, I could feel the acceleration as our bodies tumbled to the ground at over 120 miles per hour, terminal velocity. It didn't feel particularly fast and it was a strange experience, like I was floating; because we were so high up, the ground wasn't rushing up on us. I think it wasn't such a big deal for me as I was used to racing motorbikes that would do in excess of 170 miles per hour. Most weekends, prior to having my accident, I was riding quite a bit faster than my body was falling now.

Without a helmet, I could really feel the wind smothering my face as I was falling through the clouds. Before I knew it, I felt a violent jerk as the parachute opened and the other guys who were freefalling around us shot away underneath my feet. It suddenly went virtually silent. I could hear a slight whistle, as the air was passing over the wing of the parachute. Apparently we had been in freefall for 60 seconds but it had felt like only a couple of seconds, it was over so quickly.

When the parachute opened, we were still a few thousand feet above the ground. The view was fantastic as I surveyed the open flat, parched landscape. It took a couple of minutes to float down to the safety of solid ground. My instructor handed over control of the parachute to me: "Pull this cord and you go that way, pull the other cord and you'll go the other way." It was great fun spiralling down, looking below my feet at the airfield. When I landed, I handed my kit back in and sat down for a few minutes to look at the footage from my GoPro camera that the instructor was wearing for me. I had some lunch and then it was time to carry on. It was somewhat of an anti-climax getting back on the bike after jumping out of a plane, to be honest.

I cycled into the evening, and noticed just how beautiful the sun set was as it disappeared behind the horizon, projecting an array of colours into the clouds above. I plugged my dynamo lights in to illuminate the road in front of me, as it was very dark. I'd been cycling for about an hour in the dark and a car pulled up beside me. It was a husband and wife who owned a farm about 50 miles down the road. They were very friendly but stopped me because they didn't think my rear light was good enough. They invited me to their farm but it was too far to make it that evening and I wanted to try and get back into a rhythm of cycling as I'd been out the saddle for a few days. Instead, I found a place to stay, which was a small, run down motel. It was sufficient for my needs. I popped down to the bar for a Coke and ordered some food. While standing at the bar, two drunk guys walked in and started looking at me. I figured they were wondering who I was, but they didn't say anything to me.

The next day, I was heading for a town called Merredin, which was just over 100 miles away. It was pretty easy cycling, all relatively flat. After cycling out of Quairading, I came across a tiny little village called Shackleton. It consisted of a train station, a grocery shop and its claim to fame was having the world's smallest bank which measures three by four metres. I decided to pop into the grocery store to pick up a drink and a few other small bits to eat on the road. An elderly gentleman welcomed me and I noticed immediately that his accent wasn't Australian but I couldn't quite work out what it was. Before I could ask him anything, he asked me where I was from and I told him. I generally told people that I was from a town not far from London. "Whereabouts?" he said, "I know London well, I lived in Streatham for most of my life." I told him I was actually from Basingstoke and then he added, "Ah, I know Basingstoke well, I had some friends who lived there and I visited many times back in the 50's - lots of roundabouts!" I couldn't believe it - I was in the middle of nowhere and this old man who was in his 80s was living and working in this tiny little place but knew of Basingstoke. The world suddenly felt a lot smaller. He wanted to look at my bike and his wife came out and took some photos of us standing proudly by his shop with my bike. He was a wonderful man.

I arrived that evening in Merredin after a lovely day's cycling. Over the next few days, I passed through Coolgardie, Norseman and out on to the famous Nullarbor Plain. This is an area of arid, flat land with temperatures that sore well over 45°C in the summer. Service stations are 100 miles apart, so cycling between them takes a certain amount of logistical planning for food and water. I was feeling strong and knew my limits and what I was capable of cycling, with or without the right nutrition. My first day on the Nullarbor was from Norseman to Balladonia, which was 120 miles. The road surface wasn't much different to what I'd been cycling on anyway so it was fairly straightforward. I decided to camp at Balladonia as the motel rate had gone up quite considerably, which was no surprise, considering it was the only one within 100 miles.

The following day would see me cross the world famous '90 Mile Straight', Australia's longest straight road. I had been really looking forward to this and I stopped at the sign and took a couple of photos and asked a couple if they would kindly film me as I cycled past the sign. I had plenty of food and water on the bike and had the most fantastic tailwind pushing me along. The winds can make or break a day on a bike when cycling vast distances, especially in open terrain like the Nullarbor Plain. For the vast majority of the year, the winds blow from the west and, much to my delight, they were blowing with a vengeance. The road surface was incredibly smooth, more so than the rest of the Eyre Highway that cuts its way through hundreds of miles.

I'd heard horror stories and been told that I must be suicidal to cycle across the Nullarbor. It was so far proving to be quite the opposite experience. I had people in cars and caravans pulling up beside me, asking if I needed anything or if they could place water for me further down the road to collect. Thankfully, it wasn't that hot and with the strong winds that had converged on my bearing, the conditions were ideal. I tucked into the aero bar position on the bike as I made my way along the 90-mile straight and was devouring the miles, averaging 22mph, which would be a half good racing speed, let alone a touring pace.

One thing I really noticed was the unexpected torrent of caravans heading west across the Nullarbor. Chatting to the retired 'grey nomads' as they were delightfully known, they explained how everyone was heading home for the summer as they had been in the north for the winter. It was a bipolar mixture of cheery waves from caravans and angry horn blasts from road trains. Most of the horn blasts from the road trains were just letting me know they were approaching, in case I was in a tired daze and drifted out in front of them to what would be an instant death. Their bull bars with the combined weight and speed would literally obliterate anything in their path. The sides of the roads were littered with road kill, mostly kangaroos or, as the truck drivers referred to them, 'roos'. In the heat, their bodies would swell up and often split open if they were still intact, giving off the most unpleasant stench I've ever smelt. It was so bad that it would make me gag. As I had a tailwind, I wouldn't smell anything until I'd actually gone past it and then I had to try and hold my breath for as long as I could until the smell had gone.

Another strange observation was the amount of bottles containing bright yellow liquid that littered the side of the roads. It wasn't until I saw a bottle come flying out of the side of a truck that I realised it was in fact urine. By urinating into the bottles, it meant that the drivers didn't have to stop and waste valuable time as they were racing precious cargo from one side of Australia to another. I was approaching the end of my day and only about 30 miles away from a little service station in Caiguna, when I heard the roar of a truck coming from behind, so I moved over slightly. I noticed that for some reason it didn't honk its horn at me. As the truck passed, the driver threw an object out of the window.

It all happened very quickly and all I saw was a white blur out of the corner of my right eye, but it hit me hard on the shoulder and liquid covered my top. Thankfully, none went on my face. I realised, to my absolute disgust, the driver had thrown a bottle of pee at me without a lid on. It absolutely stank and I was so angry. Before I thought about taking the registration plate, the truck was long gone. I can only assume the guy had a vendetta against cyclists. As it was still quite hot, I took my shirt off and cycled topless to Caiguna where I checked into the motel, having no choice but to pay their extortionate prices. I needed a shower urgently and washing facilities as my kit was now soaked in urine. I'm a true believer in karma so I would imagine that the driver got his comeuppance at some point.

The following morning, I left Caiguna with the aim of getting to Madura, which was a very easy 100 miles away. I managed it in just over six hours but for some reason, my right knee was throbbing a little so I decided to stay in Madura as opposed to going on. I called a good friend of mine, Gary, who runs a very successful injury rehab clinic and asked him for some advice as my knee had actually been playing up for a few days. He kindly talked me through some massaging techniques that he thought might help.

I was now getting pretty close to the border of Southern Australia. I'd been chasing two other cyclists down for the past few days, as some of the motel owners and people travelling the other way were informing me of two loaded down cyclists who they had passed coming my way. Over the next couple of days, I had a bit of rough weather with very heavy rain and a head wind, which had rather strangely turned on me. Luckily it didn't last too long, as pedalling into the wind was so demoralising, it cut my speed in half. I went from a tailwind and an average speed of close to 20mph to having to push hard to make an average of just 10mph. The wind was biting at my face and every time I eased the power from my legs on the cranks, I could feel the wind just grinding me to a stop. It was like riding with my brakes on. What was slightly disconcerting was the lightning that was getting closer and closer. It looked amazing in the distance but it was fast approaching me. With absolutely nowhere to escape, I had to cycle right through the middle of it, which was quite nerve-wracking, considering how flat and featureless the terrain was.

I managed to catch the two cyclists up in Eucla. They were Australian guys called Don and Steve. Steve was ex-Australian Royal Navy and Don was a production engineer. They were both in their 50s and were cycling from Perth to Melbourne, for fun. They were pretty loaded down with kit and I was surprised to find they were carrying bottles of beer and wine, although I did think that was pretty cool for two guys in their 50s to be doing. They had been covering around 60 miles a day with a mixture of camping and staying in motels. I stumbled across them right before the South Australia border as I pulled into a motel to get some food. They had a room and were drying their kit out from the previous day's soaking. They invited me in and put the kettle on for a cup of tea, which went down well.

Like all the cyclists I was passing, they were staggered at how little kit I was carrying and pretty impressed that I was going around the world. I was going to carry on that evening but they offered me the use of a fold-up bed in the room and insisted on buying me dinner. It was also an offer I couldn't really refuse as my money was rapidly dwindling. We had a cracking dinner that evening and I woke up to a lovely sunny day the following morning. It was over 120 miles to the next village and that's where I was aiming for. I wasn't sure if Don and Steve would want to cycle that far. I thought it would be nice if they did, as it would make a change from cycling on my own, but understood that it was a long way with the amount of kit they were carrying. Much to my surprise, they said they would try and push on with me.

We crossed into South Australia with no difficulty, despite being warned that border control was very strict on taking certain types of food across the border. We posed for a photo in front of the South Australia – Western Australia sign and carried on. The wind was blowing hard on our backs, pushing us along at an average speed of 16mph, which was fantastic, considering the weight Don and Steve were carrying. As my bike was so much lighter, I was free-wheeling along all day, the wind was blowing so hard. We stopped for lunch at the Great Australian Bight, looking out into the Southern Ocean, hoping to see some whales that had been recently sighted. I didn't see any but it was certainly a fabulous view as the large waves violently broke on the beach.

That evening, we made it to the motel after 122 miles. I was very impressed the guys had been able to cover the distance with no problems, and the wind certainly helped. I had to leave them the following day as I was running slightly behind schedule. I was due to meet someone who was going to cycle the last part of my Australia leg to Sydney with me. Two years prior to the world cycle, I was minding my own business on the London Underground, making my way to an Everest sponsorship meeting, when I noticed an absolutely stunning woman sitting on her own, reading a very famous book that accounts a disaster on Everest. Having read the book, I said to her, "That's a great read, isn't it?" She started talking to me and I could instantly tell she was very friendly and her accent gave away she was from Australia.

We got chatting, as there weren't many people in the carriage and she asked me how I knew so much about Everest. I told her I was attempting to climb it the following year and was on my way to a sponsorship meeting about it. She was quite taken aback and was asking all sorts of questions. Her name was Michelle and she was working as a nurse in London on a two-year visa. I gave her a card with my website on so she could follow my progress on Everest. When she got off the train, she wished me luck and smiled at me, while looking right into my eyes. I thought to myself, "Wow, you're stunning and seem to be a very genuine, friendly person." I chuckled to myself as she walked down the platform and the train pulled away. I didn't think I'd ever see her again. I soon forgot about her until a year-and-a-half later, when I announced after my successful ascent of Everest that I was going to cycle around the world.

One afternoon, I had a message from a girl called Michelle, saying that she had followed my Everest climb with interest and was asking if I'd be coming to Australia. I had no idea who this person was until the penny dropped and I realised it was the same Michelle I had met on the train that day. She had added me on Facebook and I hadn't even realised it was her, despite accepting her as a friend. I was shocked and just couldn't believe it. I emailed back and told her that I would indeed be cycling all the way across Australia if she wanted to join me. We started to Skype a fair bit and decided that she would cycle a leg with me somewhere in Australia. I was so impressed with her efforts; she had purchased a bike and was training hard. We'd agreed to meet in Port Lincoln and she would cycle to Sydney with me, which was around 1,000 miles, give or take.

JK

I needed to cover the best part of 400 miles in two days in order to get to Port Lincoln to meet Michelle on time. Thankfully, it turned out to only be 350 miles but it still meant two big days of cycling, most of which was spent in the aero position, grinding out the cranks with my head down. It was during these two days that I noticed the amount of weird and wonderful things I was coming across on the side of the road. Tools, clothes, wallets, knives and magazines, all of which had probably somehow made their way out of a car window at some point. The icing on the cake was nearly riding over a handgun that was lying in the road. I stopped to look at it and right before I was going to pick it up, realised it may not be wise. It was a bit of a conundrum, as I didn't know what to do with it. Was it a murder weapon and how did it get there? I decided the best thing to do was just to leave it, so I carried on. I spent quite a few hours pondering over what the story was behind that gun.

I eventually rolled into Port Lincoln at 9pm, meeting Michelle in a hotel. It was a very surreal situation: I was standing in the lobby of a hotel looking at this woman that I'd randomly met on a tube in London, thinking that I'd never see her again. The next morning, I helped her get her bike ready and after some breakfast, we started to make our way up to Port August which would take a couple of days. Unfortunately, it was a baptism of fire for Michelle as typically, the winds had turned on our nose and it couldn't have been more demoralising as we slogged our way up the coast. We made it to Port

August on schedule but it had taken its toll on poor Michelle and she was having a few pains in her knee. I felt quite sorry for her as she was trying incredibly hard, but it was quite a shock to her body. She wasn't carrying much kit as we agreed we would find accommodation for the days she would spend with me as it saved her carrying camping equipment, so she just had a rucksack, which I ended up carrying for her. I didn't mind at all as I'd cycled half way round the world to get there so, needless to say, I was pretty strong on a bike.

Our route took us around the coast down to Adelaide where she had to take a couple of days off due to fatigue. We agreed that we would meet each other at Mount Gambier as she was going to get a bus there. I felt bad as I couldn't wait for her because of my tight schedule and I had to get to Sydney for a talk I was giving to a sponsor. She completely understood and was very accommodating in that sense. The cycling from Adelaide down to Mount Gambier was stunning, with a mixture of steep hills through picturesque towns that wouldn't look out of place on a postcard. As I was cycling out of Adelaide, I met a group of cyclists who were supporting another cyclist on his first day riding down to Melbourne from Adelaide to raise money for charity. I cycled with them for a few hours and got chatting to a guy called Michael, who was a very keen runner and cyclist. We were talking about bikes and different setup options for long distance endurance cycling and the calories required to sustain 100-plus miles per day.

He asked what my route down to Melbourne was and I mentioned I was heading to Mount Gambier to meet Michelle. He said that he was interested in cycling to Mount Gambier with me but would need to go home first and check if it was okay with his wife. I gave him my mobile number and asked him to let me now if he was going to join me the following day. That evening, I made it to a small town called Meningie, which was just over 100 miles south of Adelaide. Michael called while I was having dinner and told me that his wife would drop him off in the morning and he would cycle to Mount Gambier with me, where his wife would collect him later. He arrived at the motel where I was staying at 6am the following morning. As it was just over 155 miles to Mount Gambier, I felt a little guilty as he would have left home at about 4.30am, but he said he liked early mornings.

We cycled for a few hours before coming across a café where we stopped and had breakfast. It was quite flat and we had a good tailwind so were averaging around 20mph and making very good progress. We spotted a group of cyclists in the distance and caught up with them pretty quickly. It was an Australian school teacher who was cycling around the entire coastline of Australia. He had a support team in a small converted van travelling with him so we stopped off for lunch with them then cycled together for a little while until their route took them a different way. We made great progress that day and covered 160 miles in nine hours. I said goodbye to Michael, after a thoroughly enjoyable day of cycling.

I met up with Michelle that evening and was pleased that the two days she had taken off had made a big difference. She was refreshed, motivated and raring to go, which I really admired. The following day, we covered just over 110 miles and crossed into New South Wales, finishing in Port Fairy. We were now approaching the famous 'Great Ocean Road', which runs all the way round to Geelong just south of Melbourne. Both Michelle and I were very much looking forward to this part of the ride as it's often described as one of the most scenic roads in the world and is widely used by cyclists, from amateurs having a gentle ride to full professional UCI teams.

Our first couple of days on the Great Ocean Road, or the B100, proved to be quite eventful. Not long after stopping to marvel at the Twelve Apostles, we noticed some very dark, menacing clouds rolling in off the ocean. Michelle and I stopped to take some photos, as it was quite an interesting sight. As they got closer, things started to change; the wind picked up dramatically and the soft patter of rain on our waterproofs soon turned to a torrential downpour. We tried to seek accommodation in Princetown but everywhere, which was basically two motels, was fully booked and they sent us packing. By now it was getting dark and we had over 30 miles to go to the next village of Lavers Hill, and Michelle was getting tired. The temperature had also dropped significantly and, with the torrent of rain that was hitting us, everything was soaked, despite us wearing Gortex jackets.

The roads started to wind through a forest with the inclines getting steeper and steeper. Michelle was very close to breaking point and was mentally struggling, biting my head off every time I said something that annoyed her. I didn't mind; in a strange way, we got to know each other very quickly as she was outside of her comfort zone and I was trying to make it as easy as possible for her, but these cold, wet conditions were proving pretty tough for her. To make things worse, my dynamo light wasn't particularly effective as we were climbing slowly up the hills and Michelle's light had run out of battery, leaving us in almost total darkness.

I knew we were getting closer to Lavers Hill but I was quite concerned for Michelle. She was shivering and extremely cold and I knew that it was quite an unpleasant experience for her. The roads were fortunately very quiet so there was no real danger from passing cars. I saw a car coming towards us quite slowly so I decided to flag it down, just to double check that we hadn't passed Lavers Hill without noticing or taken a wrong turn.

"Ah, no worries mate, it's only half a mile down the road, you can't miss it," the guy said in a broad Australian accent. At that point, I was extremely relieved as I was getting a bit anxious, plus I was cold, wet and miserable myself, but I was hiding it from Michelle.

As the lights of Lavers Hill approached, I thought about what a tough night it had been, and I hoped we would find somewhere to stay. Thankfully, we found a motel that had a spare room so I was able to get dry and ordered some food from the bar. Michelle had shown real fortitude that day and I looked at her in a totally different light thereafter. The following morning, we woke up to beautiful blue skies and glorious sunshine, a complete contrast from the previous evening. There were a lot of fallen trees and debris on the roads from the high winds, which was evident when we came across a large fallen tree that had come down, blocking an entire road. There was stationary traffic on either side of the tree and kids jumping all over it. Luckily, we were able to carry our bikes over the tree and continued on our way.

We stopped for lunch in Apollo Bay, which was a lovely little coastal town. The cycling was now absolutely stunning as we slowly made our way up the Great Ocean Road, taking in the majestic views as the famous road hugged the coastline. Michelle had organised a night's accommodation with a lovely couple she knew called Gary and Margaret, who lived just off the Great Ocean Road. They were very hospitable hosts, washing our kit and cooking us a wonderful dinner.

Over the next five days, Michelle and I made our way through Melbourne and into New South Wales. I was quite taken aback at just how hilly New South Wales was, as we got closer to Sydney. Our time together was coming to an end and, in a strange way, I didn't want to leave Michelle. We had only been cycling together for the best part of two weeks and in that time, we had had some massive arguments (which is totally out of character for me) but we also had some really great times and lots of good memories. I was under a lot of pressure from sponsors to be at certain places by a certain time, which made things difficult. I could tell that Michelle was looking forward to finishing and was excited to see her family who were making the long journey to Sydney to see her arrive at the famous Opera House. I was excited for her too as her achievement was Herculean, considering how little endurance experience she had.

Her last day was quite an easy cycle into Sydney and I was excited to be visiting the city and seeing the famous Opera House and Sydney Harbour Bridge. We arrived slightly early so we stopped to have a snack in a coffee shop and soak up the atmosphere. The sun was shining, it was lovely and warm and people seemed to be happily going about their business. As I sat eating my cake, chatting with Michelle, I could hear all the different foreign languages being spoken as people walked by; it was a truly cosmopolitan city. Michelle rang her mum to see where they were and she confirmed that they were waiting for us outside the Opera House. We finished our drinks, donned our helmets and cycled down the hill to find her parents and friends. I had no idea what they looked like so I just followed Michelle. When I heard a huge "Yay, well done Michelle!" and clapping, I assumed they were her parents and friends.

She was so happy; I could see the look on her face as she was hugging everyone. Her parents turned to me and shook my hand, thanking me for looking after their daughter and congratulating me on getting to Sydney. We found a nice bar to have some drinks and relax in. I really wanted to have a beer and chill out but I had to cycle over to another part of the city to give a talk at a sponsor's office, so had to leave after 45 minutes. I was determined to cycle over the Sydney Harbour Bridge, which I did on the way to the talk. It was quite amazing: the view was incredible looking out over the harbour. After the talk, I headed back to Michelle's uncle's house where I'd kindly been invited to stay. They were incredibly warm, friendly people, laughing and joking with me about how I was able to put up with Michelle for so long.

That evening, I caught up with a friend who was living and working in Sydney and it just so happened that there was an Australian Navy Fleet Review taking place in the harbour, with a light and firework show, so we decided to check that out. The next day, I went back to see Michelle and say goodbye to her and her family. I needed to be in Brisbane in five days' time, which was 650 miles away, so I couldn't spare another day off the bike. It was strange saying goodbye to Michelle; I wanted to give her a hug and tell her that I was going to miss her but it felt a bit awkward with her family standing there too.

I got cracking and tried to push myself hard. I wasn't carrying Michelle's kit now so that made a bit of a difference. I was heading to Lake Macquarie where I was going to stay with the family of one of my sponsors. I'd spoken to James from Balmain Asset Management who had lined-up the accommodation with his in-laws. I arrived in the early evening to the address I was given. It was a wonderful looking house that backed on to Lake Macquarie. I was warmly greeted and instantly welcomed into the house by James' father-in-law, Bob.

They were having a barbecue, which would have been fit for a king. Bob showed me to my room and I grabbed a quick shower and joined them for dinner. Bob's son was visiting with his girlfriend and her parents so there were quite a few of us sitting round the table. Most of the conversations were around my cycle and other expeditions.

"I'm sorry if we are asking you too many questions, it's not every day that someone comes into the house who's rowed the Atlantic, climbed Everest and is cycling around the world," said Bob. I didn't mind at all as I was really enjoying their company. When he realised that I was cycling up to Brisbane too, he kindly said that I could stay in one of his flats there.

I got to bed at around midnight after eating as much as I could; I knew I wouldn't be eating food like that again for a while. Bob and I exchanged contact details in the morning and I said goodbye as I made my way north. It was amazing how I was meeting so many different people through, often random, situations or through someone who knew someone. I received an email from a lady called Daniela who lived in Lennox Head, which I would be passing through in a few days. Apparently, she was sitting next to Chris on the plane from Singapore to London and Chris was chatting to her about my world cycle. She took a note of my name and website and started to track me. She asked me if I needed a place to stay when I was passing through. I kindly took her up on the offer when I arrived a few days later.

Daniela and her husband had two children and were from South Africa. They were a very friendly family and really welcomed me into their home. Daniela was an energetic person but also a very tough cookie. She told me about how her dad was murdered in front of her when she was a child by an intruder in their home. I just couldn't imagine what she must have gone through when she was describing what happened and what it was like where they lived in South Africa. They also couldn't believe that I had never been surfing in my life and thought it was shocking that I had cycled the entire length of Australia without once stepping foot in the ocean. She insisted that we all got up early the next morning to go surfing. At 6am, we headed down to the local surf spot; there were a couple of surfers out but it was pretty quiet. I borrowed a pair of swimming trunks and went in the sea with Daniela's husband, who was a dab hand at surfing.

The only board they had was a small board meant for experienced surfers so it wasn't the best start for me, but I was determined to try and stand up, at least once. Paddling out was also harder than it looked, as I was constantly getting knocked off by the waves. My stubborn perseverance paid off and I managed to get the hang of it. After almost an hour of trying, I stood up for about three seconds on a wave before falling in. I joked that we needed to be on the lookout for Great White Sharks, which was in the back of my mind, having watched many Discovery Channel documentaries about surfers who have been attacked. Daniela's husband laughed and said in his South African accent, "I wouldn't worry - if you can see them, they are not interested in you. Trust me, you wouldn't even know if they attacked you." I laughed but found it slightly disconcerting nevertheless.

We went back to the house for breakfast and I said goodbye. I was 125 miles away from Brisbane and had told Bob that I would be at his flat by the evening. I was coming to the end of my time in Australia where the summer was fast approaching and the mercury was hitting over 40°C most days. I was excited to be moving on but I was missing not having Michelle cycling with me. I found it quite amusing when she moaned at me for cycling too fast and didn't hold back when I said things she didn't agree with. It was a character trait that I'd grown quite fond of.

As I arrived into the city of Brisbane, I was blown away at the sheer size of the place and just how built-up and commercial it was. I arrived at the address of the flat that Bob had kindly said I could stay in for a few days. When I arrived, it was a little more luxurious than I had expected. It was a high-rise block of flats overlooking the main park and river that ran through the city. It was situated in the heart of downtown Brisbane, a very desirable and trendy area. It was about 10pm when I arrived and the concierge had been waiting for me. "Ah, hello Mr James, we have heard all about you," said the doorman, as I walked into the building.

They showed me to the apartment, which was on one of the top floors, with stunning views across the city. I couldn't believe how lucky I was to be staying here, before flying to the US. Bob had really looked after me by letting me use his apartment and I was grateful. The building had a fine dining restaurant, which Bob instructed me to use and put on his tab but I didn't want to take advantage of his generosity so I didn't eat there. On my second and last day in Brisbane,

Bob rang me and asked why I wasn't eating in the restaurant. He had obviously spoken to the concierge and they had told him that I hadn't been eating there.

On 16th October 2013, I flew to Chicago where I was due to give a talk at the Chicago Week of Ideas event, which takes place every year. My flight had been booked and paid for by the organisers. I arrived at the airport to make my first connecting flight to Los Angeles but quickly ran into a problem at the airport. Because I only had a one-way ticket into the US (as I wasn't sure when I would be flying to Europe), the airline wouldn't let me check-in and fly. I was told that if I wanted to fly out of Australia, I would have to purchase another onward journey ticket out of the US.

I was feeling pretty frustrated as I didn't really have the spare money to be booking a redundant ticket, but I had to sort out the situation as I needed to be on that flight. I pushed my trolley with my bike all packed up in a box over to the Flight Centre desk. I was greeted by a beautiful woman who must have been in her mid 20s. She smiled at me and asked how she could help. I explained my situation and she instantly came up with a solution. Apparently, this was not uncommon and had caught out many travellers before me. They would sell me an onward ticket from New York to Lisbon for $300; the actual value was over $1,000 but as soon as I had taken off from Brisbane, satisfying the airline that I had an onward ticket, they would cancel it. It was really just an administrative exercise that was going to make them $300. I wasn't sure if they should be doing it or not but it was going to solve my problem, so I couldn't complain. A few hours later, I was sitting on a plane heading over the Pacific Ocean to the USA.

19

The generosity of America

I arrived in Chicago and picked up a shuttle bus that the hotel ran to and from the airport. I was quite surprised at the change in temperature. I knew it would be colder but the difference was shocking. I had two days in Chicago, one to rest and one to give the talk. I was only asked to speak for 15 minutes and I originally wasn't planning on visiting Chicago at all, but as they were paying for my flight, I decided to make the detour. My plan was to fly back to San Francisco where I was going to start my US leg of the cycle when the talk was over.

I gave the talk to a packed out auditorium with a line-up of other adventurer types who all had fascinating stories to tell. The organisers wanted me dressed in my cycling kit and to have the bike on stage as I was giving the talk. I guess it added to the authenticity that I was cycling around the world and had taken time out to be a guest speaker there. Afterwards, I was standing in the lobby, chatting with guests from the audience, when I was approached by two women. They were very friendly and asked me lots of questions. One of them asked me how long I was in town for, so I told her that I was leaving the next day. I asked her if she could recommend anything for me to do or see that evening. Instantly, they both said that they would take me out and show me some Chicago sights. We exchanged telephone numbers as I'd just picked up a new US T-Mobile SIM card. I wasn't sure if I would see them again but they agreed to pick me up from my hotel that evening.

I waited at reception and was met by one of the girls, Venece. Her friend was already out and would meet us later in the evening. She gave me a guided tour of the city in her car, finishing at what she said was Chicago's best pizza restaurant. She wasn't wrong: it was my first ever, real Chicago deep dish pizza and it was amazing. During the evening, we were chatting about the cycling around Chicago and how North America had some great cycling to offer. It made me think that perhaps I should try and cycle to San Francisco as opposed to fly. It would obviously mean more mileage but it was a great opportunity to see a little more of America.

The next day, I left the hotel at 8am, planning to head west. I instantly felt at home being back on the bike, after a few days off. As I made my way out of Chicago, I passed through some very rough-looking neighbourhoods, with large groups of people hanging out on street corners. The areas I was passing through looked like they were sets from a gangster film. I had that uncomfortable feeling you get in your gut when you can sense that something's not quite right. After a few hours, I was clear of Chicago and the landscape became sparser as I passed through smaller towns. I was really struggling with the cold, as it was snowing and pretty windy. I knew I was going to need to invest in some warmer cycling kit as I was freezing.

While standing up on the pedals cycling, without warning, my pedal came out of the right crank arm, causing me to slip and go crashing to the floor. I was crossing a road at the time, and fortunately no cars were around, so I picked myself up and looked at the pedal. The threads on the pedal looked fine so I couldn't understand what had happened. I tried to thread it back into the crank and it just slid straight in as the threads were completely stripped inside. This wasn't something that could be easily fixed so I was in a bit of a dilemma. I was just outside a small town called DeKalb so I walked with my bike on the road to a MacDonald's that I could see in the distance.

While I was walking up the street, I noticed a bike shop across the road called the North Central Cyclery. I was greeted by a very friendly guy called Tobie, who asked me where I was going and where I had been. He was a real cycling enthusiast and instantly walked straight over to a display and pulled off a pair of socks.

"Hey man, put these socks on, your feet must be freezing," he said, handing me the socks. He'd noticed I was only wearing a pair of ankle socks with my shoes and leggings. He took the bike straight into the workshop and started assessing the damage. He advised me that the best thing to do would be to fit a new crank arm; luckily he had a second-hand one, which he kindly fitted for free.

The shop was well stocked and I knew I was going to need to start wearing some warmer clothes on the bike so I decided to buy a few bits. Tobie offered me some lunch and said that I could use the shower and rest in the basement downstairs. I took a shower and changed into my evening clothes and relaxed on a chair. The next thing I knew, Tobie was waking me up saying it was 5pm. I couldn't believe I'd been asleep for three hours. He'd seen me fast asleep and didn't want to wake me up. He said he'd spoken to his wife and said I could stay at their house that evening if I wanted to. I kindly took him up on the offer and was very grateful for a bed for the night.

Tobie had completely serviced the bike and cleaned it for me, which was a lovely thing to do. That night, we had dinner and chatted about the route over to San Francisco. Tobie felt very strongly that it was too late in the season to cross the Rocky Mountains. It was late October and the winter had already arrived in the northern states. That was certainly true as there was already snow on the ground in some areas and it was bitterly cold. He pointed out that the cycling would only get tougher at this time of year on the route I was taking. Being fairly stubborn, I wanted to carry on, but part of me knew exactly what he was saying was true. The next morning, I waved goodbye to Tobie and his family. They had been my guardian angels, appearing at just the right time. Had my crank sheared its threads on the Nullarbor, I would have been in big trouble.

Over the next four days, I battled severe headwinds, snow and freezing temperatures. It became clear that it was far too late in the year to cycle across the Rocky Mountains, which were still well over a week away. I decided to revert back to my original plan of starting my US leg in California. I was only in Chicago to give the talk and was going to fly to San Francisco anyway, but wanted to try something different. So I flew from Des Moines to San Francisco where I could get back on schedule with my mileage as I had dropped slightly behind while travelling from Australia and giving the talk in Chicago.

I arrived in San Francisco absolutely shattered and not feeling particularly well. Richard from Ofsure had some friends who lived in San Jose who had offered me a place to stay ever since Richard mentioned to them that I was cycling around the world. It was about 50 miles south of San Francisco International Airport and when I arrived at their house, which was at the top of a fairly steep hill, I was absolutely knackered. I felt incredibly tired and every bone in my body was aching and hurting. My throat felt like it was on fire and I was generally very run down. I'd been extremely tired at various points on the cycle but this was a totally different feeling of complete fatigue and exhaustion. I'd been very lucky up until this point with no illnesses or major incidents that had physically stopped me cycling. I ended up spending two days on their settee feeling pretty run down and exhausted. Richard's friends, Martin and Helen, were absolutely amazing and really looked after me well. I felt pretty pathetic crashing out on their sofa but they were very understanding and insisted I rest.

After a couple of rest days, my strength returned and I was feeling a lot stronger. I was really excited to be cycling down the famous 'Highway 1', which runs parallel to the Pacific Ocean along the coast, not dissimilar to the Great Ocean Road. The weather was absolutely perfect with a slight tailwind, beautiful sunshine and not a cloud in the sky. It took three fairly easy days to get down to southern California, passing through Santa Cruz, Monterey, San Simeon and Lompoc.

The following day, I was heading to Ventura when I spotted a cyclist making his way up a hill in front of me. He was moving slowly as I was catching him up quite quickly. I rode up beside him and started chatting. He had a very friendly aura about him. It turned out he was a pastor and called himself 'Spirit Rider'. He was a 70-year old Afro-Caribbean who had cycled across the US over 10 times in his life. He spent a lot of time working with young people from disadvantaged backgrounds, taking them on cycling tours. Not being religious, it was strange how this man made me feel; he spoke with a very calming voice and it made the hair on the back of my neck stand up. We chatted and I cycled with him for about half-an-hour before he stopped for a rest and told me to go on ahead. I took a photo of us both, exchanged email addresses and carried on my way.

A few hours later, as I was approaching Santa Barbara, another cyclist came up behind me and started chatting. He asked where

I was going so I told him I was heading for Miami and that I left London four months ago. He was gob smacked at the distance I'd cycled. We were both heading in the same direction so we cycled together. His name was Brad and he had recently relocated from Sacramento to the Santa Barbara area with his family, after selling his business. He was in his early 50s and was in excellent shape for his age. He was riding a lovely, race spec Cervelo bike with carbon wheels; it looked amazing.

Brad was really interested in my adventures and we chatted for quite some time before heading off. He asked me if I had anywhere to stay in Ventura, which I didn't, as I had only just planned to stop there. It was just over 100 miles from Lompoc where I'd started that morning. He then asked me if I wanted to stay at his house as he had plenty of room available. It did mean stopping slightly short of my target distance but I thought it was a very nice offer so I took him up on it.

Brad lived in Carpinteria, which was a lovely area. While chatting over dinner with Brad and his family, he asked me if I needed to do any maintenance on my bike. As it happened, I did. The current sprockets and chain rings had over 11,000 miles on them and were starting to slip. I was currently on my fourth chain of the trip even though I'd been changing it frequently and cleaning it where possible. I carried a bottle of chain lube and some degreaser so I could clean the chain on an almost daily basis. I stayed the following day and we worked on the bikes, giving my bike an almost full rebuild and clean up. Brad was a pretty good mechanic and I think he enjoyed working on my bike. His garage was so clean you could eat off the floor and every tool had its place.

Later that day we went out for a ride and Brad said I could ride one of his bikes. Even his number two bike was a lovely Scott that wouldn't have looked out of place in a Tour De France peloton. It was absolutely staggering how fast it felt, riding a 6.8kg race bike after riding a setup that was almost four times the weight over half way around the world. It was quite an amazing experience. Brad was seriously considering riding some of my route with me and was talking about cycling to Texas, which would have been great, but in the end he couldn't really take the time out from his other commitments.

I left Brad's house the following day and carried on cycling, around the coastline towards Los Angeles, passing through Malibu, which is home to many film stars. As I was getting closer to Los Angeles, it started getting much more built-up and I could see the tall buildings in the distance. Cycling through Venice Beach was quite an experience: people of all shapes and sizes were walking along the sidewalks and beach. I was surprised at the amount of homeless people who were living rough, although thinking about it, the climate is perfect all year round, so it's no wonder they flock to the area. I'd probably do the same.

I had to cycle inland briefly to get down to Huntingdon Beach and on to the road that was going to take me south to San Diego, which was still Highway 1. In order to get to San Diego, I had to cycle through Camp Pendleton, which is a US Marine base. I arrived at the security gate and handed in my ID, which was my passport, for the guard to look at. There were a few other cyclists who were passing through at the same time who I cycled with because they knew the way and I didn't want to get lost on a military base that was bigger than my hometown of Basingstoke.

I was heading for my friend Vicki's house, who I'd met on my previous cycle across the US. She lived in Carmel Valley, which is just north of San Diego, in a beautiful residential area. I was pretty tired when I arrived as I'd pushed a 180-mile day. We just had time to go out for something to eat and Vicki knew this great place for tacos. Afterwards, we went to an ice cream parlour, where I ordered an absolutely massive chocolate ice cream. It was something that you'd only find in America, the portion size was so big.

I was now going to be following the same route that I'd cycled back in 2012 across the US so I knew exactly where I was going. I headed out of San Diego and within a few hours, I was climbing a 4,000ft pass that would then drop me into a desert environment that was below sea level. It was a great day's cycling and I was amazed at how I breezed over the climb without any real difficulty. Thinking back to when I cycled the route a year earlier, I had been exhausted.

That evening, I stayed with a husband and wife in Brawley who I'd found on a website called warmshowers.org. It was a website for cyclists who host other cyclists as they are passing through their town, very similar to couch surfing. A friend of mine had suggested using it, to keep my costs down. I was running very low on money and was still going to be on the road for another couple of months before I was due to finish.

The next day, I cycled on Route 78 to Blythe, which was all flat and almost 100 miles. I passed some sand dunes that people were using to race motocross bikes and beach buggies across. It looked so much fun as they were screaming around, up and over the dunes. While I was in Brawley, I managed to line up a place to stay in Blythe too. When I arrived, it was a fishing tackle shop with a large mobile home on site that was for guests. The owner wasn't there but the lady working in the shop was very friendly and offered to help with anything I needed. Another 160 miles away was Phoenix, which I was going to aim for the following day. I had a look on warmshowers and found a couple of people who were registered and offering a place to stay.

I got up early and headed off. Blythe was right on the border of California and Arizona, separated by the Colorado River. My route took me along the I10, which is a freeway that runs from the West to East coast. In some places, there are no other parallel roads so cyclists are allowed to use them. Just after I crossed into Arizona, I thought I'd try calling a couple of guys from warmshowers to try and line something up for that evening. I left a voicemail with a guy called Phil and then tried the other contact called Bob, who answered the phone straight away. He was very friendly and told me it would be fine to stay. He asked me where I was and I told him I had just left Blythe.

"Ah wow man, I don't think you will make that today, it's over 150 miles away."

I told him that I would be with him for about 9pm. He sounded quite shocked.

"Okay, call me if you need anything." What a wonderful man to be so friendly and he doesn't even know me, I thought to myself.

It was a fairly straightforward day, impossible to get lost as there was only one road to Phoenix. Although it was a freeway, it was only two lanes and wasn't particularly busy. Every now and then, a large truck would whizz by and the wind from it would suck me along as it passed for a second or two.

Almost bang on 9pm, I was at Bob's flat in downtown Phoenix and had covered just under 160 miles. I called him and told him I was downstairs. It was a really nice high-rise block of flats, not dissimilar to the one I stayed in while in Brisbane.

Bob came down to the reception to greet me. He was a short, stocky guy and softly spoken. We went upstairs and he showed me around the flat and introduced me to his wife Jessy, who was a very glamorous-looking air hostess for an American airline. They were very friendly and I instantly felt very comfortable around them. It turned out that Bob ran a not-for-profit group called 'We Cycle USA', which took young people off the streets and gave them the opportunity to work on bikes and learn new skills. If they donated a certain amount of time to the club, they could build and keep their own bike. It really was a fantastic organisation, giving young people structure and the feeling of accomplishment that they were not necessarily getting elsewhere. I really loved the work that Bob was doing and admired his passion for it.

It was now the day before Thanksgiving, which is almost as big as Christmas in America and celebrated all over the country. Bob suggested I stay for another day, as there was a ride that had been taking place since 1980 every Thanksgiving Day called the Phoenix Turkey Ride. It was a 40-mile ride from downtown Phoenix to the top of South Mountain which, as its name suggests, is a mountain to the south of Phoenix. I decided that it sounded fun so I stayed with Bob and Jessy for another day. While I was there, I had a call from Phil who was the first guy I'd reached out to on warmshowers. He was a British guy living in Phoenix so we met up and he rode the Turkey Ride too. After the ride had finished, I carried on cycling, exploring the city. It was like a ghost town, not a person or car in sight.

That evening, we all went out for dinner to a steak house. It was a wonderful evening and I felt like I'd known Bob and Jessy for a lot longer than 36 hours.

"James, I'm going to fly over to London to see you cycle your last day and finish this amazing ride," said Bob over the dinner table. It was a lovely thing to say but I very much doubted it would happen. The following morning I needed to move on and was heading for Tucson. Bob joined me, along with some other guys that I'd met on the Turkey Ride, for a couple of hours before needing to turn back. I'd managed to line up another family to stay with who looked after me like I was their own. I was blown away by the kindness of everyone I was meeting. I personally didn't think it was a big deal that I was cycling around the world but I would spend hours answering questions on what it was like, as well as recounting tales from Everest and the Atlantic.

JK

Over the next four days, I piggy-backed from one family to another as I made my way along the I10 through Arizona, New Mexico and into Texas. Most families would always know someone in the next town where I was stopping and they would phone ahead, often telling me that their friends would be delighted to host me. I stayed with one family in a small town called Willcox in Arizona, who worked in the cattle industry. They were a proper cowboy family, with spurs on their boots and, for fun, they attended rodeos and entered lassoing competitions. I had a go at lassoing, which was pretty tricky despite them making it look so easy. They were a lovely family and gave me a set of spurs as a souvenir. I unfortunately didn't have room for them and felt bad when I said I didn't have a way of carrying them.

My first stop in Texas was El Paso where I was going to stay with Shannon who I'd randomly met on my previous trip. I met her in the evening after she had finished work at UTEP University. I hadn't had a particularly good day as I'd cracked my tooth in California and it was starting to play up. I thought that perhaps it would settle down but it was actually getting worse. That evening, I was in so much pain that I didn't sleep for the entire night. It was unbearable: just breathing with the air passing in and out of my mouth on the exposed tooth was excruciating. I said to Shannon that I needed to see a dentist urgently. Thankfully, I was able to get an appointment at 8.30am so I headed straight down to the surgery.

I was greeted by a dentist who was bursting out of his T-shirt, with arms bigger than my thighs. He had a surprisingly soft handshake for his enormous stature. I sat in the chair and he examined my tooth, and told me that I needed a root canal. He wasn't able to do it but he rang a friend of his who could. He was into bodybuilding on a competitive level. He couldn't believe it when I told him what I was doing. His surgery was the coolest surgery I'd ever seen, with lots of sports memorabilia hanging on the walls, signed by famous sporting stars. I asked him how much I owed him.

"Man, I'm not going to charge you, I just want to help you. I think it's going to cost a fair bit for the root canal though," he kindly replied.

I headed over to the other surgery that had squeezed me into their schedule and I'd been quoted the best part of a thousand dollars to do the work. I was fast running out of money so I called Richard from Ofsure to let him know about the unexpected expenditure. A few weeks prior to this, I was explaining to Richard that I was running out of money. He kindly agreed to fund me if I ran out to ensure that I could complete the cycle and my overall goal. I was very conscious of not taking advantage of his kind generosity, however I had no choice but to spend the money in this case.

After a short wait, an assistant led me into the room to meet the dentist.

"Why on earth are you in cycling kit?" he asked.

"Ah yes, sorry, I'm cycling around the world."

"Ah, that explains why you stink!" he exclaimed.

I wasn't sure if he was joking or being serious so I just chuckled and smiled.

The whole process took the best part of 40 minutes; he was asking the usual questions that I'd answered hundreds of times before. After he had finished the procedure, he disappeared for about 20 minutes, leaving me in the chair. I was wondering what an earth he was doing, when he eventually came back into the room.

"Wow, what you're doing is amazing!" he told me.

It was a little strange as we had already been talking about it. I think he probably went off to Google me, perhaps to see if I was telling the truth or not. I thanked him, and he said that he wasn't going to charge me for the work. I couldn't thank him enough and we joked that the healthcare system in America is great: all you need to do is cycle around the world and you get free treatment. I took his photo, shook his hand and cycled back over to Shannon's house.

By now, most of the day had gone, so I decided to stay in El Paso for one more night. Shannon was busy that night so I stayed with one of her friends, a guy called Don, who ran a magazine company. I was telling Don about the sequence of events with the two dentists who'd looked after me. I thought it would be a nice idea to go back to the first dentist, Scott, and give him one of my new cycling tops that I hadn't worn yet to frame and put on the wall along with his collection of other signed tops. Don thought it was a great idea so we drove over to give it to him. Scott was over the moon and really happy with the top. We took a picture together with the cycling top and he assured us he would frame it.

That evening, I was desperate to try out Don's Jacuzzi in his garden, so while he watched American football with his wife, I wallowed in the hot tub. I spent a sublime half-an-hour relaxing in the warm water. The following morning, Don cycled with me for 25 miles as I headed south, skirting the Mexican border adjacent to the I10. We stopped for an early breakfast before he turned around and I carried on. I was heading for a small town called Van Horn, just over 130 miles from El Paso. I was about 50 miles away when someone in a car started waving at me as it drove past and then proceeded to pull over further down the road. As I got a little closer, I realised that it was Cameron and Maggie, who were friends of Don's he had introduced me to while I was staying. Cameron had a bag of cakes that he passed to me, and said, "Hey James, how's it going, you need these more than we do." I took a couple and chatted to them for a few minutes before carrying on. They were heading to Austin and told me to call them when I got there.

Over the next three days, I covered 320 miles, passing through the picturesque town of Alpine as I made my way to Del Rio. Every now and then, military fighter jets would roar overhead, flying very low to the mountains. It was funny to think they would cover the distance I cycle in a day, in less than 10 minutes! I often wondered where they were going or what they were doing and the stunning views they would have from the cockpit.

I was about 70 miles from Del Rio when I noticed a cyclist travelling in the same direction as me, standing by the side of the road with his bike. As I approached, I saw he was carrying quite a lot of kit and was dressed quite scruffily. He wasn't cycling for fun; it was quite obvious that he was homeless. Nevertheless, he was very polite as he slowly made his way along the road. I asked him if he knew if there was a service station ahead; it was marked on the map but I wasn't sure if I had passed it or not. He didn't know but wanted to offer me some of his bread if I was hungry. I politely refused, telling him I was just wondering and I wasn't hungry. I wished him well and carried on. For the next couple of days, I couldn't stop thinking of that man's kind nature; he had absolutely nothing but was still prepared to offer me his food. What a truly selfless human being.

I wasn't far from Austin and was approaching San Antonio so I called Cameron who said he would come down to San Antonio to join me for the ride up to Austin. Maggie drove him down where I met them both by Lackland Air Force base. It was just under 100 miles into Austin and it was a fantastic ride. I didn't need to worry about the navigation, I could just ride and enjoy the scenery. Austin is an incredibly hilly place but has so many nice, smooth roads that are brilliant for cycling. Although I'd already been to Lance

Armstrong's shop on my previous US cycle, Cameron suggested we should have a coffee there as it has one of the best cafés in town. We arrived about half-an-hour before it closed.

That evening, the three of us went out to a Texas-style ranch house restaurant. I ordered the biggest steak on the menu, which happened to be a 25-ounce T-bone. They were both shocked at how quickly I consumed it. I was ravenous and my appetite was insatiable. With the amount of cycling I was doing, I physically couldn't eat enough. My body weight had stabilised at around 75kg, 15kg lighter than when I left London.

All of the roads I was cycling were surprisingly familiar. I was impressed at just how much of the route I remembered, even something small like a little turning or building that I'd remember seeing before. I now didn't have any more contacts on the rest of the route until I got to Florida so I reached out to a few people on warmshowers. One lady offered me a place to stay in Opelousas, Louisiana. She told me to call her on her cell phone when I was about an hour away. I gave her a call and informed her of my position, giving a rough ETA. She unexpectedly told me that she wouldn't be home until later that evening as she was watching a football match but had left a key out for me and dinner in the fridge. I thought this was a little strange and felt very uncomfortable knowing I was going to let myself into a stranger's house. She was in her early 30s and living on her own, that's all I knew about her. At one point, I thought I should perhaps decline the offer and find a motel but money was tight and I ended up becoming intrigued to meet this person. I gave her one final call before arriving and she told me to go straight into the house and make myself at home, use the shower and do whatever I wanted to do.

When I arrived, the house was a mobile home that had been permanently fixed in place, along with all the others in the street.

I let myself in and found the room that she told me to put the bike in. There was a collection of bikes in the house so I placed my bike alongside them. I decided to jump straight in the shower so I was fresh and didn't smell when she came home. I heard movement in the house while I was washing myself so I quickly scrubbed myself clean, but before I could get out of the shower, she opened the door and just walked into the bathroom to say hi. There was a frosted pane of glass that went around the shower so luckily she didn't see me standing there naked. I was pretty shocked but thought it was quite funny. I dried myself and got dressed and went into the living room. We chatted for a bit, then she offered to drive me to the grocery store where I picked up some protein drinks and snacks for the following day.

When we got back, she asked me what time I was getting up in the morning. I told her that I'd be out of the house by 7.30am, and she said that was fine and she was going for a bike ride as well. The following morning, I woke up at 7am and was up and dressed within five minutes. I took my bike out of the room and the woman had disappeared out of the house, leaving the door open. It was very strange; she didn't even say goodbye.

It was a very cold and cloudy day when I left but I was looking forward to crossing the famous Mississippi River just before Baton Rouge, the capital of Louisiana. It was a straightforward cycle along the Ronald Regan Highway, otherwise known as Highway 190. The amount of cars on the road was certainly building as I got closer to Baton Rouge and I could see the bridge in the distance. As I cycled onto the bridge, the hard shoulder that I'd been cycling on disappeared and it just became two lanes of traffic. It was a very long stretch of road and cars and lorries were roaring past me. I felt safe but realised this would be the worst place to get a puncture as there was nowhere to stop. Literally thirty seconds later, I ran straight over a massive gap where two bridge sections joined together. It was such a big gap that I could see the water below and my front wheel crashed down it with a violent thud. I knew instantly that it would blow the tyre out and a big bang promptly followed. I wasn't able to lift the wheel over in time, so the front wheel sustained some damage but it was nothing that couldn't be sorted. Sadly the inner tube had snapped the valve so it was useless and I wasn't carrying any spares.

I had to walk the bike across the remainder of the bridge while the traffic whizzed by within a few feet. I was in what looked like a pretty rough area and was a long way from a bike shop. I didn't really want to be walking through this area on my own with my bike and equipment. I called a guy up who lived locally whose details I'd found on warmshowers and asked his advice on where I should go and whether it was safe. He kindly said he would drive his truck out and give me a lift to a good bike shop that he used. It was another random act of kindness from a total stranger. I reflected that I'd be paying forward favours for the rest of my life to pay back the kindness that had been bestowed on me.

When I arrived at the bike shop, the mechanic took the bike from me and set it up on the stand. He took the wheel off and began working on it. It needed to be trued as the impact had buckled the wheel. While I was waiting in the shop, a chap who was chatting to the staff asked me where I was from and did I know a British guy called Mike who raced around the world setting the record for the fastest circumnavigation on a bike. As it happened, I did, and he also knew another good friend of mine called Sean who had also cycled around the world. I thought it was quite amazing that he knew the same people I knew from back home. Mike had even stayed with him while passing through Baton Rouge.

After the bike had been given some attention, I was back on my way. I wanted to be in Florida for Christmas and Pensacola was just over 200 miles away, which was two fairly easy days if I didn't have any problems. On Christmas Eve, I arrived into Pensacola. My parents had kindly transferred some money for me to stay in a slightly nicer hotel as I was away for Christmas. I managed to get into a Hilton, which was right on the sea front. I needed to be in a hotel on Christmas Day as the PR Director of the Scouts, a fantastic guy called Simon, had arranged for a Skype call with the BBC. The theme was 'What are you doing this Christmas?' Obviously they wanted to talk to me about my world cycle.

The call was arranged for the following morning, Christmas Day itself. That evening, I went down to the restaurant, thinking it would be really quiet but I was quite amazed at how many people were around. I ended up sitting at the bar, chatting to the sushi chef. He asked me if I had tried sushi before, and I deliberately told him that I hadn't and wondered what it was like, in the hope that he might give me some to try. My strategy paid off and he was plying me with sushi for most of the evening.

I went to bed that evening after a few beers and slept like a log. I woke up and wished myself a happy Christmas before calling my parents. Afterwards, my phone rang and it was the BBC trying to line up the Skype interview. I'd managed to acquire a Father Christmas hat and thought it would be quite fun to wear it for the interview. I announced on Twitter and Facebook that I was about to be live on the BBC news. After the interview, loads of messages from friends came through. Apparently the hat looked cool so I was pleased I'd pulled it off.

Before I left the hotel, I called Andy, who I hadn't spoken to for a few months. It was great hearing his voice and we chatted about what was going on at home and in the gym we both trained at. Christmas Day was a wonderful day: lovely sunshine, hardly any traffic on the roads and a great tailwind pushing me along. Over the next four days as I passed through Panama City, Tallahassee, Live Oak and St Augustine, before heading south to Miami. I was asked if I was married by a waitress in MacDonald's when I stopped to use the Wi-Fi and order a milkshake. Apparently I was the most handsome man she had ever seen. I was pretty shocked at her forwardness but took the compliment graciously as I stood there, sweating.

When I arrived at the pier in St. Augustine, there was a fireworks display being set up for New Year's Eve so the pier was closed to the public. There was a large police presence around the area and I got chatting to one officer. I told him that I'd cycled from the West coast and was hoping to get to the end of the pier. When he realised I'd cycled from San Francisco, he told me he would make an exception and escorted me to the end of the pier. I took a couple of photos and carried on. I was now on one road all the way to Miami, the A1A, 300 miles of flat, smooth road that hugs the coastline, passing through some of the most affluent areas in America. I was having fantastic luck with the winds and was benefiting from a lively tailwind that was enabling me to average almost 20mph. I pushed 150 miles, stopping at a motel in Cape Canaveral.

The following morning, I decided to have a bit of a lie-in, as it was New Year's Eve and I was determined to be on my bike cycling as the clock struck midnight and the New Year rang in. I left the motel at around 11am, after spending some time trying to book a flight from Miami to Lisbon. Everything was totally booked up and I couldn't get a flight for almost a week.

That afternoon, I stopped for lunch and while I was eating, a family came in and randomly started chatting to me. My bike was leaning up against the window outside so they asked me where I was going. I told them I was heading to Miami, they then asked where I'd cycled from. I was eating so couldn't be bothered going through the whole story. When they heard that I'd come from San Francisco, they said, "What? You've cycled from San Francisco?" They started going crazy, wanting to shake my hand, announcing to everyone in the shop that I'd cycled from San Francisco. They then asked if they could have their picture taken with me. I didn't tell them that I'd actually cycled almost around the whole world in the last six months but I did wonder what their reaction would have been to that. Before leaving, they warned me that I needed to be careful on the roads, as there would be a lot of drunks about on New Year's Eve. I was pretty confident that I could look after myself but I appreciated their advice.

As it started to get closer to midnight, I cruised along, not really pushing myself, just enjoying being out in the fresh air. It was a beautiful night, not a cloud in the sky, with the moon shining bright and reflecting off the ocean as the waves lapped at the shore. I thought back to all the wonderful people that I'd met during my time on the road and how far I had travelled. I was now getting pretty close to the end, with only Europe left to cycle through.

I looked down at my iPhone in my frame bag as I cycled to watch it switch from 23.59 to 00.00 and into a New Year. In the blink of a second it was 2014 and I had seen the New Year in, sitting on the saddle of my bike, just how I'd intended to spend it. I was pretty tired, as I had already covered 147 miles, so I looked for a motel. I found a Super 8, which is an American budget chain of motels that I'd frequently used before. I went in to the reception and the guy behind the counter was fast asleep, snoring. I thought he would wake up if I just coughed, but it wasn't happening. After about 10 minutes of trying to wake the guy up, he finally came to and was one of the rudest people I'd ever met. I couldn't believe the way he was speaking to me and I was a paying customer. However, I was very tired so I didn't really care.

The next day, I had a place to stay, thanks to a guy called Juan who I'd met in Phoenix. He introduced me to Daniel and Patricia who lived in Fort Lauderdale, and they kindly said I could stay with them. I arrived at their house in the afternoon. Daniel had some amazing bikes in his house hanging on the wall and was a very strong cyclist who used to race but now just rode for fun. They were a wonderful couple and told me to make myself at home. I told them I wasn't flying for a few days and they said I could stay for as long as I wanted.

I wanted to keep cycling as I found it mentally very difficult to get back into a rhythm when I took any days off. Daniel joined me for a day and we covered just over 100 miles, exploring Miami and all the places that I'd never have been to without knowing about them. For the other couple of days, I cycled up and down the A1A; it was such a great road that had a dedicated cycle lane built in and was used by plenty of other cyclists. I ended up randomly chatting to a guy who was out training at a set of lights, while waiting for them to change. His name was Ernie and he was a really nice guy. I ended up spending the day with him.

Richard from Ofsure sent me an email to tell me that he was going to part-fund a PR company to promote my arrival back into the UK, with James from Balmain Asset Management. I hadn't really been getting much press coverage apart from in India where I was very well received. I wasn't overly fussed, as I wasn't doing it for the PR opportunity. Richard and James had been doing some research and it turned out that, when I crossed the finish line in Greenwich Park, I would be the first and only person to have rowed an ocean, climbed Mount Everest and cycled around the world. Apparently the media was very keen on the story from the initial conversations with the PR firm. I was slightly anxious about promoting this accolade in case someone had in fact already achieved this but had chosen not to promote themselves. In my experience, some of the most amazing people, doing the most amazing things, are the people who go about their business quietly.

As I had the ELIFAR Foundation aligned to the cycle, I knew the PR would benefit them too, so I was all for promoting my arrival back into the UK. James had pulled in a favour from a guy called Euan who worked for the PR firm, Innesco. I had a conference call with Richard, James, Pru and Euan to discuss the details. I instantly liked Euan's style: he was extremely enthusiastic and was coming up with some great PR angles. They all told me to just concentrate on the cycling and they would deal with the PR for me. I didn't really know what sort of take up we would get on my arrival to the UK and I didn't give it too much thought.

20

Homeward bound

The time came to fly to Lisbon where I would meet my parents. It was my birthday and my flight arrived before theirs so I checked into the hotel they had booked, before heading back to the airport to meet them. As they walked out of the arrivals hall, they didn't see me waiting, so I sneaked up behind to surprise them. It was great seeing them after six months on the road. My brother had also flown out with his girlfriend, Yasmin.

We spent the day walking around Lisbon, gazing at the different shops and drinking hot chocolate. That evening, we all had a family meal together. I asked my dad to bring a few bits out for the bike, one of them being a new cable for the dynamo as it snapped in Fort Lauderdale. Without it, my lights wouldn't work, which were one of the most important bits of kit on the bike.

The next day, I said goodbye to my family and left the hotel to start the last leg back to London. It was pouring with rain and utterly miserable; I just couldn't get into a rhythm. Having seen my parents, it felt like I should be finished and not still 1,000 miles away. I had been reluctant to see them before I actually finished in London but I knew they wanted to come out to see me, so didn't want to disappoint them.

My first day in Europe wasn't great. It rained all day, not letting up once and it was also pretty cold. I had the right kit to wear; it just didn't make for particularly enjoyable cycling. As dawn approached, I was riding along and I heard a loud bang before my rear tyre instantly deflated. The side wall of the tyre had split, leaving the inner tube exposed, which exploded after a few seconds. I knew the tyre was worn but I was surprised it had actually split. It took almost an hour of faffing around in the rain using energy gel wrappers to try and cover the tear to create a temporary fix so I could carry on.

Over the next four days, I worked my way up through Portugal and crossed into Spain at the border town of Badajoz. I started making my way north through Salamanca and Valladolid, to Aranda de Duero, where I was giving a talk to a local school. I was greeted by a wonderful woman who spoke perfect English. We took my bike into the classroom and I set my laptop up. The teacher told me to speak slowly in English and they would understand me. The children were only about 10 years old but I was very impressed with their behaviour and understanding of English. At the end of the half hour presentation, I spoke a few sentences in Spanish, thanking them for having me. Their faces dropped and they looked bemused to hear me speaking in Spanish; I wish I could have captured the look on their faces. I spent a short while chatting to the children afterwards. That evening, I stayed in the town and was taken out for dinner by the people who had organised the talk. Aranda de Duero is famous for its underground wine caves, through which I was taken on a tour.

I now intended to carry on cycling with no days off until I finished, as I still had around 600 miles left before I was in Caen where I would pick up the ferry to Portsmouth. It only took two days to get to France after leaving Aranda, although it rained every day. The cycling in Spain was fantastic: there was nowhere near the amount of cars on the roads that I'd experienced in other countries and car drivers appeared to be quite courteous to cyclists. I crossed into France at the small town of Irun and started heading to Bordeaux. France was fairly easy to navigate, as all the roads are very well sign-posted. The next town after Bordeaux was La Rochelle, where Euan had lined up an interview for me with a French newspaper. The media interest was starting to build and Euan alluded to the fact that it was going to be a national story when I arrived back and I wouldn't be disappointed.

While I was in La Rochelle, I received an email from Bob in Phoenix. He had been following my journey and informed me that he had booked a flight and was on his way to London to see me cycle my last day, as promised. I was shocked, as I really didn't think he was going to keep his word and had quite honestly forgotten that he even said he would. I was looking forward to seeing him again though, so I put him in contact with my parents to help plan his arrival.

I was only a few days away from Caen now and hadn't even booked my ferry. I asked Pru to look into it for me, who had been such a massive pillar of support throughout the duration of the cycle. She came back with the ferry times and kindly booked the night ferry that I needed. I was starting to get incredibly excited as I was only a few days away from finishing. The plan was to arrive into Portsmouth and cycle to Brighton, stay the night in Brighton and then cycle the last leg from Brighton to Greenwich Park. As I was cycling to Caen, I had a phone call from Euan, informing me there would most likely be multiple news channels sending camera crews along to greet me off the ferry. The media was fast picking up on the story, thanks to Innesco and the fact that I was going to be the first person to complete all three challenges.

My ferry didn't depart Caen until 11pm but I ended up arriving at the port for 7pm so I had plenty of time to kill. By now, I was incredibly excited. I was starting to get phone calls from media agencies who wanted interviews with me. I had no idea how they got hold of my contact details but it was a good sign the level of interest was escalating. I felt like celebrating, as I knew I'd just cycled the last day of the world cycle. The next two days would be quite different: I wouldn't be on my own, with various people joining me as I made my way up to London. I decided to have a beer and ordered some fries from the bar. I thought that a beer might help me sleep, as Pru had kindly booked me a cabin on the ferry so I could try and get some rest before the madness of the next few days.

I boarded the ferry at around 10.15pm and secured my bike in the hold where the cars and lorries were parked, before making my way up to the top deck. It was all very surreal that the journey of the last six months was coming to an end. I started thinking about all the people I'd met and the different experiences I'd had. My phone rang and it was Euan asking me how things were going and telling me that a journalist would be calling me, probably trying to find a silly angle to the story, so to be mindful if she started asking bizarre questions. I took the call with the journalist who was actually very pleasant and didn't ask too many awkward questions. By now it was past midnight and the ferry was due to arrive at 6am, so I thought I'd head to my cabin to get some rest.

It was a tiny room with a single bed and a shower. Thankfully, the water was hot so I cleaned myself up and lay on the bed in the hope of catching a few hours' sleep. I just couldn't sleep at all. My head was a rollercoaster of emotions: I was happy to be finishing but slightly sad at the same time. I kept wondering what the next couple of days would be like. I managed about an hour of sleep before being woken by music that started coming out of the speakers in the cabin walls at 5am. I put my cycling kit on, packed my kit and headed to the below decks where my bike was secured. I phoned Euan to tell him that the ferry had arrived and the cars were about to disembark. He told me to make sure I was the last one off the ferry. I waited until all the cars and the odd motorcycle had driven off before slowly making my way out. It was cold and very damp so I was very careful cycling off the ferry and down the ramp. I knew that media crews were waiting for me at the bottom of the ramps but had no idea how many or what it would be like.

I cycled very slowly down the ramp, which felt like I was in slow motion. My heart was racing, then I saw a large group of people at the bottom of the ramp. About a second later, flashes started to light up the whole area as the journalists started taking photos as I was cycling towards them. It was a bit like a scene from the red carpet of a Hollywood blockbuster. There were photographers shouting my name, clicking off hundreds of photos, and I could see loads of crews with all their sophisticated equipment. I stopped in front of them when I got to the bottom of the ramp and remember saying, "Hi guys, thanks for coming, bit nippy this morning, isn't it!" They laughed and started asking me to pose in certain positions for the cameras and wanted me to cycle back up the ramp for more shots. I repeated that five times before a reporter from Channel 5 wanted to interview me.

I was then ushered through Immigration with a representative from the ferry company. She told me there were quite a few people waiting for me in the terminal. I knew there would be some Scouts. I couldn't take my bike through Immigration so just before I walked out into the terminal, I was given my bike by a cargo handler. There were loud cheers from the Scouts who had got up early to come down to welcome me. My dad was standing in the background with Bob standing next to him, with a massive smile on his face. The Scouts had a photographer with them called Pete who I knew, so we took some photos with everyone. After 45 minutes, the crowds started to disburse. Most people had to get to work and most of the Scouts had to get to school. It really was fantastic seeing Bob again; I could see that he was really excited to be there.

I also met Euan from the PR company Innesco for the first time. It was strange as I felt like I'd known him for quite some time as we'd been chatting on the phone a fair bit prior to my arrival. After giving another couple of interviews outside the terminal, it was time to get moving, as I was cycling to Brighton and the weather forecast was atrocious in the afternoon. Euan had a radio interview lined up in another part of Portsmouth at a shopping complex called Gunwharf Quays. It was only a few miles away so didn't take long to get there. My dad drove Euan over from the ferry terminal and we both went into the studios. The guy who was interviewing me offered me a cup of tea, and I joked that this was my first cup of tea back in England. "Don't worry, I'll make you a good one," he said, smiling.

After the interview, I met a couple of friends who were cycling with me. Chris who was cycling with his sister to Brighton, Bob and another friend called Ian, who was a strong cyclist. It was only a small group, compared to the amount of people who were intending to join me for the last day to London. The route took us out of Portsmouth through Chichester, Bognor Regis and Worthing, before reaching Brighton. About an hour into the ride, it started to pour with rain and it was getting incredibly cold. Bob was really starting to struggle as, living in the deserts of Phoenix, he just wasn't accustomed to our bitterly cold and wet environment. His legs were cramping up quite badly and I could see he was in a lot of pain. We still had around 25 miles to go, which would have been very slow and painful for Bob. Thankfully, we had a photographer who was taking photos along the way, using his car to leap frog in front of us. We asked if Bob could jump in the car and we agreed to meet at the hotel in Brighton.

Soon after Bob left, the weather started to deteriorate even more and the winds started to become dangerously high, battering us all over the road. Chris was now pretty tired and made the decision to jump on the train and meet us in Brighton. It was now just myself, Ian and Chris's sister Yvonne. We were five miles from Brighton when my rear tyre exploded with a loud bang. It was raining hard and I was soaked through but for some reason, I had a smile on my face. I'd been on the road for just over half a year and had over 100 punctures. I thought to myself that fixing one more really didn't matter and soon I'd probably miss fixing punctures at the side of the road. This time the bead on the tyre that runs around the rim had split so the tyre was pretty useless. I Googled 'bike shops near me' and miraculously found that there was one two minutes away. I bought a new tyre and inner tube and the owner kindly let me use the workshop to fit them.

As we were running behind schedule, Yvonne had to leave us and be collected by her partner as she needed to be somewhere else that evening. I thanked her for cycling with me and carried on with Ian. We got our heads down and pushed hard for the last five miles to the hotel on the seafront where we were staying. When we arrived, we quickly got inside to warm up. Euan told me that the interview I'd given that morning was going to be on the five o'clock news, according to the reporter. Another cycling friend, Tony, and his wife Shelly, had driven down to Brighton especially to see me, as they couldn't make Greenwich Park the following day. Other friends had also made the trip down to Brighton, for which I was grateful.

The evening news came on and there I was being interviewed. Everyone in the hotel bar starting cheering. It was very surreal standing in the hotel with everyone looking at me. People who weren't even part of our group were offering to buy me a beer and wanting to have their photo taken with me. There was a hen party in the bar and the bride-to-be, along with her mum, took a particular liking to me for some reason. As the evening progressed, other friends started to arrive who were going to cycle the last day with me. I didn't intend to really drink, as technically I still hadn't finished. It didn't help my good intentions when the hotel manager gave me a magnum of Champagne, which was a very kind gesture. I decided that we all needed to have some so I shared it out among my friends. That evening, I got to bed at about 2am, much later than intended.

The following morning I felt much better than I thought I would when the alarm went off at 6am. I was sharing a room with Bob, who gets up at the crack of dawn every day. We headed down to breakfast and then made our way over to Brighton Pier for 8am, which was the meeting place and start time for anyone who wanted to join me on the ride up to London. Euan had arranged for another news channel to shoot an interview with me that morning and they were waiting at the pier. There were about 20 of us cycling up to Greenwich Park, most of whom were friends, but some people joined us who I'd never met before, who had been following my journey via social media and wanted to come along. It was great.

We had planned my arrival into Greenwich Park for 2pm so we had plenty of time to cover the distance. I wasn't going to lead the route, as I wanted to cycle up and down the group with everyone, so Ian and Richard (another of my sponsors) offered to lead. We managed to stay together as a group and stopped for a quick lunch at the halfway point, which consisted of a few flapjacks and chocolate bars. Euan had taken a train from Brighton to London and was waiting in Greenwich Park along with everyone else. He called me to tell me not to cycle up to the finish point, which was by the General James Wolfe Statue next to the Royal Observatory, without calling him first.

We arrived at the gates to the park at 1.30pm, so decided to grab some coffees and wait until the agreed time of 2pm. I had a lot of adrenaline running through me and had wondered what this day would be like since setting off. So far, it was everything I'd imagined. I was very anxious about the weather as the previous day was horrific and the forecast for the last day was just as bad. Almost as if someone was looking over me, the clouds separated and by the time I arrived at Greenwich Park, it was lovely and sunny with not a cloud in the sky.

We all made our way over to the gates for 1.55pm and I called Euan to let him know we were ready. He told me at exactly 2pm to start cycling up towards the finish line. I took my jacket off so my cycling jersey would show my sponsor branding when I crossed the line, however it was a very cold day and, despite the blue sky and sunshine, I was absolutely freezing. The five minutes from 1.55pm to 2pm felt like they passed in a few seconds, and off we went, cycling towards the top of the hill in an arrow formation, with me at the front.

I was totally blown away when I saw the size of the crowd waiting for me. There were hundreds of people: friends, family and Scouts. A ribbon had been stretched across the finish line and was being held by the children of my main sponsors, Richard from Ofsure and James from Balmain Asset Management. A massive cheer erupted as I crossed the line with everyone following me. There were loads of photographers who were taking pictures and various film crews had turned up. It was quite an amazing experience; everywhere I looked I could see the different faces of everyone that I recognised.

I couldn't believe the wonderful support I was receiving, especially from the Scouts. It was important to me that, as the Hampshire Scouting Ambassador to 22,000 fantastic Scouts, I did them all proud. While I was away, they were fundraising for my chosen charity, the ELIFAR Foundation, and they had a cheque that was going to be given to Paul who represents the charity. We all posed for photos together, along with some Scouts who had earned their Captain Ketch Ambassador Challenge badge. I had carried my own badge around the world and wanted to give it to Fi, who had orchestrated the Ambassador Challenge badge. Without Fi, a lot of things would not have happened and I was very grateful for all her support.

James and Richard had very kindly arranged for a small after-party at a venue in central London, so after I'd spoken to everyone who had made the effort to come and see me, I headed over. Close to Green Park, it was full of close friends and family. The room was buzzing with excitement; James made a short speech and toast. It was great meeting up with everyone again and it was the first time all those who had supported and encouraged me over the years were in the same place at the same time. I wasn't there for long as the BBC had confirmed they wanted me in the studios the following morning in Manchester. Euan, myself and Bob (who was very much enjoying his whirlwind tour of the UK) had to catch the train that evening in order to make the breakfast show the following morning. There wasn't a great deal going on in the media when I finished my cycle. However, the news of my arrival, and the fact that I had become the only person to have achieved all three challenges, was spreading fast.

The following morning, we arrived at the BBC studios in Manchester. I had given quite a few interviews over the years and was fairly confident in front of the cameras but I was slightly thrown when the presenter asked me if I'd missed my wife and kids. Instantly, she knew something wasn't right, but it was live TV and I didn't want to embarrass the presenters, so I had to quickly think on my feet. "I missed everyone and am glad to be back now," I replied. It turned out that the researcher had made an obvious mistake: the presenters were not at all happy about it and apologised profusely. I told them it didn't matter and that I thought it was quite funny. As soon as the interview had finished, my phone started going crazy, with messages from friends, asking me who my wife and kids were, just teasing me.

Later that afternoon, we got the train back to London. Richard was still staying in London so Bob and I headed over to his hotel. When we got into the city, I was sitting on the tube and noticed that I was in the Metro newspaper. I was quite shocked. Euan was sitting in front of me at the time and I showed him the piece. "Amazing, they ran the story!" he said. The guy sitting to my right turned to me and said, "Is that you?" I replied that it was. "Ah fantastic, well done mate, I read about that this morning!". It was strange to see all the commuters reading the newspaper with me on the front of it. The term 'Global Triathlon' had been adopted by most of the national newspapers and I was completely blown away by the interest in my story.

That evening, Richard, Bob and I went out for dinner at a roof top restaurant, it felt quite relaxing after all the madness of the past 24 hours. When Bob and I returned to the hotel he asked me what I had learnt from travelling the world, meeting different people and experiencing diverse cultures. Of course, I could have talked for hours to answer his question but the first thing that came into my head was this: "Everything works out in the end. If things aren't working out, it's because it's not the end!" Everyone has the capability to be whoever they want to be.